BUDGET REFORM POLITICS

POLITICAL ECONOMY OF INSTITUTIONS AND DECISIONS

Editors

Professor James Alt, Harvard University
Professor Douglass North, Washington University in St. Louis

BUDGET REFORM POLITICS

*The design of the appropriations process
in the House of Representatives,
1865–1921*

CHARLES H. STEWART III

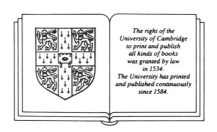

The right of the
University of Cambridge
to print and publish
all kinds of books
was granted by law
in 1534.
The University has printed
and published continuously
since 1584.

CAMBRIDGE UNIVERSITY PRESS

Cambridge
New York   Port Chester   Melbourne   Sydney

Published by the Press Syndicate of the University of Cambridge
The Pitt Building, Trumpington Street, Cambridge CB2 1RP
32 East 57th Street, New York, NY 10022, USA
10 Stamford Road, Oakleigh, Melbourne 3166, Australia

© Cambridge University Press 1989

First published 1989

Printed in the United States of America

Library of Congress Cataloging-in-Publication Data

Stewart, Charles Haines.

Budget reform politics : the design of the appropriations process
in the House of Representatives, 1865–1921 / Charles H. Stewart III.

p. cm. – (Political economy of institutions and decisions)

Bibliography: p.

Includes index.

ISBN 0-521-35472-2 hard covers

1. Budget – United States – History. 2. Budget – Law and
legislation – United States – History. 3. Government spending policy –
United States – History. I. Title. II. Series.
HJ2050.S74 1989
353.0072'2 – dc19   88 – 38677
                                                              CIP

British Library Cataloguing in Publication Data

Stewart, Charles H.

Budget reform politics: the design of the
appropriations process in the House of Representatives,
1865–1921. – (Political economy of institutions and
decisions).

1. United States, Congress. House of Representatives.
Budgeting. Reform, 1865–1921
I. Title II. Series
328.73'07412

ISBN 0-521-35472-2 hard covers

Contents

Tables and figures

TABLES

Tables and figures

FIGURES

Series editors' preface

This Cambridge series, Political Economy of Institutions and Decisions, is built around attempts to answer two central questions: How do institutions evolve in response to individual incentives, strategies, and choices; and how do institutions affect the performance of political and economic systems? The scope of the series is comparative and historical rather than international or specifically American, and the focus is positive rather than normative.

Charles Stewart's work has two important features. One is his use of rational models of congressional changes in budget procedures between the Civil War and the end of World War I. Linking congressmen's career objectives to their local constituencies, he applies the modern Congress model in which a decentralized electoral process leads congressmen to prefer particularistic, localistic policy production over national-interest legislation. He shows that this demand for localistic policy leads to institutional or structural fragmentation, and conflicts with existing leadership and committee structures as well as with the centralizing demands of war and other crises. The political economy of this conflict, which produces opportunities for countervailing reforms, explains the evolution of budget procedure in the long run.

The other prominent feature of the book is Stewart's careful quantitative modeling of budget and spending decisions and outcomes with explicit reference to the impact of institutional constraints. Analyzing the devolution of budget powers of 1885 and its attendant surges in spending, he argues that rather than devolution of power causing spending, both follow from broader social and economic changes that increased demand for spending.

Stewart's original fusion of quantitative and historical analysis shows both how institutional procedures changed in response to legislator preferences and broader social and economic developments and how these procedures shaped congressional policy.

Acknowledgments

As with any study of this scope, I could not have finished without the help I received from numerous individuals and institutions, the entire list of which would be a small book in itself. A few deserve special mention, however. John Chubb, John Ferejohn, and Terry Moe read and guided the first version of this work. Subsequently, the following individuals contributed by reading parts or all of the manuscript: Walter Dean Burnham, Josh Cohen, Peter Lemieux, Mathew McCubbins, Richard Samuels, Kenneth Shepsle, and Eric Uslaner. Mark Reynolds provided key research assistance for the completion of Chapter 4. James Alt was also instrumental in encouraging me in the final months. Elisabeth Case saved me from embarrassing myself too much in my use of the language as she edited the final manuscript. As well, three institutions have nurtured me while this manuscript has sprung up: the political science departments of Stanford University and the Massachusetts Institute of Technology, as well as the Governmental Studies Program at the Brookings Institution. The dean of Humanities and Social Sciences and the provost at MIT provided finances to help finish the project. To all of these individuals and institutions I owe a tremendous debt of gratitude. Of course, I absolve them of all the errors of judgment and fact that might be found in what follows.

And then there was Kathy, who provided aid beyond what mere words can describe. . . .

PART I

Issues in the study of budgeting

Introduction

Those who have lived in the United States during the post-World War II era have witnessed a considerable amount of tinkering with the procedures Congress uses to appropriate public funds. Each decade seems to bring a structural fix for the budgetary problems that ail us. Four "reforms" in recent decades particularly stand out: the creation of a joint budget committee under the Legislative Reorganization Act of 1946, the experiment with an omnibus appropriations bill in 1950, the passage of the Congressional Budget and Impoundment Control Act (CBICA) of 1974, and the passage of the Gramm-Rudman-Hollings deficit reduction act in 1985. The shift of billions of dollars of expenditures away from the annual appropriations process toward "entitlement" and "backdoor" spending during the 1960s also counts as an important, if informal, alteration of congressional procedures. In addition to these procedural changes that have actually been enacted by Congress within the past generation, countless other schemes have been proposed to change the budgetary process even further, only never to get out of committee.

To most people, all of this tinkering (or tampering) is yet another indication of the increased complexity of our age. The necessity to deliver more government services to more people requires Congress to expand its institutional and analytical capacities. More people rely on government spending for their livelihoods, and both they and their representatives try to structurally shield spending of interest to them from close public scrutiny. The seemingly insatiable appetite of modern governments for spending tax dollars (or borrowed money) prompts some politicians and activists to try to rein in spending through even more structural plans. In short, as more and more people have ideas about what government should and should not do with public funds, they are driven not only to try to win budgetary battles on their merits in the halls of Congress, but also to try to make their victories even more enduring by changing congressional structures. The increased complexity of budgetary politics leads to the increased complexity of budgetary structure.

All of this complexity and acrimony seems to call for simpler days, when budgets were small, the national government relatively inactive, and the budgetary process a reflection of those simpler times. It is the point of this book, however, that such simpler days were not so simple after all.

This book is an examination of seemingly simpler budgetary times. It is about the development of the budgetary process in the House of Representatives, beginning with its simple childhood in 1865, when the House Appropriations Committee was created, and ending with its relative maturity and complexity in 1921, when the Budget and Accounting Act was passed, ushering in the modern appropriations process. Throughout the period bounded by these two landmark events, members of the House engaged in numerous struggles about how the federal government's spending decisions would be made.

By analyzing this period, using the theoretical and methodological tools of modern political science, we shall gain a better understanding about how the budgetary process has developed over time, and therefore gain a better understanding about the budgetary politics that occupy our attention today. A strong assumption that I make in this investigation is that we can learn much about the appropriations process that began to be developed in the late nineteenth century by focusing on the goals of individual legislators and then tracing how those goals became transformed into structural preferences, legislative strategies, and finally reform outcomes.

Although setting spending and taxing policy is arguably the most important thing that Congress does, it is surprising how little we know about congressional budgeting in previous eras. Among those who watch national politics with any regularity, there may be a dim memory about how things were done at the end of World War II; but rarely does collective memory about budgetary politics go back any further. One indicator of this paucity of historical knowledge about congressional budgeting and budget reform politics is that while one can locate several important studies about postwar spending and taxing,[1] and even more about budgetary politics in the aftermath of the 1974 CBICA,[2] it is

---

1 Wildavsky (1964), Fenno (1966), and Manley (1970).
2 Among the books that have appeared in recent years with a focus on the politics of the budgetary process within the framework of the 1974 CBICA are Havemann (1978), LeLoup (1980), Schick (1980), Ippolito (1981), Penner (1981), Congressional Quarterly (1982a), Committee for Economic Development (1983), Shuman (1984), Wander, Hebert, and Copeland (1984), and Wildavsky (1984). This list,

necessary to scrounge far and wide before even the most cursory of treatments is available concerning congressional budgeting before World War II.[3] The first goal of this study, therefore, is to examine a fuller range of reform politics than has ever been scrutinized, as a remedy for our glaring ignorance about congressional budgetary history.

The question of *what* happened before World War II is joined in this study by the second question of *why* these things happened. The emphasis on the explanatory arises because simply describing what happened a century ago when the House was developing its modern appropriations process would fail on two points. First, simple description would be inadequate because theory-less story telling can lead us down blind alleys. The period under study here is so intrinsically fascinating that we need a theory of congressional behavior to guide us away from simply considering fascinating personalities and intriguing strategic situations. Second, simple description would be inadequate because ultimately we need to draw conclusions about how the development of the House appropriations process in its infancy and adolescence can inform our understanding of budgetary structural politics today. In order to do that we need to develop a theory of congressional budgetary behavior that explains budget reform in such a way that the commonalities between the past and present are made clear.

THE HISTORICAL STUDY OF CONGRESSIONAL
BUDGET REFORM

Ever since political scientists abandoned the legalistic, constitutional history frame of reference in studying American politics early in this century, examining the historical development of formal institutions has held a low priority. We have been much more interested in studying and explaining the actual behaviors of political elites, the more current the behavior the better. Such a focus on actual behavior and the eclipse of normative constitutional concerns revolutionized the study of Congress, as it revolutionized the study of politics more generally and provided a

of course, does not mention the various budget analyses published annually by think tanks such as the Brookings Institution and the Urban Institute. Nor does it include the literature appearing in journals and other periodicals, which is simply too voluminous to even attempt listing here.

3 The standard source on prewar congressional budgeting is Fisher (1975), but as the title, *Presidential Spending Power*, implies, the book takes a presidential perspective and deals with congressional developments primarily as they have affected executive spending decisions over time. Studies that deal with pre-World War I congressional budgeting have only recently begun to appear with any frequency; a few are generally available. See Brady and Morgan (1983, 1987), Wander (1982a,b), Schick (1984), and Stewart (1985, 1987a, 1988).

"great leap forward" in our understanding of political institutions and behavior.

The number of scholars studying Congress and the number of journalists covering it are one tribute to the increased level of sophistication we can now bring to understanding what goes on in our national legislature.[4] But focusing so much attention on current congressional behavior has come with a price. Scholars and journalists are on the one hand continually rediscovering patterns of congressional behavior that have recurred over the decades, while on the other hand making severely time-bound "general" conclusions about Congress.

One of the most well-known and now repudiated time-bound generalizations about Congress enjoyed wide currency during the 1960s: The Senate was inherently more liberal than the House because all senators had to accommodate more interests into their electoral coalitions than did House members and because all senators represented at least one urban area, while many, if not most, House members represented none. Of course, to anyone living in the 1980s, such a conclusion seems preposterous. A political scientist would now be hard put to make a generalization about the relative liberality of the House versus the Senate, other than to note that it must fluctuate over time, given the variation of other politically relevant variables.

My point here is certainly not to denigrate the study of contemporary Congresses – far from it. It is to suggest that the current behavior of members of Congress (MCs)[5] can be understood only in reference to

4 The 1985 directory of the American Political Science Association lists 640 members who study legislative politics, out of a total association membership of 9,450. Unfortunately, detailed statistics about what political scientists study do not go back far enough to document a long-term historical trend. The number of journalists accredited to cover Congress provides a historical trend to gauge how much we know about current congressional behavior. The *Congressional Directory* for the 87th Congress (1961) listed 1,516 members of the working press who were accredited to cover Congress, including 829 people who were accredited to the House and Senate press galleries, 98 who were accredited to the press photographers galleries, 235 accredited to the radio and television galleries, and 354 accredited to the periodical galleries. By the 99th Congress (1985), the *Congressional Directory* reported that 4,529 members of the working press were accredited to cover Congress: press galleries, 1,439; press photographers, 306; radio and television, 1,477; and periodical, 1,307.

5 In recent years, writers in the social sciences have had to deal with sexist assumptions that pervade our language, and congressional scholars are no exception. The generic label for members of the United States national legislature has for decades been "congressman." That this label assumes that the generic legislator is a man is pretty clear. What to do about this? Some writers convert this term to "congressperson" – a word I personally find inelegant. Inelegance can be preferable to sexism when there is no choice. Yet there is a more elegant solution at our disposal. The solution I propose, and use in this book, is that of "member of Congress," abbreviated MC. This solution has two advantages. First, it bears a direct analogy to members of

other behavior. In the same way that the shape of a purely white circle is imperceptible when set against a purely white background, the behavior of MCs is also imperceptible when purely self-referenced. To the statistically minded, studying only one Congress or a limited range of Congresses needlessly reduces the natural range of variation in the dependent and independent variables. One way of setting congressional behavior within a meaningful political context is to compare it to that of other contemporary legislatures; another way is to compare it to past congressional behavior. This latter option is the direction taken in this study.

Those desiring to understand Congress historically are not totally at a loss in finding useful sources to consult. While there is as of yet no recognized definitive history of Congress – Galloway's now-outdated classic is the closest thing we have to such a history – three superb monographs by James Sterling Young (1966), David Rothman (1966), and David Brady (1973) deal with aspects of Congress before the twentieth century.[6] Rothman addresses questions of power and institutional development in the Senate between 1869 and 1901, Brady explores the nature of heightened partisanship in late-nineteenth-century Houses, and Young examines the power relations among the earliest inhabitants of the capital city of Washington.

These studies are especially good models for those desiring to do historical congressional research because not only do they pay particular attention to the events of the periods they describe – Young calls doing so "portraiture" – but they also bring modern advances in history and political science to understanding past Congresses. Brady brings the tools of quantitative roll call analysis to describing and explaining party cohesion. Young takes cues from sociological group theorists to explain the nature and exercise of political power in the earliest years of the Republic.

By using modern theoretical and methodological means, these scholars have been able not only to explain aspects of congressional behavior during their periods, but also to make the understanding of these periods relevant to modern political analysis. These works of congressional history point to some important fundamental parallels between past and current congressional behavior. For instance, the historical congressional literature shows that the unique fragmentation of political institutions

the British Parliament, who are referred to as "members of Parliament," or MPs. Like its British counterpart, the abbreviation MC is terse and to the point. Second, the abbreviation MC is the term that members of the House use when they sign their mail. Thus, not only does "member of Congress" have a convenient analogue to another national parliament close to us in tradition, it is a term already in use among members of Congress themselves.

6 In additional to Galloway (1976), serviceable general histories of Congress, along with helpful bibliographies, can be found in Josephy (1979) and Congressional Quarterly (1982b).

that was created in the Constitution, separation of powers and locally oriented elections for national legislators, has had a strong influence on national politics throughout our history. If we currently experience difficulties with developing coherent national policies that are immune from the tugs of special interests and localistic concerns, we are not alone historically. Certainly there have been times in our nation's history when local concerns have dominated national vision more than others – Brady in fact studies a rare period when national concerns were relatively dominant, but for reasons easily traceable to local factors – but some things never change in the basic driving forces of congressional politics, which makes the historical study of the institution continually relevant to those interested in the present.

As with these other works just mentioned, this project sets out to examine the past in order ultimately to understand the present. Given the distance of years, the task is formidable, yet still important. As one might expect, when we look at the development of the appropriations process in the House between 1865 and 1921, there are details of the landscape that look unusual to anyone used to following Congress only in the daily papers. MCs talk in archaic and flowery language – even more flowery than today. They talk meaningfully and lovingly about party loyalty and responsibility. Staffs are nowhere to be found, except for the occasional clerk in the more overworked committees. Congressional membership is a revolving door. Speakers rule the House floor as dinosaurs once ruled the earth.

Yet, as one might *not* expect, once we peer below these landscape differences, we see a basic political process at work that is easily discernible to modern eyes: Legislators do all they can to please their districts and quickly desert the party when they have to. Committees follow a territorial imperative and continually try to expand their jurisdictions. Members are not randomly distributed among committees, but agency "friends" are appointed to legislative committees and "responsible legislators" are appointed to guard the purse strings. Party leaders continually try to please disparate factions of their congressional parties, with varying degrees of success.

In short, while the legislative landscape of a century ago was different from that of today, the differences can generally be traced to differences of degree, not of kind. Idiosyncratic details of any congressional age are a product of how that age's uniqueness in terms of social structure, political issues, and economic development gets filtered through a few basic, enduring American political truths, such as locally oriented national elections, separation and distrust between the governing branches, the fragility of party power, jealousies over committee jurisdictions, and hunger for power. The congressional past is highly relevant in reaching an understanding of the congressional present.

THE HISTORICAL CONGRESS AND RATIONAL ACTORS

I have chosen a theoretical course in this study that assumes that MCs are, and have been, rational actors. That is, I assume that the politicians I am studying acted out of a pursuit of personal and political goals; that they could roughly rank those goals in priority; and that the higher the goal, the more diligently they worked to achieve it. This orientation is a familiar one to those who have even casually consulted the recent congressional literature.

The utilization of pure and strong behavioral assumptions within the rational choice tradition is frequently a useful tool when the exercise is to push the bounds of theory along certain narrowly defined frontiers, but the exercise here is to explain a fairly wide range of behaviors among a large number of actors in a disparate collection of strategic and objective situations. Therefore, this study is an exercise in *applied* theory, rather than in pure theory, and thus I do not engage in theorizing using formal techniques. Taking a rational choice frame of reference helps us to narrow the explanatory focus among a few key variables and relationships; sticking to an informal use of the paradigm allows us greater flexibility in effectively handling a number of disparate situations.

Applying the rational choice framework to historical congressional research is bound to be controversial. The controversy arises not so much because we might assume that MCs were once irrational and now have found rationality, but because rational choice approaches when applied to Congress have focused on goal pursuit within one activity – reelection. In David Mayhew's well-known formulation, MCs have been said to be "single-minded seekers of reelection." This is clearly theoretically plausible in the modern-day Congress; it is less clearly plausible in the earlier Congress, with its high turnover rates. I cannot address the full range of objections here – they are handled in later chapters – but let me lay out a couple of ways in which I believe that goal pursuit is still a relevant way in which to study historical congressional behavior.

First, as I shall argue in Chapters 1 and 2, the extent of the nineteenth-century congressional revolving door has frequently been overinterpreted. The high turnover rates mask the extent to which late-nineteenth and early-twentieth-century MCs were professional politicians, but politicians with a higher priority on local careers than on national ones. Thus, the "election pursuit" hypothesis that drives current congressional research in this tradition can be applied to past congressional behavior if the conceptualization of election pursuit is made more general, allowing for a broader notion of what MCs wanted to do with their future careers.

Second, goal pursuit is a helpful theoretical vehicle for studying the essentially internal institutional behavior of MCs. While the major engine of congressional behavior has always operated along a constituency-legislator axis, other significant goal pursuit has occurred within Congress itself. To cite only two significant areas of institutional goal pursuit: (1) Members of congressional committees have strong incentives to pursue a goal of jurisdictional expansion and protection, what Shepsle (1984) refers to as the "jurisdictional imperative." (2) Leaders of congressional parties have strong incentives to accommodate various factions of their parties in order to survive in party caucuses in the future. While institutionally oriented goal pursuit can ultimately be related back to reelection, sometimes it is much more useful to appreciate it within a more limited institutional context. Even if one wants to dispute the importance of electoral pursuit in explaining the late-nineteenth-century Congress, it is still highly plausible that the simple power-oriented goals of party leaders and committee members have survived essentially intact over the past century.

One pertinent criticism of the "electoral connection" research has been that it often assumes that legislators engage in essentially unfettered atomistic goal pursuit, when in fact congressional behavior is significantly channeled by the set of formal structures confronting MCs and the informal distribution of power residing in Congress. The institution creates many powerful constraints on an MC's behavior given his or her preferences. Or, to quote the rock classic: "You can't always get what you want." In the development of the House budgetary process between 1865 and 1921, the independent effects of preexisting structures were continually evident and served frequently to thwart or alter the "state of nature" structural preferences of the rank-and-file. I see the theoretical focus on goal pursuit as an important way to address what happens once "MCs meet the institution," by noting that committees and party leaders have goals that arise *in part* independently of short-range electoral demands. The story of budget reform, therefore, becomes one of competing goals being resolved by a dialectic, interactive process. Sometimes conflict among goals is resolved by brute force, but more often it is resolved through a process of exchange.

To put this another way, I am interested in more than just the atomistic behavior of election-seeking politicians as they try to do well by their electoral supporters. I am also interested in seeing what happens when their election-seeking behavior meets an ongoing institution characterized by elements of committee and leadership power that can significantly alter the preferences and strategies of rank-and-file legislators. This preference-altering behavior of leaders and committee members can also be understood under the general rubric of "goal pursuit." The continual trade-off between institutional goals of jurisdiction and power and the individual goals of reelection are a recurrent theme in the development of the appropriations process in the House between 1865 and 1921.

By focusing on the goal-directed behavior of MCs, we are better able to see the parallels between reform behavior of a century ago and reform behavior of the present. It turns out that this story of the development of the House appropriations process *can* help to explain modern structural politics, and some of those parallels are explored in the conclusion of the book.

The study that follows is divided into three parts. Part I provides a theoretical and historical overview of the narrative to follow. Chapter 1 begins by noting the intellectual tradition that has sought to reform and explain the budgetary process and ends by specifying key elements of a theory of budget reform politics. For heuristic purposes, I begin this theory development by focusing on the electoral process, tracing how the fundamental characteristics of that process lead to preferences for localistic policy production, and how these electorally induced policy preferences in turn induce structural preferences for fragmentation. But I then continue by noting how the pursuit of locally oriented policy and fragmented institutional structure generated by the electoral system is constrained by a set of powerful institutional and economic forces: the "budgetary problem," preexisting structural arrangements defining the committee and leadership systems, and presidential-legislative relations. Chapter 2 turns to the historical period, considering related societal, economic, and institutional developments that affected the course of the evolution of the House appropriations process between 1865 and 1921.

Part II explores the cases in which an effort to change budgetary structure reached the House agenda between 1865 and 1921. Included are such well-known events as the creation of the House Appropriations Committee in 1865 and the passage of the Budget and Accounting Act in 1921, as well as the lesser known running feud among five different committees over the jurisdiction of rivers and harbors appropriations in the 1870s and 1880s, and the thwarted effort to remove spending for public buildings from the Appropriations Committee in 1880. Because the cases encompass all efforts at reform – successful and unsuccessful, major and minor – we can go beyond past descriptions of what happened when major changes occurred and draw some conclusions about why

reform fails at some times and succeeds at others, and why reform coalitions evolve as they do.

The exposition of the cases in Part II is essentially chronological, with
a major stutter-step in the middle. Chapter 3 covers the cases from 1865
to 1885, a period defined by the creation of the House Appropriations
Committee (HAC) at the beginning and a major successful attack on the
HAC's jurisdiction at the end. This latter attack creates what I later refer
to as the "devolution of 1885" and the "regime of 1885." Chapter 4
interrupts the chronological story to explore the substantive spending
changes that ensued under the regime of 1885. The conclusion in that
chapter – no secrets need be hidden – is that although the devolution of
1885 was so widely supported in part because it was predicted to loosen
the purse strings, and although later opposition to the regime occurred
for the same reason, in fact the relationship between decentralization in
1885 and subsequent spending acceleration is complex. Chapter 5 picks
up the chronological narrative a few years after 1885, beginning with
activity surrounding the formalization of the Reed Rules, and ending
with the description of the drawn-out, nip-and-tuck process that ultimately led to an overturning of the regime of 1885, and also to the
institution of independent budgetary power and capacity in the
presidency.

Part III contains the conclusions of the study. I recap some of the more
central theoretical points I made in Chapter 1 and note how they help
to explain the events described in Part II. I also strike a more modern
note in the conclusion and specify how the events from 1865 to 1921,
and the general theory that was used to understand them, can inform
our understanding of budget reform after 1921, and especially reform
activity in the past two decades.

I

Understanding budgeting and budget reform
in Congress

In the next few pages I shall develop a theory to explain why members of Congress (MCs) create specific budgetary structures. Basic to this discussion is the identification of salient budgetary actors and processes, identification of the goals and constraints facing budgetary actors, and the specification of the key relationships among actors, processes, goals, and constraints. My aim is to lay the foundation of a theoretical explanation that is relevant to Congress over a long sweep of history. My focus, therefore, is on what has been common to congressional politics over the past century, not on the idiosyncrasies of any particular age. The exploration of unique elements of budget reform politics occurs in later chapters. Once the common elements of structural politics have been identified and the relations among them specified, then we shall be able not only to understand the important recurrent themes in reform debates over the years, but also to judge the relative importance of other causal dynamics that may have been unique to a given era, be they past, present, or future.

The importance of developing a theory to explain the genesis of decisionmaking regimes is clear, once we accept the conclusion that ongoing budget making is typically incremental. Incrementalist strategies operate through simplifying uncertainty and conflict, and structure is the most important formal mechanism by which such simplification occurs. The parameters of budgetary regimes – such as committee structures and jurisdictions and rules of floor debate – help to limit the types of budgetary decisions that legislators are likely to make. Structure in no way eliminates the inherent conflict created in budgeting, and it very rarely makes outcomes certain. But formal structure can serve to simplify budgetary politics in crucial ways by, first, assigning a higher probability that certain types of spending decisions will enter the congressional agenda and, second, making it more likely (though not certain) that the conflicts that make it onto the agenda will be resolved in a certain way.

13

Developing a theory of budgetary structural reform is both possible and necessary because of the type of work that has been done previously describing budgeting in Congress. A theory of budget reform and regime evolution is *possible* because we know a great deal about how Congress has in fact made budgets over the past couple of decades; we can add to this specialized knowledge about budgeting the enormous amount of information we have about congressional politics generally. A theory of budget reform is *necessary* because regardless of the breadth of our knowledge about congressional budgetary politics, scholars have paid less attention to how Congress goes about setting the broad parameters of budgetary debate and how the apparatus for making budgetary decisions has developed. What little attention has been paid to the development of budgetary structure has been primarily descriptive and normative, and rarely theoretical.

STATE OF OUR KNOWLEDGE ABOUT CONGRESSIONAL BUDGETING

A tour through the scholarly budgetary literature is also a trip through a century of American political history. Whether they focused their efforts on the Budget and Accounting Act (1921) or on the Congressional Budget and Impoundment Control Act (1974), those who have written about budgeting have influenced the development of reform while simultaneously adding to the cumulative knowledge about reform dynamics. To read the budgetary literature of the past century is also to catch important glimpses of the development of political science as a discipline: the traditions of constitutional history and progressive reform of the end of the past century,[1] the casting off of normative presumptions and looking to the sciences for analytic categories and methodologies in the middle of this century,[2] the development of the behavioral revolution,[3] and the recent interest in politicians as rational actors.[4]

So that we can appreciate the uniqueness of the explanatory model I develop and its relationship to what we already know about Congress and budgeting, I shall begin this discussion by examining the ways that others have studied congressional budgeting. Many of these perspectives will be used to supply pieces to my own model of budgetary structure. Because much of this literature was aimed at reforming Congress, some

---

1 Key (1940), Wildavsky (1964), Taft Commission (1912), Collins (1915/1916, 1917), Willoughby (1918), and Cleveland and Buck (1920).
2 Key (1940), Wildavsky (1964).
3 Wildavsky (1964), Davis, Dempster, and Wildavsky (1966a,b,1971), Fenno (1966), and Manley (1970).
4 Niskanen (1971), Ferejohn (1973), Arnold (1979).

of it will be reexamined later in the study as I assess the extent to which it was effective.

The passage of the Congressional Budget and Impoundment Control Act of 1974 (CBICA) provided us with a rare opportunity: the chance to observe a fundamental rearrangement of the distribution of power within Congress. Armed with the knowledge accumulated through two decades of intensive theoretical and empirical research into Congress, congressional scholars could now apply the accumulated wisdom of the ages to the analysis of events yet to come. Unfortunately, those who have chosen to study budgeting in Congress since 1974 have chosen largely to ignore the theoretical advances of the previous generation and therefore have left us with less cumulated knowledge than the physical bulk of the studies would lead us to believe.

Congress will always figure prominently in budgetary politics, and this prominence has shown through in the budgetary literature. At times the budgetary and congressional literatures have intersected directly to yield the best of both traditions, the most important examples being books by Richard Fenno (1966), Aaron Wildavsky (1964), and John Manley (1970). Unfortunately, the issues of congressional *structure*, its reform, and budgetary politics have not been integrated well when the two literature streams have merged.

There have generally been two distinct ways of understanding congressional budgeting over the past century. The first way has been in the reform tradition of political science, while the second has been in the realpolitik tradition of the discipline.

REFORMERS AND NORMATIVE QUESTIONS ABOUT BUDGETING

As American political science has evolved into a "value-free" discipline, it is interesting to note that the very first academic interest expressed in budgetary politics occurred not in the empirical study of budgetary decisionmaking but through agitation in favor of budget reform. The earliest academic literature on the problems of budgetary structure appeared at the turn of the century. The budget reform literature emerged as businesspeople and academicians sought to rid all levels of government finance, from municipalities to the federal government, of the antiquated practices and outright corruption that characterized early industrial America.

The business tie to budget reform ironically provided reformers inspiration for their basic ideas. The justification for the rise of big government had an uneasy relationship with the rise of big business during this period. On the one hand, much of the reform movement's energy was spent trying to mitigate the aggregate social consequences of the growth of large private organizations. On the other hand, the movement was impressed with the great advances in efficiency these organizations embodied. While being alarmed at the power of the "trusts," few reformers would dispute Woodrow Wilson's claims when he wrote:

The field of [public] administration is a field of business. It is removed from the hurry and strife of politics; it at most points stands apart even from . . . constitutional study. It is part of political life only as the methods of the counting-house are a part of the life of society. (Wilson 1887, 209–210)

The growth of large private corporations meant that owners and managers could no longer interact directly with most workers. Therefore, one of the most important questions confronting businesspeople was that of controlling the actions of subordinates. The guiding organizational principle that was developed to effect this control was that of centrally directed hierarchy. Scholars and practitioners argued about how "wide" or "tall" the hierarchy should optimally be, but the consensus that emerged early in this century assumed that regardless of the specifics, orders and actions should flow down successively from superiors to subordinates while information should flow in the opposite direction. It is not surprising that the groups held up as examples of proper, effective organization were the army and the Church (see Mooney 1947).

The ideas of unity of command and hierarchy were conspicuous in the prescriptions for budgeting before 1921 because federal government budgeting was anything but unified. On the congressional side, taxing and spending had been separated in the House since 1865, in the Senate since 1867; spending had been further parceled out to legislative committees beginning in 1877 in the House and in 1899 in the Senate. Centralization in the executive branch was even less apparent. The closest thing to a unifying executive budget officer was the Treasury secretary; but he could do no more coordination than to issue an annual report to Congress estimating forthcoming revenues and to bind together agency spending requests and forward them *unchanged* to Congress.

Not surprisingly, the scholarly reform prescription for federal budgeting at the turn of the century was to centralize.[5] But while centralization

5 In this study, I will frequently make reference to the concept of centralization and its antonyms "decentralization" and "fragmentation." Because "centralization" is a very slippery term in political science, I should specify what I mean when I use it. Smith (1985) provides the best discussion of centralization in the congressional context. He defines centralization as a system that minimizes both the number of effective decisionmakers and the number of decisionmaking units. Decentralization maximizes both elements simultaneously.

I should note that decentralization has rarely been an absolute concept in congres-

naturally meant restoring lost authority to the Senate and House appropriations committees, reformers outside Congress focused primary attention on the ultimate centralization of budgeting in the president, who was said to preside over the most business-like part of the federal government. The models developed to describe the ideal government organization were based on theories of trusteeship and analogies to corporations. The president of the United States, in addition to sitting formally at the top of a hierarchical organization like the president of a large corporation, was also argued to be the best situated to exercise legitimate judgments about competing budgetary claims because he was the only nationally elected political official. While Congress had the role of final legitimizer in the executive budget model, much like a corporate board of directors, it was clear to most reformers that the presidency was the only office legitimately and effectively able to set the initial parameters of budgetary debate (see Taft Commission 1912; Cleveland 1912).

Just as the principles of classical organization theory have greatly influenced various government commissions from Keep to Grace, so too have the presumed virtues of centralization continued to reappear whenever budget reform has been contemplated by either the executive or legislative branch. The criticisms leveled against the congressional process in 1919 have reverberated throughout the budgetary literature, were frequently repeated in the debate over the 1974 CBICA, and continue to be heard to this day. Consider the following quote from the 1919 House Select Budget Committee, which sounds much like the complaints voiced in the 1960s and in the early 1970s:

Expenditures are not considered in connection with revenues; ... these requests have been subjected to no superior revision with a view to bringing them into harmony with each other, to eliminating duplication of organization or activities, or of making them, as a whole, conform to the needs of the Nation as represented by the condition of the Treasury and prospective revenues. (U.S. Congress 1912, 4)

The reform movement left its imprint on the academic study of budgetary politics in two ways. First, the reformist orientation instilled in many scholars a normative preference for centralization, either centralization

---

sional institutional development. What might seem like decentralization at one point may have been considered centralization at another. The important characteristic, however, is not the absolute placement on the continuum so much as the *direction* in which structure appears to be moving at any given moment. It is this relative sense in which the term will be employed in most of the book. For theoretical purposes, however, it will be necessary at times to abstract out structure and talk in terms of absolutes for the ease of exposition.

in the office of the president or, at the very least, centralization through powerful appropriations and budget committees. Such preferences prevail to this day.[6] Second, it provided for a strong structuralist orientation in studying budgeting. As with so much of the reform movement, budget reformers assumed that justice was equated with proper rules, procedures, and structures. The ongoing attempts to alter budgetary structure led to a formal, institutional, and structural orientation to budgeting that was deemphasized in the coming behavioral revolution, but which has been reactivated in recent years.

BEHAVIORAL QUESTIONS ABOUT BUDGETING

The second main stream of the budgetary literature arose as a reaction to reformism through a deemphasis of the normative – although such concerns have never been completely excised – and by studying budgetary politics on its own terms. Behavioralism thus turned away from the formal budgetary questions toward behavioral ones.

In the 1940s classical organization theory, which undergirded reformist writings, came under persistent attack. Herbert Simon led the way by arguing that the principles of administration set down by classical organization theory were truisms – "proverbs" – and his textbook on public administration broke ground by putting politics, not "neutral" management principles, at the analytical center of public administration (Simon 1950, 1957). The attack on classical organization theory's specific answer to budgetary politics was severe, and also owed much to Simon.

Political scientists attacked the reformers' centralization assumptions by applying the advances of the infant behavioral sciences, arguing that decentralization was a natural response to the limited human capacity to process large amounts of complex data. The infusion of politics into budgeting was also taken to be a natural way of adapting to complexity; it was through repeated playing of the budget game that budgetary actors learned about budgeting and about each other, and managed to handle a potentially overwhelming task (Lindblom 1959; Wildavsky 1964).

The first attempt to apply principles of behavioral science to budgeting led to the founding of the *incrementalist* school. Incremental behavior – which here Wildavsky defined as the practice of making small changes to an existing budgetary base – occurs because people are uncertain about what the consequences of policy change will be (Wildavsky 1964, 13–16). Small, incremental changes are made so that if the results are un-

---

6 A recent expression of this centralization preference is Shepsle (1984). An interesting series of counters to this conventional centralization preference can be seen in Fisher (1984, 1985).

18

desirable, policymakers can easily alter course, minimizing detrimental effects; success can be gradually compounded, creating major long-term changes out of many minor short-term adjustments.

The *politics* of the budgetary process occurs as participants along the way – bureau chief, Office of Management and Budget (OMB) budget examiner, members of the House Appropriations Committee (HAC), the House rank-and-file, and the like – adjusted their behavior in response to the behavior of those with which they interact. Over a long period of time budget participants develop a set of expectations about one another. That is, not only does everyone play a distinct budgetary role, everyone knows everyone else's lines, and responds accordingly. For example, agencies and the OMB assume that the HAC cuts budgets, so they pad; the HAC assumes the OMB pads and that the House will add, so they cut; the House assumes the HAC has cut too much, so they add; and so forth. All along, each actor is seeking to produce a policy outcome favorable to his or her position, and no other – "Where you stand depends on where you sit." There are elements of a game in this, but more importantly, a good number of potentially overwhelming decisions and interactions are handled in small increments by all actors pursuing narrow personal or institutional goals and interests.

The same phenomena – mutually adjusting budgetary behavior and incrementalism – were explored in Richard Fenno's classic *Power of the Purse* (1966). Fenno's theoretical tack took off from mainstream sociology, but Fenno's conclusions are almost identical to Wildavsky's. Fenno's prime interest was to understand the House Appropriations Committee: how it integrated itself internally and how it responded to its environment. Fenno's chief question was: How does the HAC balance the internal desires to cut budgets, thus establishing its appropriation power, with the higher spending desires of the rest of the House? Too heavy an emphasis on one side would lead to a loss of prestige, while emphasis on the other would result in House sanctions against the Appropriations Committee. It was the tension between internal institutional desires and environmental demands that explained so much of the HAC's decision process and outputs.

The behavioral literature had an important impact on our understanding of budgetary politics in two ways. First, it prompted scholars to concentrate on the mutually adjusting behavior of individuals who were members of groups that were not experiencing immediate crises of legitimacy.[7] Second, the concentration on mutually adjusting behavior led

---

7 Fenno's HAC *was* concerned with balancing its role as guardian of the purse with the constraint of not harming programs. Thus, there was an underlying concern with legitimation. The point here, though, is that the HAC had found a set of stable

scholars to deemphasize the extent to which structure shaped the decisions that politicians made. These research tendencies arose because budgetary behavioralism emerged during a period when the concern over structure was relatively tranquil. The budgetary regime of the 1950s and early 1960s was essentially centralized, so that the normative outrage of scholars was not aroused as it had been in the 1910s. And, the centralized regime existed in a Congress effectively controlled by conservatives, so for the time being there were few serious institutional challenges to centralization. Thus, what scholars saw was stability. The turmoil in congressional structure that followed in the late 1960s and 1970s changed the extent to which scholars took the exogenous effects of the status quo budgetary regime for granted and reawakened dormant questions about how Congress decides to decide.

THE REEMERGENCE OF STRUCTURE AS A CONSIDERATION

The great electoral and societal changes that overtook Congress in the late 1960s and early 1970s reverberated throughout congressional life. Many of these changes were reflected in the budgetary process and in its outputs. Spending levels and priorities changed, generational turnover infused the institution with new political priorities, new MCs took the place of old in positions of authority, and the growth of entitlements severely reduced the institutional prerogatives of the previously centralized appropriations regime. Major policy changes and efforts to reform the budgetary process naturally attracted the attention of political scientists.

The fact that Congress once again began to change budgetary structure forced political scientists to alter their orientation in studying congressional budgeting. As soon as incrementalism was established as hegemonic budgetary theory, Congress began to act in many nonincremental ways. Thus, attention shifted away from studying decisions made in legitimated structures to asking questions about the nature of those structures, including: From where does legitimacy arise? How and why are budgetary regimes destabilized? What factors mold the development of new structures? How do MCs adapt to radical shifts of budgetary regimes?

The amount of paper used to describe budgetary changes after 1974 must have required the destruction of a small forest. Almost all attention was focused on the passage and implementation of the CBICA.[8] By far

solutions to this balancing act that were altered on the margin with each transaction with the environment; legitimation was a secondary, not an ongoing, concern.

8 The literature on the 1974 CBICA is enormous. Among the best of the literature is contained in Rudder (1978, 1985), Ellwood and Thurber (1977, 1981), Wil-

the most comprehensive and most influential treatment of the 1974 act was Allen Schick's *Congress and Money* (1980).

What is surprising after over a decade of operation under the CBICA is that we still know very little theoretically about why Congress reforms budgetary structure or why it chooses the structures it does. Thanks to the rich description that Schick and others have left us, we have a good idea about the explanation for one particular reform. But neither have old theoretical ideas been brought to bear to explain these changes, nor have new ones been developed to take their place. And the tremendous attention paid to studying one case of reform can only indirectly be useful in developing a general reform theory.

Thus, the development of a budget reform theory is still nascent, as is the unified explanation of budgetary politics over the past century. There is hope, however, for developing a comprehensive theory of budget reform, by building on the existing theoretical traditions (e.g., reformism and behavioralism), utilizing our descriptive knowledge about Congress as a dynamic institution, and expanding the historical scope of our research enterprise.

A comprehensive theory of budget reform must consist of three major components. First, it must explain the origin of individual preferences across conceivable structural arrangements. Second, it must specify the mechanism through which the constellation of individual preferences is transformed into the collective choice to change structure. Finally, it must specify the environment in which legislators act and choose and the constraints that help to govern the process of choice and decision. These elements are the focus of the next section.

TOWARD A THEORY OF BUDGETARY STRUCTURE

The dynamic unfolding of congressional budgetary structure can be explained by beginning with the assumption that MCs are rational, goal-oriented politicians. That I begin with assumptions about rationality and goal pursuit should not surprise anyone who has read the congressional literature of the 1970s and 1980s.[9] But there is more to explaining Con-

davsky (1979, chap. 7), Schick (1981), and Shepsle (1984). The three standard book-length treatments are Havemann (1978), LeLoup (1980), and Schick (1980).

9 Mayhew certainly deserves credit for bringing congressional scholars firmly into the rational choice school, with his *Congress: The Electoral Connection* (1974). Mayhew's theoretical insights primarily owe themselves to the earlier work concerning interest group formation advanced in Olson (1965). Other relevant foundational works in the social choice paradigm relevant to Congress include Downs (1957), Luce and Raiffa (1957), Riker (1962), and Buchanan and Tullock (1962). For reviews of this literature as it relates to Congress, see Ferejohn and Fiorina (1975), Sinclair (1983), Shepsle (1985), and Panning (1985).

gress than simply saying that MCs are single-minded reelection seekers.[10] Three basic components are required in order to build any purposive behavior theory of congressional activity that is meant to be applied in a rich way: (1) the nature of the goals of relevant individuals, (2) the nature of the technology through which the goals are pursued, and (3) the nature of the constraints faced by the relevant actors in achieving those goals. In the case of budgetary structure, the *goals* ultimately concern reelection and career advancement, the *technology* is the budgetary process itself, and the *constraints* are primarily defined by the institution of Congress that MCs find themselves in at any moment.[11]

The rest of this chapter specifies my theoretical assumptions about how goals, technology, and constraints have interacted in the development of the congressional budgetary process. This theoretical development proceeds through the justification of five assumptions that seem key to explaining why the congressional budgetary process has emerged as it has: (1) Budget reforms have been instruments and symbols of substantive policy change; (2) congressional behavior is fundamentally driven by the requirements of the fragmented American electoral system; (3) budgeting inherently involves conflict between the demands of the whole and those of the parts; (4) budget reform politics is constrained by the nature of the ongoing institution itself; and (5) congressional budget reform is affected by the separation of powers and the necessity to deal with an executive branch that is "wholly other."

Structure and substance

The relationship between budgetary structures and outcomes frequently seems so obvious that it goes unexamined. Yet by assuming (1) that the type of structure one has materially affects probable outcomes and (2) that politicians go about changing structures in order to change substance, we are first of all making structural decisions explicitly political and, second, relegating to secondary theoretical status other reform moti-

---

10 There may be questions at the outset about applying a theory to nineteenth-century congressional behavior that assumes reelection seeking. This issue is directly treated in the following chapter.

11 It should be clear that the theory of budgetary structure is a special case of the general theory of legislative structure. In the theory-generating process here I have confined myself to the specific case, rather than to the general, simply to make the following discussion more manageable and to the point of the historical data explored later. Developing either a general theory or a specific theory for another broad area of congressional activity (such as substantive legislation) would involve changing the specifications about the nature of the technology. In all cases of structural politics, both the nature of the goals and the constraints remain the same.

vations, such as personal animosities. Thus, our first assumption is nontrivial.

Because the assertion that "structure matters" has a certain face validity, it need not be explored too extensively.[12] Yet if we assume that reform occurs for substantive reasons, we must know why legislators might prefer structural change to the more direct route of changing policy itself.

The first reason legislators might prefer a structural route is that policy majorities in Congress are ephemeral by nature. Even if an overwhelming majority exists to change budgetary outcomes in one Congress, there is no guarantee that the majority will last past the next election. In fact, if there is a guarantee, it is that the majority will not last. Thus, a structural change on the heels of a major concurrent policy shift can serve to entrench policy outcomes long after policy majorities have vanished. For example, the budget reforms enacted between 1919 and 1921 to effect postwar retrenchment and frugality have had repercussions for over fifty years of budgeting. Even after the frugality mood of the 1910s and 1920s had passed, the appropriations process continued to exert a conservative influence that directly conflicted with occasional liberal congressional majorities. Many balanced budget activists have justified their support for the constitutional amendment route against the statutory one precisely because they want to lock in this constraint against new high-spending policy majorities that might be elected to future Congresses.[13]

Second, the symbolic uses of structural reform are not to be overlooked. Even if there is widespread consensus to alter budgetary policy outputs one way or another, actually effecting change typically requires hundreds or thousands of low-visibility decisions. Reform can be a sym-

---

12 Inquiring into the effects of structural arrangements has been given new life in recent years by formal modelers of the legislative process, who have followed up on Gordon Tullock's question of "why so much stability" in legislative decisions? Tullock's question was prompted by the fact that early work on pure majority rule voting models predicted tremendous instability, cycling, and chaos. The most persuasive answer to Tullock's question has been associated with Shepsle and Weingast, whose answer consists of the concept "structure-induced equilibria." They and others demonstrate how common legislative devices, such as committees and floor amendment rules, restrict the domains of possible legislative outcomes, leading to greater stability than originally predicted (Shepsle and Weingast 1981; Shepsle 1986). The following discussion draws a good deal of inspiration from the Shepsle-Weingast tradition, but proceeds much less formally (mathematically) than the literature that they have spawned.

13 The Reagan policy of restricting revenues through massive tax cuts in 1981 has frequently been interpreted in this manner. Even if the consequence was not fully foreseen at the beginning, the reality of stagnant federal revenues brought about by the 1981 tax cut will have the effect of restricting the size of federal spending long after Ronald Reagan has left office.

bol to constituents of the general direction their MC has chosen to take and serve to publicize the larger pattern of policy change that legislators are supporting.

By concentrating here on the policy origins of structure, I am relegating to secondary status other common explanations for why reforms typically occur. The most common alternative explanations for reform are the *functional* and the *personal.*

Functionalist explanations of structural reform as they have been applied to Congress assume a general search for functional congruence between the budgetary task and budgetary structure.[14] That is, it is sometimes argued that the search for congressional reform occurs because Congress is trying to meet the challenge of new policy demands more effectively. Such explanations generally hold that the purpose of congressional reform is to bring structure into congruence with pressing budgetary problems. Whenever Congress confronts a new budgetary problem, it reaches into its bag of appropriate solutions and adapts accordingly. For instance, problems brought on by recession and war are solved by centralization; troubles created by spending complexity bring on subcommittees and larger staffs.

Under this type of explanation, Congress is a cipher responding to environmental problems. While it is clear that certain budgetary "problems" are widely acknowledged to exist and that reform movements typically coincide with the appearance of these problems, functionalist explanations go too far in assuming that Congress is continually trying to achieve an optimal match between pressing problems and structures. They therefore imply degrees of synopticism and unity of purpose that are totally alien to the congressional environment. And, functionalist explanations ignore the genesis of the search for congruence in the first place.

I deal with the functionalist explanation by unpacking the assumptions lying therein and subsuming them into the goals of MCs and the constraints facing them. To the extent that the search for optimal structures serves a function, it is as a tool for more direct political goals, for example, reelection and constituency satisfaction. To the extent that budgetary problems affect reform, they do so as a constraint on the pursuit of purely individual goals. Both of these statements will be explored in depth.

---

14 "Functionalism" is another slippery term in social science, with many connotations (see Cancian 1968; Levy 1968). Functionalism as applied to American legislative behavior, and budgeting in particular, has been less grand than the classical applications of Weber, Parsons, and Durkheim. By functionalism, I am simply referring to that class of explanation that assumes certain functions "must" be performed by Congress and that MCs consciously search out the optimal solution for performing those necessary activities.

Personal explanations are more appealing than the functional because personal factors loom large upon an examination of any body of political elites. Still, we should not let our fascination with interesting political characters interfere with our primary interest – explaining reform over time. An explanation of structural change over decades or centuries must necessarily look beyond specific personalities in order to be generalizable and predictive.

This is not to say that personalities are trivial – they are not. But given everything else that prods reform along, personalities are rarely primary. Key budget reform dynamics recur regardless of who the individual players are at any given time. Personalistic factors determine characteristic details of particular reforms, but they rarely determine whether the time is ripe for reform. Thus, saying that individuals shape the details of reform that arise out of predictable exogenous events is different from saying that reform occurs primarily due to the jealousies, rivalries, and alliances that periodically (and randomly) arise in Congress.

Federalism and its structural implications

Students of American politics have known for some time that the mechanism of federalism that arose in the Constitution of 1787 was the product of both political theory and expediency. The theory behind federalism emphasized the ability of dispersed, overlapping sovereign entities to dissipate destructive political energies. The expediency behind American constitutional federalism arose out of the "Great Compromise" and the desire to create a stronger national government that would nevertheless be supported by enough small state legislatures to ensure ratification. Regardless of *why* the United States has federalism, the effect of federalism on Congress has been to fragment the political interests of its members, hindering mutual action in the chamber and undermining the bases for coherent policy formation and implementation generally associated with most capitalist parliamentary systems.

Placing the locus of congressional representation in the states has encouraged MCs to pursue the interests of the localities they were elected to represent rather than to conceive of the national interest more broadly. They are "delegates," not "trustees." The fragmentation engendered by federalism has not been overcome by the development of strong political parties. The ability of the parties to exert an independent influence on their members has paled in comparison to their European counterparts, even when the American parties have been at their strongest.[15] The ab-

---

15 Strong federalism does not always guarantee weak parties, as the Canadian case suggests. The persistence of liberalism in the United States also helps to keep

sence of a natural centralizing mechanism in the constitutional system has prompted American politicians to innovate over the past two centuries in order to create incentives for mutual action and support at the national level. But these contrivances have fallen significantly short of creating a sense of unified political purpose in Congress.⌡

The first major "solution" for fragmentation in the federal government was the spoils system, which helped to maintain the strength of parties from the Jacksonian Era to the Age of Reform (Skowronek 1982). Patronage was an important element in keeping the parties fairly unified, especially following the Civil War. Yet even in this partisan era, the fragmenting pull of constituents was great. As the historian Henry Jones Ford, a contemporary observer, wrote:

> The House of Representatives takes its character from the fact that it represents, not the nation, but the districts into which the nation is divided.... The consequence is that, when the House is not acting under party mandate, it is a scuffle of local interests in which every member must take his part under penalty of losing his seat. (Ford 1898, 239)

As Ford implies, the fate equal to death for MCs is electoral defeat. In order to pursue any higher policy goal, legislators must gain admission to the legislature through elections. Election, thus political life, comes through pleasing parochial voters. This basic local orientation of congressional elections obtained in the nineteenth century as it has in the twentieth, even though the structure of localism has altered over time. In more recent years it has been popular to conceive of this election-seeking enterprise as if MCs were "single-minded seekers of reelection" (Mayhew 1974, 5). Although the electoral connection will not explain all congressional behavior, or even perhaps most of it, the structure of electoral expediencies has explained more behavior than other alternatives. Because election looms so large to politicians practically, and to all Democrats normatively, the consequences of election are the natural starting point for theorizing.

In order to understand how electoral politics fundamentally affects congressional behavior, one must begin with the requirements for reelection. Beginning with these requirements is important because merely noting that members are "single-minded seekers of reelection" does not automatically lead to specific conclusions about congressional behavior; it especially does not lead directly to a conclusion that structure will tend

---

national conceptualizations of the public interest of secondary importance (Hartz 1955). Liberalism also undergirds the belief that legislators should represent "people with interests" rather than act for "unattached interests" (Pitkin 1967). Finally, the strong contrast between the American and Westminster party models may be diminishing (Cain, Ferejohn, and Fiorina 1987).

toward decentralization. For instance, members of the British Parliament (MPs), no less than members of the U.S. Congress, prefer reelection; yet each set of legislators exhibit important and well-known differences in the ways they structure themselves and in how they behave. As the electoral landscape has changed in Britain in recent years, so too has the parliamentary behavior of MPs as a consequence (Cain, Ferejohn, and Fiorina 1987).

The chief difference between the U.S. Congress and most parliamentary democracies is the way the respective constitutions, written and unwritten, structure electoral incentives. In most parliaments, party officials typically control future electoral chances by controlling nominations. While American politicians may create ad hoc centralizing mechanisms, as the patronage-based party system was in the nineteenth century, those mechanisms are necessarily fragile and are predicated on being able to affect local electoral conditions. Thus, congressional electoral attentions have been directed away from the center and national concerns back to the individual constituencies and parochial issues.

The tendency of the American electoral system to accentuate the local has a direct impact on the types of policies MCs tend to pursue. The reelection chances of MCs are enhanced to the extent they can convince their constituents that they (the constituents) are getting more from government than they are giving to it. Convincing constituents that their MC is working diligently on their behalf involves working to "bring home the bacon" and then claiming credit for the pork (Mayhew 1974, 52–61).[16] But, even if a member is not fully successful in pursuing the district's interests in Congress, all is not lost. This is because members are able to put a less negative face on failure, either through demonstrating eternal vigilance to their districts' interests or through blaming failure on other MCs. In any case, members are reelected for the *perception* that they are working hard to bring their constituents the public goods most of interest to them. In other words:

We do not ordinarily think of losses as being politically harmful. We can all point to a good many instances in which congressmen seem to have gotten into trouble by being on the *wrong* side in a roll call vote, but who can think of one where a member got into trouble by being on the *losing* side? ... That the pressure to win is only modest is an enormously important fact of life in Congress and

16 In this discussion I shall usually be speaking in terms of the pursuit of tangible rewards as the basis for congressional activity and reelection. I focus on tangible goods simply for clarity of discussion and because budgeting, more than other policy areas, involves questions of tangibles. In Mayhew's terms, this means focusing on "credit claiming." Certainly many of the fundamental dynamics seen in budgeting recur in other policy arenas that are concerned with intangibles, and thus apply to "position taking."

doubtless in assemblies generally. If members had to win all the time, they would tear each other to shreds. (Mayhew 1974, 118–119, emphasis in original)

We can extend this discussion and examine the relationship between members and constituency policy preferences, and how that relationship can generate specific structural preferences, by simplifying the discussion for a moment to cost-benefit terms. Consider a situation where the government produces one good that is paid for through general taxation. At a minimum, the individual MC should expect to be punished electorally if total taxes imposed on his or her constituents exceed the benefits they receive. Thus, if constituents and the member have full knowledge of these benefits and taxes, we would expect the member to try to make sure that the benefits that flow into the district exceed the taxes that flow out: (benefits − taxes) > 0.[17] Let us term the situation where benefits exceed taxes the district's "social profit."

Even creating a net social profit for one's constituents is not necessarily enough to ensure reelection because a challenger could come along and argue that the profit, while positive, could be higher than it currently is, and that the challenger would provide a higher social profit if the incumbent were turned out of office. Thus, if all governmental costs and benefits were perfectly known to citizens and controllable by politicians, we would expect each individual incumbent MC to try to maximize the social profit of his or her district in order to maximize the chance of reelection and to minimize the chance that a challenger might arise.

In this simple, state-of-nature example, we can see how a member's most preferred mix of costs and benefits would be the allocation of all governmental benefits to his or her own district along with the distribution of all costs to all other districts. This situation, in which district benefits are very large and taxes are zero, would give the member the maximum chance of reelection. However, in a multimember legislature there is no way that this situation could occur without our member becoming a dictator. But there are ways, given the constraints imposed by other members' preferences, to come closer to this most preferred allocation of public goods.

The classic manner of maximizing net benefits to constituents under a

---

17 Of course, constituents and MCs *do not* have full knowledge of benefits and taxes, in part because of the sheer difficulty of getting such information in the first place. But also, information about taxes and benefits is provided through a political process in which incentives exist to manipulate "objective" information for partisan gain. The end result is that most often politicians and constituents act on the basis of *perceived* costs and benefits. Considering the process through which these perceptions emerge is another study in itself. The key elements of the budget reform process can be fruitfully explored by assuming perfect information for the moment.

majority rule constraint is through the creation of a minimum winning coalition (MWC), where $(N/2) + 1$ of the legislators vote their districts all public goods and tax only the $(N/2) - 1$ districts of the losing coalition (N being even). Of course, we can also show that MWC arrangements are inherently unstable since members of the losing coalition at time t could bid away a few members of the MWC at time $t + 1$, creating a series of cyclical majorities. These cyclical majorities, in turn, make the policymaking process a rocky road for each MC, as he or she is able to bring home substantial positive net benefits half the time while having to endure substantial negative net benefits the other half. The aversion to weathering alternating booms and busts is sharpened given the "negativity bias" in the perception of costs and benefits: Legislators will be punished more severely during lean years than they will be rewarded in fat ones (Weaver 1986). Therefore, MCs have a strong interest in finding institutional ways out of the boom and bust cycles generated by the dynamics of minimum winning coalitions.

There is a widely recognized solution to the cycles created by MWCs – universalism. Universalism can be defined as the practice of allocating spending and taxing based on egalitarian criteria. All districts pay approximately equal taxes and receive equitable, if not equal, benefits. Under universalism "there are no losers ... though some winners do considerably better than others" (Arnold 1979, 12–13). The drive to enact and enforce universalism is said to come from the risk aversion of legislators. "Legislators who regularly seek reelection generally prefer bringing home a modest amount of bacon each year to acquiring nothing some years and subsequently facing their opponents' charges of powerlessness" (Arnold 1979, 12). Hence, under universalism, social profits are not maximized, but maximum social deficits are minimized.

The significance of the universalism that arises due to logrolling for building structures is clear when we move away from the simple model and its assumption that government provides only one good. As soon as the government provides more than just roads (say) and begins to produce goods that widely vary in their immediate utility to different types of geographic constituencies – for example, farm price supports, dams, urban renewal projects, and money for civil rights enforcement – the road is open to asymmetries of spending and structural preferences among members of Congress. A legislator from a farm state has no real interest in sharing an equal share of urban renewal funds, just as an urban legislator has little interest in sharing equally in crop price supports. Rather, rational legislators pursue only those goods that would most benefit their constituents. The farmer and city dweller will trade support for each other's programs. The farmer will give up his fair share of urban renewal in return for the urbanite's fair share of agricultural programs.

And the urbanite will trade her fair share of agricultural programs for more urban renewal. Thus, within the broader assumption that districts overall should be treated equitably (i.e., universalism), some districts receive more of some goods and less of others. It is through this asymmetry of demand for government programs that legislator spending preferences help to determine legislator structural preferences.

The structural result of universalism and logrolling is the privatization of particular governmental goods by interested (i.e., "high demand") members of the legislature. Legislators with keen interests in a particular program will tend to dominate the committees and other agenda control mechanisms of policy planning in order to create the most benign environment for the development of their most cherished programs. For instance, farm-state legislators will want to decide among themselves how much spending on price supports will be recommended before they begin negotiating with the urbanites. And they will also want to have an upper hand in deciding the opening bargaining moves around those issues ancillary to aggregate spending, such as questions of geographic and programmatic allocation, mixes of technologies, and the weights applied to long- and short-range goals. The converse will hold for the urbanites in their dealings with the farmers.

The upshot in this example is that the farmers will prefer the creation of a farm committee, dominated by farmers, to oversee farm programs. In general, members whose constituents have particular interests will prefer the creation of committees that give them and like-minded legislators an advantage in setting the agenda for their favorite programs. Therefore, geographic electoral fragmentation leads to policy preference fragmentation, which ultimately engenders congressional preferences for structural fragmentation.

The practical application of these general comments about policy universalism is difficult to miss in even the most cursory of glances at Congress. Although there are a few broad policy committees in both houses, such as the appropriations and taxing committees, most committees are created for the oversight of particular programs, and the members and leaders of those committees have intense prior interests in the activities overseen by those committees. Urbanites have dominated the banking and currency committees over time, just as farmers have dominated the agriculture committees and lawyers the judiciary committees.[18] Even the

---

18 On self-selection, see Shepsle (1978). This tendency to self-select has also shown up in recent research on the nineteenth-century Congress. For instance, Wilson (1986a,b) has shown that members of the Rivers and Harbors Committee in the past century were drawn from members who represented districts that *already* received above-average water project allocations. That is, the causal arrow ran

broad policy committees have not been immune to policy parochialism and particularism, though the levels of particularism have been somewhat muted. The special attention paid to the oil depletion allowance by members of the Ways and Means and Finance committees has been legion, for instance. And members of the appropriations committees have been known to help channel added spending to their districts, though to lesser degrees than their counterparts on legislative committees.

Thus, the decentralized electoral system drives legislators to emphasize local responsiveness over the general interest. The emphasis on particular interests ultimately leads to programmatic universalism. And programmatic universalism leads to a preference for fragmentation of spending structure.

Theories of congressional structure typically stop here with the structural fragmentation engendered by the demands of electoral fragmentation. But, when we add the effects of the four other theoretical assumptions raised at the beginning of this section, conclusions about the inevitability of fragmentation become less clear.

Budgeting and the case of the whole against the parts

The ability of MCs to get what they want structurally, and therefore substantively, is partially determined by the nature of budgeting itself. Budgeting as a whole can be thought of as the confluence of two problems: distributional and aggregational. The *distributional* problem refers to the fact that spending decisions are answers to questions about who gets what.[19] The *aggregational* problem concerns what happens when all of the budgetary pieces are added together. This latter problem is directly derived from Allen Schick's well-known characterization of the distributional and aggregational problems as that of the "parts against the whole."[20]

The previous section discussed the genesis of the distributional prob-

from constituency interest (measured by existing spending levels) to committee membership, but not vice versa.

19 One must be careful not to characterize the distributional problem as one of "carving up the pieces of the budgetary pie," although such an analogy is frequently a convenient shorthand. As I suggested in the previous section, if budgeting is generally bottom-up in origin, the process will not resemble the carving up of anything; it will resemble the adding together of disjointed pieces. Budgeting thus resembles less the slicing of a pie than the mythical construction of a horse by a committee, which yields a camel.

20 Schick (1980) sets the "war" of the whole against the parts as the engine that drove reform in 1974. Here, I treat it as a constraint on the reelection engine that generally drives congressional politics.

lem. Because MCs are electorally rewarded for the quality of their advocacy for their own constituencies, and not for the quality of their advocacy for the nation as a whole, there are strong forces pushing budgeting toward a bottom-up process. Congressional budgetary practice over the years, even when there have been strong control mechanisms, has tended to arrive at aggregate spending decisions by passing appropriations bills seriatim and then adding them up at the end, and to consider taxing separately from spending altogether.

The bottom-up tendency of congressional spending decisionmaking conflicts directly with the other inherent property of budgeting – its top-down quality. "While legislative norms propel Congress toward the fragmentation of power, budgeting invites the concentration of power. Budgeting necessarily involves the pulling together of disparate interests and perspectives in a reasonably comprehensive and consistent decisional process. Budgeting demands attention to the relationship of the parts and the whole, to the linkage of tax and spending policies, as well as to the priorities accorded to the competing claims for public resources" (Schick 1980, 6).

The belief that spending and taxing should be properly balanced has been embodied in the spending ideologies that have guided the general behavior of representatives for the past two centuries. The more enduring spending ideology is the pre-Keynesian belief that budgets should always be balanced – a balanced budget is a moral budget. But even the upstart Keynesianism did not deny that spending and taxing should be coordinated, just that balanced budgets were good per se. The move from *budget policy* to *fiscal policy* between 1930 and 1965 involved a redefinition of the proper relationship between spending and taxing, but not a denial of the utility of budget balancing under certain predefined conditions.

The difficulty with meeting the normative requirement that spending and taxing be somehow coordinated is that coordination is not automatic in the bottom-up budgeting exercise that MCs most prefer. Although it is widely recognized that spending and taxing totals must be coordinated, control mechanisms clash head on with universalistic impulses. Control is difficult to obtain because it requires spending cuts and revenue increases, both of which bear negatively on the electoral reward structure facing individual MCs.

Yet MCs do control themselves. Why? MCs agree to constrain universalism because the nature of the aggregational problem provides positive and negative incentives for support of budget control. The strength of these incentives will rarely match that which accompanies distributing benefits to constituents; but the incentives will always be present, even if in microscopic amounts.

Spillover effects and the particular interest in the public interest. Some inducements to control the level of budgetary fragmentation and privatization spring from the existence of spillover effects. Although it is convenient to think of government spending as having effects only in those districts where money is spent, in fact real programs have costs and benefits that spill over into adjacent districts, and ultimately the effects of all individual projects and programs aggregate into effects on the entire macroeconomy. A dam, for instance, benefits citizens for miles around, even those from other congressional districts, and imposes costs on many others, most obviously those up- and downstream. A program that engages in the construction of dozens or hundreds of dams not only affects the livelihoods of the residents of the districts in which the dams are built and the thousands who live up- and downstream, but also affects the overall health of the macroeconomy. As government does more and programs expand, it becomes more likely that the *aggregate* consequences of all federal spending will materially affect the well-being of millions of people, as the more direct consequences of individual programs become more difficult to contain strictly locally.

Because the aggregate consequences of constituency service can be so dysfunctional for the health of the macroeconomy, MCs have a "particular interest in the public interest." Members know that unless a certain minimum level of fiscal health is maintained, the financial underpinnings of the universalism on which they so depend will be destroyed. As the time horizons of legislators expand, and they have varied over time, it is more likely that legislators will support at least the minimum level of budgetary control and coordination necessary to allow them to live to spend another day (Mayhew 1974, 145–146).[21]

Gaining this level of control is not easy, of course. Mayhew points out that the provision of budgetary control runs into classic public goods problems and that budget control will generally be underprovided in Congress. This is true enough. But, as Mayhew also points out, most members have substantial resources with which to purchase control from a small group of members who serve on "control committees." These resources include added power, prestige, and the ability to divert an added

---

21 The issue of the time horizon of MCs has particular bearing on the relative weight MCs put on the aggregate consequences of their actions. An MC who has no interest in making national politics a career will weigh long-term consequences less heavily than an MC who has made national politics a career. To this extent, ceteris paribus, modern MCs should be more "responsible" than nineteenth-century MCs. And, indeed, one consequence of increased seniority around the turn of the century may have been the willingness to take seriously efforts to centralize the budgetary process in the 1910s.

increment of federal spending to constituencies of the members of the control committees. Olson also noted that many public goods problems could be overcome by the operation of small group dynamics (Olson 1965, chap. 2). It is an empirical question whether the House and Senate can be considered Olsonian small groups. If they can, then the social pressures defining the "norms" and "folkways" of the two chambers might also operate to pressure some members into taking seats on control committees and other positions of control, such as party leadership.

In a related vein, political elites – legislators included – generally have more broadly conceived views of what constitutes the public interest than do most citizens, and thus are likely to take national concerns into account in making their decisions.[22] The local orientation of MCs is substantial, but not total. The awareness of the broader national interest is heightened for MCs by their working environment, in which they are in the midst of the clash of local interests. It would be a dullard indeed who continually interacted with 534 aggressive, opinionated, and successful people from all over the country and did not develop a feel for the problems that beset the nation generally. The national interest that is conceived of by any given MC is no doubt filtered through a localistic lens. Nevertheless, there is an understanding of larger national problems within the cognitive maps of individual MCs, and thus the basis exists for developing some structural solutions that bring about a degree of budgetary control.

Another factor that may increase the willingness of rational MCs to take into account aggregate budgetary conditions is the tendency of constituents to be sociotropic. That is, citizens show a surprising tendency to judge the government's handling of the economy based on perceptions of the public good, in addition to their own direct, personal experience with the economy. Again, perceptions of the national interest are undoubtedly filtered through localistic lenses. Nevertheless, the fact that constituents consciously try to evaluate the effectiveness of government simultaneously on two levels, the private and the public, provides a basis for MCs to be able to sacrifice short-range localistic gains for long-range rational economic health without being *inevitably* punished at the polls (Kinder and Kiewiet 1981).

I want to make it clear at this point that the impulses MCs might have toward supporting action congruent with the national interest do not have to derive from altruism. Rational MCs have several reasons to choose the long term and national over the short term and local. But the frequency with which the national and long term *dominate* the parochial and short term are rare. Because budgetary decisions are being made

---

22 Stouffer (1966) still remains the classic work in the comparison of political attitudes of American elites and masses on general policy questions.

continually, however, even rare events can occur with some regularity. Given institutional predispositions toward inertia, these rare bits of national concern can get enacted into law and remain in effect for a long period of time.

Thus, the aggregational and distributional problems exist in continual tension, and therefore preferences for centralization and fragmentation must also exist in continual tension within each MC. Because parochial pressures are generally more salient to MCs, the tension will typically be resolved in favor of universalism and thus in favor of fragmentation. But, the nature of the tension is dynamic and that dynamism brings opportunities for centralizing preferences to become ascendant.

Economic crisis and demands for centralization. Students of organizations have long noted that the options of disjointed versus coordinated decisionmaking are useful for organizational survival under different conditions. The superior functional utility of centralization and coordination has been conceded, even by devout incrementalists, under conditions such as rapid changes in an organization's environment, overwhelming concern with a few pressing problems, situations involving a long series of weak causal relationships that have a strong cumulative effect, and resource scarcity (Lustick 1980). The more that any of these conditions obtains in the congressional budgetary environment, the more likely it is that the fragmentation and centralization tensions will be resolved in favor of centralization.

The factors making centralization a rational structural choice are all too familiar in budgeting. Rapid environmental changes are attendant to major international crises, such as wars. The federal response to the OPEC oil embargo is an example of a system accustomed to handling many low-intensity conflicts being overwhelmed by a single high-intensity disruption in such a way as to affect budgeting. The problems of managing the cumulative effects of complex, interrelated processes are substantial in all economic planning. And resources allocated to the national government frequently become scarce during deep recessions or budget deficits. Thus, centralization is more likely to present itself as the rationally strategic structural choice under conditions such as wars, international trade difficulties, increasing economic interdependence, recession, and deficits. Under these conditions, legislators will be more likely to view centralization as electorally rational.

The conclusion that centralization is individually rational under "crisis" conditions may also be reinforced by the electoral process. MCs are more likely to centralize in response to economic crises because voters tend to vote retrospectively based in part on the condition of the macroeconomy. Centralization is widely believed to promise a better opportunity for improvement of an economy under crisis than does fragmentation. And even if centralization has an effect on the crisis only over the long run, the fact that centralization was *supported* by members in the short run can serve the electorally useful purposes of symbolic politics and position taking. Thus, during economic crises MCs may support centralization in anticipation of negative electoral consequences if they do not.

But if MCs do not centralize right away in response to crisis, the dynamics of the electoral system may still work to produce structural coordination. Regardless of what legislators do during economic crises, there is still a great possibility that some incumbents, especially members of the president's party, will be turned out of office at the next election. It is likely that the new first-term members will have been elected on promises to address the economic crisis through (among other things) working to rationalize budgetary decisionmaking. The classes of new Republican House members who entered following the 1918 and 1920 elections could be considered to fall into this category. Thus, if MCs do not actually act to centralize at the beginning of an economic crisis, centralization may be subsequently facilitated through the infusion of new members into the legislature who were elected promising support for reform.

Thus, we see how the nature of the budgetary problem creates a structural tension that is resolved at any given moment, but that is never resolved for good. Because parochial concerns are more immediately felt in the electoral process than are national ones, we should expect fragmentation typically to prevail among MCs individually and collectively. But national pressures and crises do periodically impinge upon local concerns, and those are the times when centralization will be more preferred.

So far I have dealt with the purely exogenous factors that shape the structural preferences of MCs. It is now time to bring the institution of Congress into the calculus and specify how it alters the nature of the tension between fragmentation and centralization.

The interaction between member preferences and the ongoing institution

The inherent tension between localistic constituency service and nationalistic fiscal responsibility gets played out in an immensely complicated, vital institution: Congress. The central dynamics of structural politics that I have already specified – the drive to please local constituencies, the logic of substantive universalism, the establishment of structural fragmentation, and the utility of central coordination – are also shaped by the nature of the ongoing institution. Another layer of complexity must be added to the relatively simple dynamic tension between control and fragmentation.

The fact that struggles over structure are pursued in an existing institution, not in the state of nature, means that the simple calculus that ties the demands of local constituents and the national economy to an individual MC's structural preferences is also heavily influenced by perceptions about the existing power structure. Because a status quo structure vests interests in a given set of institutions and rules and creates institutional resources that can be mobilized to fight for or against structural change, rank-and-file MCs must add to their structural preference calculations perceptions about the institutional strength of the status quo before they proceed with any attempt to institute reform.

The two most salient institutional components in this regard are the committee and leadership systems. They are the most salient for two reasons. First, the committee and leadership systems are frequently the *targets* of reform proposals. The committee system is frequently assaulted head on through attacks on jurisdiction and membership. Leadership is rarely attacked frontally, but reformist attention to the rules that govern legislative consideration and committee appointments serves to define the discretion that party leaders have in pursuing independent policy directions. Second, the committee and leadership systems are frequently the *sources* of reform proposals and are often the primary sources of reform opposition. To understand the extent to which the committee and party systems mold the development of reform, we need to explore briefly (1) the costs and benefits these systems bring to rank-and-file members and (2) the resources these systems have to further and resist reform efforts.

Committee system: benefits. To an individual member, the existence of a committee system carries the benefits deriving from a division of labor: Members are able to focus their attention on a narrow range of issues, thus allowing the institution to function more expeditiously than if each member had to meticulously study each issue that confronted the legislature. The emergence of the standing committee system can be attributed directly to dissatisfaction with the cumbersome early congressional practice of considering legislation *first* in committee of the whole, *then* in select committees of detail (Sklandony 1985). Division of labor is also beneficial to members because it allows those not interested in certain subjects to direct their energies elsewhere. Thus, the most obvious benefits a committee system would have to rank-and-file members, considered at this basic level, are (1) the facilitation of the body's work and (2) the compartmentalization of work to allow those with the greatest interest to focus on a particular issue. Also of interest to members, though less

37

obvious to the outsider, are the services that committees can perform to build coalitions.

The provision of technical expertise through a division of labor has a long tradition in Congress that derives from the raw electoral incentive as well as from the fact that individual MCs benefit when the institution as a whole can hold its own against the executive branch. Technically expert committees are beneficial to all MCs because without them legislators would have a difficult time translating their localistic policy preferences into action. If members of Congress could not turn legislative posturing into some sort of tangible, visible outcome, future promises to constituents would ring false, and constituents would have little reason to believe their representatives' credit claiming (Fenno 1966, 1973; Mayhew 1974).

Not only do individual MCs have an interest in rewarding technical expertise to directly facilitate effective localistic spending, they also have an interest in doing so in order to maintain congressional strength against the president. This is not to say that Congress is a unified, anthropomorphic actor who is "jealous" of the chief executive. Rather, it is to say that there is a great potential for presidential and congressional policy preferences to clash, and MCs have an interest in prevailing in such clashes. As far as individual legislators are concerned, the president is the most powerful rival in the budget priority-setting game. Members assume that the president would want to turn the appropriations process to his own advantage, and that should he gain greater control over budgeting, their own political futures would be in the hands of someone else. Because the president formally has greater access to executive branch information and because the OMB serves as a powerful budgetary analyst on his behalf, individual MCs have reason to fear that the president will indeed gain great control over budgetary decisions that affect them directly (Wildavsky 1979, 35–42).[23] Because individual MCs fear that another politician (the president) may be in a position to manipulate spending for his – not their – advantage, they may also be interested in creating powerful centralized structures to develop expertise comparable to that of the executive branch. One of the most important ways of doing that is through the committee system.

The practice of sustaining technically expert committees to do battle against the executive has been demonstrated not only through the perpetuation of relatively stable subject-specific legislative committees over

---

23 Of course the OMB/BOB became a factor only after 1921. Still, the general point can be applied to budgeting before 1921 by noting that Congress has always had to rely on the executive branch for information to guide its decisions. To the extent that Congress can rival the executive branch in information, it can hope to direct agency behavior, rather than merely ratify executive branch preferences.

the years, but also through the practice begun by early Congresses of setting up committees specifically to investigate the executive departments. Such committees emerged as a consequence of congressional suspicion of executive power claims and have reached their greatest levels of activity during periods of split partisan control of government. The best known of this type of committee, though it represented an extreme excess of activity and deficit of expertise, was the Joint Committee on the Conduct of the [Civil] War (McConachie 1898; Smith and Deering 1984).

In addition to providing general benefits to MCs, the committee system allows members from areas with keen particular interests to pursue those interests. More will be said about this below. For the moment it is sufficient to note that a technically expert committee system that allows interested members to serve on relevant committees overcomes at least some motivational problems associated with getting members of the House to do the chamber's work.

In addition to enhancing expertise and allowing interested members to oversee programs of interest to their constituents, the committee system also carries an important function that is often overlooked: coalition building. To some extent, each committee can serve as an exchange forum for overcoming the fragmentation generated by localistic constituency pressures. Even expert decisions cannot be passed in Congress unless parts of the body can come together to engage in logrolling and police compliance with coalitional arrangements.

The paradox of the committee system is that even while it has the tendency to fragment authority within Congress, it can also serve to unify certain other elements that might otherwise be fragmented even further. Consider the following example. Assume for the moment a three-member legislature representing three regions of equal size, wealth, and so forth. All members are single-minded reelection seekers who act in the economic interest of their constituents. Also assume that any taxation to pay for the projects is divided evenly among the regions. Member A comes from the North and favors spending $15 to purchase public works projects for the North; B comes from the South and favors $15 of southern public works projects; C comes from the Midland, which was long ago developed and thus puts no value on adding any more public works to its region. Members A and B can get what they want if they trade their votes: A coalition of A + B beats C alone.

But also assume that the legislature is structured so that there are two public works committees and two public works bills, one for A's projects and one for B's. A logrolling arrangement in which A votes for B's projects and B for A's will result in a net gain of $5 each for A and B ($15 in benefits − $10 in taxes) and a $10 loss for C ($0 in benefits − $10 in taxes). But absent an enforcement mechanism, there could be problems in keeping this coalition together.

If the two public works bills are voted on sequentially – A's then B's – A and B could combine to vote to give A $15 of benefits, taxing A, B, and C each $5, creating net benefits of $(10, -5, -5)$ for A, B, and C, respectively, after round 1. Member A then could renege on the vote trade, vote with C to deny B its projects in round 2, and come out 5 units ahead: $(10, -5, -5)$ versus $(5, 5, -10)$.

Legislators realize this potential problem, of course, and usually avoid it in practice. But the scenario does have a probability greater than zero. The scenario has a greater-than-zero probability because the electoral benefits should such defection occur are often substantial and tempting. The necessity to keep fragile coalitions together is also important because the existence of a low-demand group like C is common in most legislatures. For instance, in the nineteenth century, one-quarter to one-third of the House typically voted to oppose *any* spending on internal improvements, citing extravagance, unconstitutionality, or both (see Table 3.5). A minority of this size can be especially troublesome when confronting the possibility of presidential veto.

The solution to the problem presented here is to *force* A and B to vote together by making a vote against A also a vote against B and vice versa. This can be achieved through a number of instruments including amendments, omnibus bills, and threats. Structurally, the way to do this is to create one public works committee that produces one public works bill. Thus, if A wants to vote against B, it must also deny itself funds.

Examples of this type of structural behavior arise in legislative as well as appropriations areas. One of the best examples is the coalition created by the placement of the food stamps program in the Agriculture Committee; this coalition has been fashioned by urban liberals who back crop supports in return for the support of food stamps by rural MCs (Ferejohn 1986). A centralized appropriations committee can provide the opportunity for coalition building within the confines of a structured environment. Limiting decisions to a small number of bills provides an opportunity to build coalitions around divisive areas. And because the coalition building process takes place in a smaller group than the entire chamber, retribution against broken promises can be swifter and more direct than such activity in the context of the entire chamber.

Committee system: costs. While committees provide the benefits of expertise, interest segmentation, and coalition building, the committee system also exacts costs from each rank-and-file member. These costs are primarily incurred by those not on particular committees and are derived from (1) agenda control and (2) substantive biases.

The cost of agenda control arises because committees generally have control over the pace of their work and substance of their outputs. Therefore they may choose to delay legislation not in accord with the overall committee preference. This could be seen as beneficial at an aggregate level in many cases, but to any member with a special interest in legislation that must be approved by a committee on which she or he does not serve, this represents a distinct cost in added organizing efforts. By having almost complete control over outputs, committees have strong procedural advantages when their legislation gets to the floor. An important advantage comes in the rules governing amending committee legislation on the House floor. "Closed rules" give committees almost complete agenda control over substance. Lacking a closed rule, the House rule that amendments adopted in the Committee of the Whole must be passed a second time in the full House, while amendments defeated in Committee of the Whole may not be reconsidered again, gives the committee two guaranteed shots at defending their position while giving opponents only one guaranteed shot at the committee.

The two-edged sword of negative agenda control was frequently demonstrated by the House Rules Committee in the 1950s and 1960s when its conservative membership bottled up widely supported progressive legislation. On the one hand, the Rules Committee's conservative bias allowed House members to pursue legislation about which they were skeptical, relying on Rules to bury the measures when they left the legislative committees – the so-called heat shield role of the Rules Committee. But, the Rules Committee also buried social legislation about which most legislators were confident, delaying the implementation of popular social and civil rights laws by a matter of decades. The delay in action over genuinely supported bills may not have cost MCs electorally, but it did thwart the principal policy goals of hundreds of legislators.

The second cost that committees can impose on the rank-and-file is related to agenda control. Substantive bias, embodied in most committees, derives from the basic division of labor that allows members to concentrate on those areas in which they are most interested. For example, farm-state legislators are more likely to be on the agriculture committee than on the banking committee. This allows urban legislators to pursue things other than farm policy, but it also leaves farmers able to use their positions to allocate more resources to their districts than they could have gotten if the committee were representative of the chamber's preferences. This bias has the effect of increasing the benefits to constituents represented on a committee while increasing the costs to everyone else. That is, it guarantees that government will ultimately be "too big" (Niskanen 1971).

Committee system: resources that further or obstruct reform. To summarize, then, the committee system imposes costs and produces benefits for all members. The benefits lie in the facilitation of work, the development of expertise, the ability of MCs to minimize their attention to issues of little interest and electoral reward, the creation and maintenance of winning coalitions, and the potential to extract added benefits for one's own district by serving on a locally useful committee. The costs are incurred when these committees delay legislation of interest to members and when they succeed in altering the distribution of outcomes away from the chamber median toward that of the committee's median.

In a simple cost-benefit framework, we would expect any individual legislator to tolerate a status quo committee system so long as these costs in skewed outcomes and delays were overcome by the benefits gained through expert work and the pursuit of particularistic programs. Once the net benefits generated by the committee system become negative to any given member, that member would begin wishing for a change of structure. This preference for structural change could also occur because an entrepreneur claimed that he or she could organize committees in a way that would increase the net benefit to the member's district. In any case, if costs exceed benefits, the individual member would begin to consider whether or not to support a challenge to the status quo.

Yet once the member begins to consider whether to support a structural change, she or he comes up against another important aspect of the committee system: Committee members have more institutional resources than nonmembers. Further, committees have chairs who have enhanced resources of both a strategic and a tangible nature. The strategic resources of committee chairs include such things as influence over the committee agenda, while tangible resources include augmented staffs. The scope and nature of these two resources have changed over the years, and as they have changed, so has the ability of committee members and their chairs to prevail in structural matters. Committee members also have the additional resource of being able to promise any member that it will consider legislation of interest to that member that is under the committee's jurisdiction. The existence of these resources can be very important as a given member decides whether to support or challenge the status quo committee system.

The fact that members have differential resources that are a function of their committee memberships can help to influence outcomes when their structural prerogatives are threatened. Consider a situation in which it is proposed that spending jurisdiction over a program be transferred from committee X to committee Y. Committee Y in this case claims that the change will increase the net benefit to the constituents of member A. Both committees have certain resources at their disposal to be used to persuade member A to support one committee or the other. Committee X could perhaps appeal to member A, noting how past spending decisions had been favorable, thus calling in bargaining chips. Both committees could promise member A added benefits in the future. And each committee could threaten to punish member A if the challenge should go in that committee's favor, with A voting on the losing side.

Thus, committees are likely to use their decisions as resources to get members to side with them in questions of structure. It is likely that members will be more retrospective than prospective, emphasizing the past behavior of committee X (in our example) rather than concentrating on the promises of committee Y. If members vote in structural matters retrospectively and if committees, knowing this, are strategic in their decisions, we should expect most challenges to existing structural arrangements to fail. That is, knowing that a dissatisfied chamber could strip it of its power, committee X should behave in such a way that its natural friends are continually rewarded and that borderline members are especially courted, leaving only a small group of dissatisfied members.

Finally, it should also be noted that the committee system not only endows people with resources, it also encourages the further development of acute interests. This is true, to begin with, because people with acute substantive interests tend to gravitate to committees that are related to that interest. But the nature of committee work is to concentrate added attention to that interest. Consider the following hypothetical experiment. Take two members, A and B, with identical interest in a particular issue, and put A on a committee that deals with that issue, leaving B off. We would expect A to develop an even greater interest in the issue over time than B, based largely on the added time and effort that A has spent attending to the issue.[24] This interaction between substantive interest in a committee's subject area and attention paid to the subject area by virtue

---

24 The classic example of how energy and attention paid to an issue can serve to expand an MC's interest is contained in Fenno's description of the "Socialization of Fred Santangelo" onto the agriculture subcommittee of the House Appropriations Committee (1966, 215–219). While Santangelo, who represented Harlem between 1957 and 1963, actually had no real interest in agriculture at the start, he realized early on that there were things of direct interest to his constituents that relied on the vitality of agriculture (school lunches and meat inspection). Santangelo began with a concentration on these more parochial programs, expanded his attention to broader agricultural issues, and became a major exponent of agricultural programs to other urban members of the House. Had Santangelo never been appointed to the agriculture subcommittee, his interest in and attention to agriculture would have been at least an order of magnitude less.

of being on a committee should cause committees that already have control over a subject to be more reluctant to relinquish that control than committees without existing appropriations authority would be eager to seize such authority: another example of the negativity bias in the operation of institutional development.[25]

Thus, while merely concentrating on the member's preferences before entering an ongoing legislature may lead us to conclude that each member would want a fragmented committee system, we see that once an MC is within an ongoing institution, there are other considerations that help to alter those initial preferences. Regardless of initial structural preferences that MCs might have, final preferences can be greatly influenced by the activity of those already benefiting from an existing committee structure, who use the resources they have accumulated through their positions not only to prosecute their policy preferences, but also to protect their institutional authority.

Party leadership. While the committee system developed its great complexity early in the House, party leadership in its most basic form was created even earlier through the Constitution. The precise details have varied over the years, but the locus of party leadership in the House has remained focused on the Speaker for the past two centuries. And, while most of a committee system's benefits and costs derive from disintegration, the virtues and decrements of a party apparatus lie in integration.

Party leadership: benefits. Committees and electoral concerns have tended to fracture Congress; but in order to pass legislation, these disparate elements must somehow come together. As I have already argued, committees can serve a limited role in unification. But it is still the party leadership that stands in the best position to unify disparate policy elements over time.

The benefits that party leaders bring to rank-and-file party members are based on the leaders being in the middle of an otherwise fractionated system. Leaders are in the middle both in terms of communications and

25 A good object lesson in how these acute interests can be reinforced is NASA's action allowing two influential MCs, Sen. Jake Garn (R-UT) and Rep. Bill Nelson (D-FL), to fly on the space shuttle. Both men had acute interests in the space program to begin with, developed through their career and constituency backgrounds, and reflected in their committee assignments. But the flights seemed to have heightened their interest in and support of the shuttle program, as was indicated in their responses to the explosion of the *Challenger*, compared to other MCs of similar interests. Most committee members do not get to go on the "ultimate junket" as a consequence of their committee's work, but the Garn/Nelson shuttle affair is a dramatic, if unusual, public example of the symbiotic relationships between committee members and the programs they oversee.

in terms of policy preference. That is, by their very identification as party leaders, they become an obvious focus of attention when particular policy minorities begin to build coalitions leading to passage. And because leaders must be at least satisfactory to divergent elements of their party in order to be elected, there is a good possibility that the policy preferences of leaders reside somewhere near the median of members of their party (Truman 1949; Ripley 1969).

The purpose of the leadership-supplied unification is ultimately to help members of the party survive politically. In practice, the dynamic of this unification has usually relied on the party leadership positioning itself as a broker between various interests. The brokerage function has led successful party leaders to understand the disparate needs of their followers and to bring together politicians who have something to trade. This brokerage role is reportedly the chief way in which Lyndon Johnson came to be regarded as the quintessential party leader. By being the one who knew the political needs of the senators in his – and to a good extent the other – party, Johnson was able to bring senators together for their mutual benefit. Thus, to the extent that party leaders can bring about mutual exchange and bargaining among members, they can help each member and each member's own district (Fenno 1965; Huitt 1965; Evans and Novak 1975; Glass 1975; Cooper and Brady 1981; Kingdon 1981; Calvert 1987).

Party leadership: costs. The brokerage process implemented by party leaders is not a free service to backbenchers since they become reliant on the judgment of the leaders – the power that comes from knowledge can be substantial. But leaders also have expressed powers that give them resources not only to facilitate *member* preferences, but also to facilitate their own *leadership* preferences.

The most important expressed power that party leaders have had to facilitate their own policy preferences has been the committee appointment power. In the House, this power has vacillated within and away from the Speaker's direct influence. Yet, *somebody* in a leadership position, be it the Speaker, the Ways and Means chair, or members of the executive committee of the Republican committee on committees, has had a great deal of influence through this authority, both in molding the biases on committees and in bargaining based on promises of committee assignments.

Likewise, being at the center of an otherwise fragmented system puts party leaders in a particularly good position to be aware of the indirect costs and benefits that accrue because of the disconnected search for district benefits. Being in the center of bargaining among many different members with widely divergent interests means that leadership is more likely to be aware of the externalities generated by individual member actions. Being more aware of the cumulative effects of externalities than most members means that leaders are likely to weight more heavily the consideration of indirect costs and benefits than are other members when they function as party leaders.

Party leadership: independent use of resources. It should finally be noted that leaders are likely to use their institutional resources to fulfill their more intermediate power goals. That is, they will use their resources to aid in their reelection as party leaders. But, assuming that leaders want to remain leaders, they have a balancing act to maintain as they use their institutional resources. On the one hand, they must use them so that the rank-and-file members of their party believe their own policy interests are being furthered. Thus, any party leader must be a willing and effective go-between, and he or she must be willing to assign institutional perquisites, such as committee seats, so as to involve the greatest number of party followers in the oversight of programs of interest to them.

On the other hand, strategically dispensing perquisites means that party leaders must use their resources to mitigate the disintegrative tendencies of the institution. In the realm of making committee assignments, leaders mitigate disintegration by taking particular care to sustain "control committees" and also by providing some degree of substantive balance on all committees (Masters 1961; Fenno 1966, 1973; Mayhew 1974, 147–158; Shepsle 1978). And mitigation of disintegration also requires party leaders to appoint a few "low-demand" members (i.e., members without acute policy interests) to all constituency-oriented committees so that the preferences of "interested" members are tempered.

As with the committee system, then, party leadership has certain resources at its disposal that it can use to further the particular interests of its immediate constituents (namely, party members) as well as the more general interests of leadership. In effectively using these resources, leaders remain leaders.

The decision on the part of any rank-and-file member to challenge party leadership on a structural matter, whether it be a threat to depose party leadership all together or a threat simply to oppose leadership on some other structural issue, must be based on a calculation that has two distinct parts. The first part is the calculation of the expected substantive gains to the member if the challenge is successful. The second part of the calculation is that of determining "disloyalty costs" incurred for opposing leadership.

Disloyalty costs are likely to be exacted whether or not a challenge to leadership is successful. If the challenge is successful, leadership, while unlikely to impose immediate sanctions against disloyal members, will still be inclined to reward supporters. Thus, if the challenge succeeds, the net disloyalty cost is the difference between the level of future leadership assistance that would have been received if the member had been loyal and the future leadership assistance actually received.[26] If the challenge is unsuccessful, the disloyalty cost is likely to be borne more directly and exacted through overt leadership sanctions. What the nature of the disloyalty cost calculus comes down to is that unless success is assured beforehand, it will be very difficult to get party followers to support structural change if it is opposed by party leadership. Support among the rank-and-file for a leadership-opposed structural change increases to the extent that (1) the probability of success is high or (2) other indirect benefits, such as benefits to be gained from position taking, vastly outweigh the immediate disloyalty costs. Thus, the disloyalty costs associated with challenging, and the even higher disloyalty costs associated with challenging and losing, mean that any direct public challenges to leadership must rest on a rate of dissatisfaction such that the expected substantive gains exceed the disloyalty costs absorbed by angering leadership.

On the whole, the operation of the substructures of Congress dampens the tendency of MCs to challenge formal arrangements when members are dissatisfied with this behavior. This dampening effect is closely associated with the phenomenon of "equilibrium institutions" discussed in the formal public choice literature (Shepsle 1986). Because structural preferences are so closely correlated with substantive ones, the potential exists in theory for congressional structures to continually change, or cycle, just as substantive decisions can fall prey to cycles under certain theoretical conditions (Arrow 1951). Yet compared with substantive decisions, which are typically immune to cycles in real-world legislatures, legislative structures are even more stable in practice. This structural stability arises mainly because those who benefit from the status quo typically have sufficient resources to stave off reform attempts. From an institutional standpoint, then, successful reform is truly an extraordinary event.

The separation of powers and budgetary politics

As if the complexity of the internal power structure were not enough, members of Congress must also contend with the effects of the separation

---

26 An example of disloyalty costs at work following a *successful* leadership challenge is Rep. Les Aspin's (D-WI) challenge to Melvin Price's (D-IL) incumbency as chair of the House Armed Services Committee in 1985. Aspin unseated Price in direct defiance of Democratic party leadership. Speaker O'Neill subsequently was cool toward Aspin and favored later attempts by House liberals to unseat him at the beginning of the following Congress.

of powers when they go about choosing budgetary structures. Of course, the level of influence that presidents have exerted in congressional budgetary politics has varied over the decades, but it has never been completely absent – the veto precludes this – as it has never been all-powerful. The fact that the president shares an important component of the legislative process, with no guarantees that presidential policy preferences will even approach congressional preferences, leads to real budgetary conflict and, in structural matters, even more complexity for MCs to consider when they evaluate calls to reform.

Students of American political institutions are fond of anthropomorphizing the differences between the executive and legislative branches. Congress is said to be jealous of its prerogatives and wary of presidential usurpations. While it is convenient to use such anthropomorphisms as shorthand, congressional "jealousy" is ultimately an aggregate expression of an *individual* political phenomenon. The congressional-presidential rivalry fundamentally rests on factors that do not require a conception of a collective congressional consciousness. In fact, assuming a collective congressional consciousness actually hinders a full understanding of congressional-presidential relations. Rivalry between Congress (seen individually and corporately) and the president is derived from two causes: (1) The political interests represented in the presidency are likely to be different from those represented in Congress and (2) the greater organizational capacity of the executive branch increases the chance that the president will prevail when his policy preferences clash with majority preferences in Congress.

Constituency differences create different predominant institutional perspectives in both Congress and the executive branch. Congress's bottom-up representational scheme generates a congressional preoccupation with particularism that was explored earlier in detail. The presidential constituency is argued to be unitary, as is revealed in the common assertion that the chief executive is "president of all the people."

The characterization of the presidential constituency as inclusive and national is accurate to the extent that presidents must transcend state and congressional district boundaries in order to be elected. In the process of gaining nomination and election, presidential candidates must bring a wide variety of policy interests under their wings. The president enters office with a fairly broad national coalition already built. When MCs enter office, they represent only their own districts and must work to achieve broad national coalitions after the fact of election. Inclusive, national consensus building is entirely foreign to congressional races and vests in the person of the president greater nationalistic legitimacy than that which rests in any individual in Congress.

But because no president has ever received anything approaching a unanimous popular vote – a mere 60 percent majority of voters and 30 percent plurality of eligibles constitutes an extraordinary landslide – it is clear that presidential coalition building is exclusive just as it is inclusive. Therefore, while the president's electoral coalition is wider than that of Congress, it does not necessarily entirely overlap the aggregate electoral constituencies of all MCs. The fact that the president's mass political base may be wider than Congress's should not blind us to the fact that it is not all-encompassing. The types of political interests that are under the president's wings may or may not be replicated in Congress, even when the executive and legislative branches are controlled by the same political party. Such differences in policy coalitions led early students of "parties-in-government" to differentiate between the presidential and congressional branches of the two political parties. The congressional wings of the two parties were said to be dominated by rural and conservative interests while the presidential wings were urban and progressive. Although experiences with Congress during the Carter and Reagan administrations have put this specific characterization of the differences in doubt, it is clear that congressional and presidential parties are different animals, even if the nature of the differences has a habit of changing over time.

The upshot of these constituency differences is that Congress (aggregately) and the president have frequently disagreed over spending policy. Cleveland's disagreements with Congress over internal improvements and pensions, Eisenhower's clashes over recession-fighting mechanisms, Carter's attacks on water projects, and Reagan's defense of military spending are some instances. The president's preferences cannot be ignored by Congress because of his potent veto power. The president's positive success against Congress also partially depends on his ability to go over the heads of MCs – a practice engaged in with varying success since Andrew Jackson. The more enduring way with which the president can get his way is through the executive branch's superior institutional capacity.

Thus, presidential influence in the politics of budget reform is twofold. On the one hand, the inherent clash of presidentially and congressionally oriented constituencies will often compel MCs to be attentive to those parts of congressional structure that help legislative majorities prevail against presidential policy preferences. The historic strength of the House Appropriations Committee and the Joint Committee on Taxation staff are just two congressional responses to this clash. On the other hand, the superior ability of the president to rally the support of voters on policy questions can have an impact on congressional thinking about budget reform. This ability to rally popular support has varied over time, of course, running the gamut in more recent years from Richard Nixon's ability to use popular sentiment to goad Congress into actively pursuing reform in the early 1970s to the persistent inability of Ronald Reagan to rally citizens to his side in his efforts to force Congress to endorse a whole host of reforms in the late 1980s. Thus, although its influence has varied greatly over the decades, because the presidency is an institution that is largely independent of Congress and potentially its superior in arousing popular support, the presidency itself can become an important exogenous factor in the development of the congressional budgetary process.

SUMMARY

The goals and incentives, the technology, and the constraints involved in structural development are easily specified. Rank-and-file MCs and party leaders, as well as the president, rely on different constituencies to gain reelection, while congressional committees desire greater authority over the development of programs under their jurisdiction. Budgeting itself creates tensions between distribution and control. Rank-and-file MCs are constrained in pursuing most-preferred structural arrangements by the existing institution and by presidential goals; leaders are constrained by the preferences of their followers; and committees are constrained by the preferences of the whole chamber. In all, while the number of places on which we should focus our attention in observing structural development and institutionalization are well-defined and controllable, the resulting relationships and interactions are myriad and complex. All of the exogenous and intervening processes involved in producing budgetary structures vary, and vary widely. We shall spend the rest of the book studying the interactions of these varying processes.

This theoretical discussion about the origin of structural politics should finally alert us to how the development of fiscal structure proceeds on a number of different levels at all times. It proceeds both institutionally and individually, and it involves both reform leaders and followers. Failing to distinguish between the various levels of reform activity can lead to confusion when we go about actually describing and explaining the politics of institutional development.

The most important of these simultaneous tracks are the individual and institutional. At the individual level, we are interested in why some members propose reform, why others actively fight it, and why still others in the middle choose sides. The discussion so far has suggested some cross-sectional differences among members that lead to differential structural preferences: Dissatisfied members are more likely to support change than satisfied members; high-demand members are more likely to support fragmentation than are low-demand members; leaders are more likely to favor centralization and control than are nonleaders; and committee members are more likely to see the usefulness of their overseeing more programs than are nonmembers. But the simple existence of preferences does not automatically produce positive actions congruent with those preferences.

Thus, at the institutional level, we are interested in explaining why some reform proposals pass and why others are defeated. The success or failure of reform is partially determined by the aggregate mix of cross-sectional characteristics. For instance, the more high-demand members there are in the House, the more likely it is that the House will actually enact fragmentation. But factors only indirectly related to preference mix, such as the internal distribution of power and institutional norms, also partially determine structural outcomes. In explaining why the institution of Congress changes, which is a distinct issue from explaining why its members *prefer* change, we must be attentive to all of the processes that alter policy preferences, internal power distributions, and political goal structures across time.

The second set of parallel tracks describing the development of congressional structure are leadership and followership.[27] The incentive and institutional structures of Congress encourage some members to pay particular attention to structural design, leaving others to follow their lead.

Because challenging the status quo is always potentially costly in terms of institutional status, we should expect structural challenges to emerge from those who have the most to gain, or least to lose, from reform. Because of the nature of the division of labor in Congress, those who have the most to gain are generally already members of easily identified organizational units. Thus, we should expect reform to be initiated by members with the most acute policy or institutional interests, or both. Similarly, because most rank-and-file members most of the time have more to lose than to gain in challenging the status quo, the coalition-building process on the way to reform passage should be slow and uncertain.

The division of labor that allows Congress to do its work also creates a division of labor in formulating and advancing structure reform. Because the most intense particularists reside in subject-matter legislative committees, we should expect fragmentation proposals to come from legislative committees. Because the greatest interest in budget control resides in control committees and in party leadership, we should expect centralizing reforms to originate from the control committees – Appropriations, Ways and Means, and Rules – or from party leadership directly.

---

27 Leadership in this case refers to *reform* leadership; leaders in reform movements may or may not be the same people as party leaders.

If reforms originate in organizational units that embody extreme interests, then we should witness "reform incubation" before any reform gets on the agenda, much less before it is actually approved. To exaggerate only a bit, control committees should always be concocting schemes to centralize budgeting even further, while legislative committees should always be scheming to fragment even more. But, rank-and-file members rarely have the incentive to consider challenging the status quo. They must be convinced that supporting a challenge is worth their while. Such convincing, called coalition building, takes a long time in most cases. Thus, we should not be surprised when reform takes a long time to consummate or when reform sentiment dissipates before enough reform followers join to form a majority reform coalition. Because control committees, legislative committees, and party leaders have special incentives and abilities to formulate reform proposals, we should expect reform activity to flow from these areas, even when there is not widespread dissatisfaction with budgetary outcomes in the chamber at large. Thus, a proposal to centralize spending structure may or may not indicate widespread dissatisfaction among low-demand members, just as a proposal to fragment spending further may or may not indicate widespread dissatisfaction among high-demand members at large. The fact that reforms are *proposed* is an indicator of the preferences of reform leaders. Whether that reform does or does not pass indicates the preferences of reform followers.

2

Setting the historical stage

The simplified contours of legislative life that I outlined in Chapter 1 are not alien to anyone knowledgeable about the modern Congress. The major actors and constraints that were discussed – constituents, rank-and-file legislators, committees, party leaders, the president, reelection, checks and balances, the state of the economy, and the budgetary problem – have all been staples of modern congressional scholarship. The theoretical tack I have taken in this study – that of constrained goal pursuit by rational politicians – is more controversial, even if it is becoming a very popular direction to take.

What is open to dispute, more than the theoretical use of rational choice, is whether the legislative world I abstracted in Chapter 1 is plausibly relevant to the legislative world of the nineteenth century.[1] After all, a century ago legislators eschewed reelection as a rule, political parties were dominant, autocratic Speakers ruled the House floor, national issues infused local congressional elections, and there was little of the structural complexity and differentiation that currently describe the modern Congress. What could be more different from the House of the 1970s and 1980s? Nevertheless, it is a premise of this study that these descriptive differences between eras are essentially epiphenomenal. It is important to pay careful attention to the changes in career opportunity structures, legislative institutionalization, and party power that have altered the description of the constraints that individual MCs have faced over the century. But these changes have not altered the fundamental fact of legislative life: The careers of politicians are primarily linked to the localities from which they come, not to the national commonweal. The aphorism "all politics is local" has not changed in relevance over the

---

1 The most forceful and persuasive argument about the dangers of importing twentieth-century assumptions into the nineteenth-century Congress is found in Price (1977).

century, even if the context in which localism has been pursued has changed.

In asserting a fundamental kinship between congressional politics of the 1880s and 1980s, we must still be very careful not to create anachronisms. We must understand how the House of 1865–1921 was fundamentally similar to the present, while at the same time be aware of the nature of the broad legislative and budgetary contexts in which MCs operated in the past. Therefore, before zeroing in on specific cases of budget reform, we must take a broad look at the House of Representatives between 1865 and 1921 and ask whether rational actor principles can plausibly explain behavior during this period, and also specify the general contextual variables in which the politicians we shall later examine lived their political lives. It is thus to the political and economic context of the House between 1865 and 1921 that we shall now briefly turn.

REELECTION AND POLITICAL CAREERS

The place to start in building bridges between our understanding of the current and much earlier Congresses is with the primary engine of legislative behavior: reelection and (more broadly) political career ambitions. Recent scholarship that has posited the reelection incentive to be the major determinant of congressional behavior has been written in the context of very high congressional reelection rates. Applying the reelection hypothesis to the late-nineteenth- and early-twentieth-century Congresses could be dangerous, however, if reelection was not a significant motivation to members of Congress at that time. It is therefore important to know the extent to which reelection was an important consideration to members between 1865 and 1921.

As many studies have shown, members of the nineteenth-century and early-twentieth-century House were not reelected at nearly the same rates as more recent MCs have been (Polsby 1968; Price 1971; Bullock 1972; Fiorina, Rohde, and Wissel 1975; Bogue et al. 1976; Kernell 1977) One way of seeing this is to look at rates of membership turnover in the House: Turnover levels were considerably higher during this entire period than in the present (Figure 2.1). But the figures also show that membership turnover had begun to drop by 1865. The decline in the number of rookie members of the House continued between 1865 and 1921, accelerating after the realigning 1896 election.

Although membership turnover is a handy surrogate to measure the extent to which MCs pursued reelection, it is not an entirely satisfactory measure. In fact, conventional measures of turnover, such as raw turnover rates or its converse, percentage of members returning, understate the extent to which an MC desired to continue in House membership. The

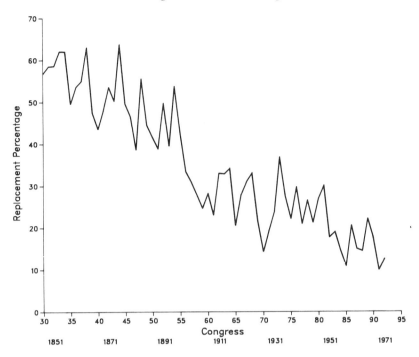

Figure 2.1. Percentage of House seats replaced, 30th–91st Congresses, 1847–1969. Data from Morris Fiorina, David Rohde, and Peter Wissell, "Historical Change in House Turnover," in Norman Ornstein (ed.), *Congress and Change* (New York: Praeger, 1975), Table 1.

ability of an MC to return to the House was determined not only by the willingness of that MC to return (which would be measured by the rate of running for reelection), but also by the type of electoral system in which he or she ran. It is true that House membership was not as attractive a job as it is today, and higher turnover in part reflects this. But it is also true that House membership was not entirely unattractive a century ago and that many MCs desired reelection but failed to achieve it. It is because of these failures, for which we have no good measure of frequency, that turnover rates certainly understate careerist *preferences* during this period.

The turnover rate understates careerist preferences because it measures reelection success, not reelection-seeking *activity*.[2] Thus, many members may have desired to be returned to the House, only to have those desires

2 Turnover rates are a function of the probability that a member of the House at time t is a member at time $t + 1$. A member who retired before time $t + 1$ is treated like a member who ran for reelection at time $t + 1$ but lost.

thwarted by (1) dramatic partisan swings in midwestern and eastern districts (especially between the 1870s and 1896), (2) the practice by which local officials were rotated through various offices, the House being just one stop on the rotation,[3] and/or (3) electoral challenges waged against victors in the House itself.[4] Also, the turnover rate does not count at all what might be called "nonconsecutive reelection," which is the process in which members, once in the House, were not reelected, but later returned to serve nonconsecutive terms. The phenomenon of non-consecutive reelection was common during the period covered by this study. For instance, over a quarter (26.5 percent) of all people who served in the House between the 41st and 54th Congresses (1869–1897) left the House for at least a term, only to return later.[5] The fact that a quarter of all members who left the House during this period subsequently re-

---

3 Rotation is one of the real *terrae incognitae* of nineteenth-century electoral politics affecting House elections. The extent to which such rotation occurred is unknown, but it is assumed to be substantial. Most of what we know about partisan rotation is anecdotal; Abraham Lincoln's experience with being allowed only one shot at a House seat is probably the best-known instance.

The practice in the districts that comprised Berks (Reading) and Lehigh (Allentown) counties, Pennsylvania, provides one illustration of rotation over time. The two counties, Democratic strongholds in an otherwise Republican state, were combined into one congressional district between the 51st and 72nd Congresses. The Democratic machines of the two counties swapped the seat between them, a compact that held until the institution of the direct primary in 1906. The pattern of county occupation of this seat up until the 1906 election is as follows: Berks, 51, 52; Lehigh, 53, 54; Berks, 55, 56, 57; Lehigh, 58, 59. During each county's "turn" at the seat, the same man was incumbent both terms, except when Daniel Ermentrout from Reading died during the 56th Congress. Ermentrout's successor, Henry Green (also from Reading), was allowed to serve another full term of his own, in addition to Ermentrout's partial term. I thank Walter Dean Burnham for pointing me toward this case.

4 Until after the turn of the century, losers of congressional races frequently appealed their losses to the entire chamber if the House was controlled by their own party. Between the 37th and 64th Congresses (1861 to 1915) there were 245 contested election cases in the House, an average of 8.8 cases per Congress (Rowell 1901; Morres 1917). Alexander (1916, 313–330) reports that up until 1916, when he was writing, 380 of the 383 election challenge cases that had ever been brought before the House since the first Congress had been decided in favor of the candidate from the majority party (also see Willoughby 1934; Barnett 1939; Dempsey 1956). The partisanship of adjudicating contested election cases is one piece of evidence suggesting that raw turnover rates underestimate the extent to which MCs valued their seats enough to prefer reelection and were skillful enough to win.

5 This analysis is derived from data made available by the Inter-University Consortium for Political and Social Research. The data were contained in the computer data file, "Roster of United States Congressional Officeholders and Biographical Characteristics of Members of the United States Congress, 1879–1985: Merged." Neither the original collectors of the data nor the Consortium bear any responsibility for the analyses or interpretations present here or subsequently in this book.

turned indicates that House service was valued more than the reelection rate would indicate.

Finally a higher turnover rate does not necessarily indicate a *disinterest* among representatives in furthering their careers through the use of their Washington influence. Even if continued service in the House had had absolutely no fascination to any MCs a century ago (producing a turnover rate of 100 percent), House membership could have still been used to pursue other electoral goals. "Potomac Fever" had not yet hit former members of the House by 1921, and almost all former members pursued subsequent careers that were rooted back home, in local or state politics or in local business and farming (Bogue et al. 1976). The political career opportunity structure was different than the present, with House membership holding a lower rating in the hierarchy of offices. Hence, House membership was frequently a springboard to more interesting and powerful careers back home.

While members may have valued their House seats less during the 1800s than MCs have since World War I, it is still clear that these nineteenth-century legislators were anything but political amateurs, unconcerned about their political futures. Even if they did not care about returning to the House itself, MCs typically had other political ambitions, such as a governorship, mayoralty, Senate seat, or judgeship, that required them to go about their Washington business with one eye always trained on the home district (or state).

And, while it is true that geographic constituents were probably less attentive to House members' activities in the nineteenth century than they have been since the advent of television, when we look at indicators of attention paid to the nineteenth-century Congress, it is surprising how much information constituents *did* have about what their MCs did. Samuel Kernell, in his study of newspaper reportage in Cleveland in the middle of the nineteenth century, shows that the majority of political news stories, both election oriented and nonelection oriented, focused on national events (Kernell and Jacobson 1984; Kernell 1986). And, while presidential politics generally dominated the election news, most national policy and institutional news was given a congressional focus. While one must approach these findings with caution, they suggest that geographic constituents had more information about their legislators' actions available to them during this period than we might expect from our initial conceptions about nineteenth-century communication.

Therefore, while it is slightly less accurate to speak of late-nineteenth-century legislators as being "single-minded seekers of reelection" when we compare them to twentieth-century legislators, it is unreasonable to argue that the localistic legislative bias induced by the electoral process was fundamentally less in the latter half of the past century. Increasingly, reelection to the House *was* a priority for House members; even before reelection became the norm, future careers of most MCs still rested on their House performance, as they sought further state or local offices or as they tried to remain generally influential in local affairs after political retirement.

CONSTRAINTS AND CONTEXT IN THE HOUSE, 1865–1921

Not only was the logic of the electoral connection descriptively different in the past century from how it is now, but many of the institutional, political, and budgetary constraints varied as well. Macroeconomics, partisanship, reformism, and structural development all had their own unique characteristics during this period, providing a different set of constraints for MCs than they face in the late twentieth century.

Partisanship

In the decades following the Civil War, Republicans held a tight rein over the federal government. This rein was the tightest in the Senate and presidency; Republicans typically controlled the House as well, but electoral swings were more likely to benefit Democratic representatives, giving Democrats an occasional toe hold in the federal government during the twenty years following Reconstruction. After the critical election of 1896, even control of the House was largely foreclosed from the Democrats.

The degree of Republican control of the Senate and presidency was imposing. The Senate was organized by the Republicans for forty-six of the fifty-six years between 1865 and 1921. During the same period, which encompassed sixteen presidential terms, two Democrats occupied the White House for four terms while nine different Republicans served the other twelve.

Even though Republicans were also the majority party in House elections, electoral swings were frequent and large enough to yield more numerous Democratic majorities in the House, especially before the critical election of 1896. Of the sixteen Houses between 1865 and 1897 (39th–54th Congresses), exactly one-half were controlled by each party (Figure 2.2). These islands of Democratic control in a Republican sea saw House Democrats experiment with the rules in order to overcome the general Republican dominance in government. Democrats were forced to resort to indirect ways of influencing policy since Democratic House majorities rarely coincided with Democratic majorities elsewhere in the federal government. Following the election of 1896, however,

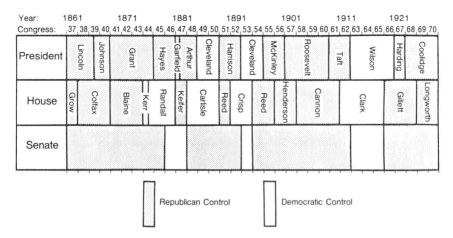

Figure 2.2. Party control of the presidency, House, and Senate, 37th–70th Congresses, 1861–1921.

Republicans consolidated their control of the House and, with it, the entire government. Of the twelve Congresses between 1897 and 1921 (55th–66th), eight were organized by the Republicans and four by the Democrats.

Before the 1896 realignment, neither of the two parties had successfully absorbed the burgeoning social protest movements of their day, and party strategies were defined in terms more backward looking than visionary (Sundquist 1983). To Republicans, the Democratic party remained the party of "Rum, Romanism, and Rebellion" – with emphasis on Rebellion. To Democrats, especially southerners, the Republican party remained the party of domination. In more pragmatic terms, the post-Reconstruction parties continued to be more interested in maintaining patronage than in absorbing social reform.

Thus, for the first half of the 1865–1921 period, most interest in appropriations control was not so much motivated by a desire to protect massive spending programs, as by a desire to control the administrative apparatus of government. Certainly pork barrel and pensions spending was near and dear to many legislators. But, the largest proportion of the budget continued to pay for the administrative upkeep of the federal government, including employee salaries and procurement. Congressional attention was primarily focused on the workings of the executive branch. But, legislative oversight was primarily aimed at ensuring that political rewards were protected, and House structure was aimed at maximizing congressional control of administrative behavior for partisan ends (White 1958, chaps. 2–4).

After the election of 1896, party alignment was further consolidated along geographic cleavages, while the concomitant rise of reform movements and their absorption into the two parties lessened the reliance on patronage as a partisan cohesive. The origins of the 1896 realignment produced socially bifurcated parties, which served to heighten and reinforce partisan cleavages within Congress (as measured by roll call votes) to heights now recognized as historic (Brady 1973, 1978).

The latter half of the 1865–1921 period was certainly the height of American Republican government, even taking into account the decade following the anomalous 1912 election. This unity of partisan control of the federal government by the Republicans after 1896 caused congressional attention to become less focused on the executive branch as a partisan enemy, although relations between individual MCs and agencies were by no means placid.

But because the Republican party, like the Democratic, remained a loose coalition of local machines throughout this period, intraparty conflict increased over time within the Republican party, as geographic interests vied for power within the party (Skowronek 1982, 168–176). By 1921, the cleavages of 1896 had begun to fray, and the parties began to take on the general shapes that characterized them after the realignment of the 1930s: Republicans became more aligned with conservative business interests and midwestern farmers, while the Democrats developed distinct branches in the North and South.

For a variety of reasons, then, partisanship played a significant role in the politics of budgetary structure between 1865 and 1921. In fact, the role of pure partisanship in determining legislative outcomes eclipsed anything experienced during the present generation: Partisanship prompted Democrats to use appropriations politics to control the Republican executive; periods of partisan hegemony lessened contention over legislative structure; the periods of split partisanship heightened structural battles; partisanship underlay differences over pork barrel spending; and the parties' separate absorption rates of reformism prompted different attitudes toward budget reform around the turn of the century.

The macroeconomy

Of the various exogenous factors affecting budgetary structural politics during 1865–1921, the ones that probably varied the most were the makeup of the economy and the composition of the federal budget. This period witnessed the transition of an agrarian nation to an industrial one and a steady increase in the size of government. While the structure of congressional budgeting arguably caused many of the changes in the

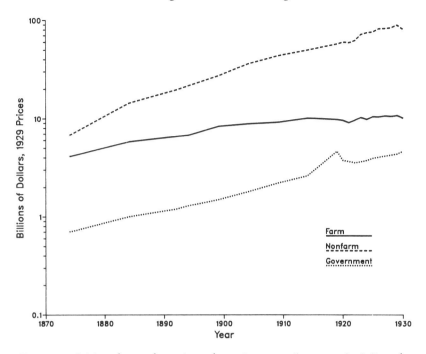

Figure 2.3. Origins of gross domestic product, 1874–1929 (in 1929 prices). Data from U.S. Census Bureau, *Historical Statistics of the United States* (Washington, D.C.: U.S. Government Printing Office, 1975), series F125–9.

composition of the federal spending and taxing, the changing composition itself also affected budgetary politics and thus requires a brief accounting.

The American economy underwent dramatic changes in size and composition between 1865 and 1921 (Figure 2.3). During this period agricultural output remained fairly steady (measured in constant prices) while government spending steadily increased. But, the most important compositional change in the macroeconomy was the order-of-magnitude increase in the size of the domestic economy attributable to the nonfarm/nongovernment sector. The importance of this change is documented by the shift in the number of persons engaged in various types of work during the period (Figure 2.4). While at the beginning of the period we are studying approximately half of all American workers were agricultural and half nonagricultural, by the end of the period nonagricultural workers had increased their share in the work place by about 50 percent while agricultural workers had decreased their share by about 50 percent.

Price trends, on the other hand, can be divided into two distinct periods (Figure 2.5). Until the turn of the century, prices exhibited a secular decline; this was reversed in the first two decades of this century. World

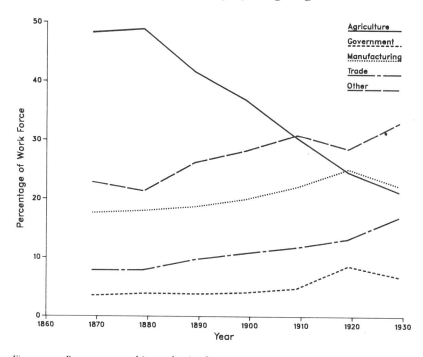

Figure 2.4. Persons engaged in production by sector, 1869–1929. Data from U.S. Census Bureau, *Historical Statistics of the United States* (Washington, D.C.: U.S. Government Printing Office, 1975), series F250–61.

War I dramatically accelerated inflation and left prices in the end on a new plateau, approximately twice as high as they had been before the war. Inflation during World War I was an important development that spawned citizen awareness of government fiscal activity, partially accounting for political interest in budget reform between 1919 and 1921.

While the political problems attending rampant inflation produced by government activity (however necessary) are obvious, the deflation experienced late in the nineteenth century was also politically problematic because it differentially affected various sectors of the economy. Most important, the dramatic collapse of crop prices severely affected farmers, one consequence being the increased agrarian activism associated with the period and the subsequent increase in demands on government to ameliorate social suffering (Wiebe 1967; Sundquist 1983).

Likewise, while the economy grew dramatically between 1865 and 1921, that growth was not without its setbacks. Major "panics" and depressions occurred during 1873–77, 1893–96, 1907–08, and 1921–22. The extent to which panics permeated the national economy, affecting the agrarian areas, remains in dispute (Studenski and Krooss 1963).

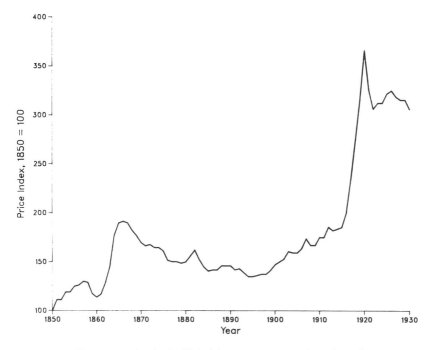

Figure 2.5. Consumer prices in the United States, 1850–1930. Data from the Economist, *World Business Cycles* (London: The Economist Newspaper Ltd, 1982), p. 27.

Nevertheless, the panics, centered as they were in cities, were highly visible to members of Congress in Washington. And because the panics especially hurt trading centers, they had great negative effects on imports. A drop in international trade, of course, meant a drop in tariff revenue. Thus, even if panics never reverberated beyond urban areas, they directly influenced budgetary politics by the resulting severe blow to revenues. In pre-Keynesian days, a drop in revenues necessitated retrenchment of expenditures to balance the budget (Kimmel 1959, 55). Thus, it should be of no surprise to us that during periods of acute revenue loss due to financial panics, congressional budgeting became more contentious.

The tariff and the income tax

The tariff was significant not only because its yield decreased during depressions and panics, but also because of the partisanship associated with its maintenance. Even though the idea of a protective tariff was at least as old as the Republic, government policy in post-Civil War America emerged more protectionist than it had ever been before. The principal reason for this heightened protectionism was the Democratic South's absence from Congress during the Civil War until the early 1870s and the inability of the northern Democrats to forcefully pursue southern Democratic interests in their absence (Stanwood 1903, vol. 1; House 1940).[6] Thus, the Civil War settled little as far as the tariff was concerned, producing continued sources for partisan animosity for the next several decades.

What made opinions about the protective tariff so important in influencing *spending* politics was the difficulty that Democrats experienced in reducing tariffs, even when they controlled the government, or some portion of it. The highest hurdle that the Democrats had to overcome before they could reduce tariff rates was the separation of powers. Under the best of circumstances before 1897, Democrats had to contend with a consistently divided government for two decades: a Democratic House could do very little when faced with vetoes from Republican Senates and presidents. Divisions within Democratic ranks also hindered tariff reform. When a unified Democratic government was finally elected during the 53rd Congress (1893–95), rifts within the Democratic party delayed reform and finally limited the degree to which tariff rates were ultimately reduced in 1894 (Stanwood 1903, II:296–352; Bauer, Pool, and Dexter 1963, 14–18).

The locus of this Democratic opposition to tariff reform centered in the Pennsylvania delegation led by Samuel Randall. While Speaker (1876–1881), Randall blocked action on the tariff. Once deposed as Speaker for his tariff views, Randall used the reporting powers of the House Appropriations Committee – to whose chair he was appointed in 1883 – to block reform.

The partisan contours of the tariff issue influenced spending preferences in a number of ways. Republicans were induced to generally favor higher spending levels; without high spending, huge surpluses would arise and make the Democratic argument in favor of a "tariff for revenue only" more appealing. Conversely, Democrats associated spending expansion with unacceptably high import duties. These pure, partisan differences were illustrated in the respective party platforms in the 1888 election, which was held in midst of the largest of the tariff-generated surpluses.

In their party platform, the Democrats attacked the system of protective tariffs, accusing the Republican party of trying "to meet and exhaust by extravagant appropriations and expenses" the surplus. The Democratic party pledged both to "enforce frugality in public expense" and to "abolish unnecessary taxation" through tariff reform.

6 One of the reasons why northern Democrats were unable to forcefully articulate an antiprotection stand following the Civil War was that they themselves were frequently split on the issue. Pennsylvania Democrats were especially notorious for being nearly as protectionist as the northern Republicans.

The Republicans had few quarrels with the Democratic characterizations. They defended the tariff system, indeed called for further barriers. And, in contrast with the Democrats' call for extraordinary frugality in public expenses, the Republican platform demanded "appropriations for the early rebuilding of our navy, for the construction of coast fortifications,... for the payment of just pensions to our soldiers, for necessary work of national importance in the improvement of harbors and the channels of internal, coastwise, and foreign commerce, for the encouragement of the shipping interests" (Noyes 1909, 128–129).

Faced with the reality of severe hurdles in lowering tariff rates, however, Democrats began to support the expansion of particular types of spending. As far as the Democrats were concerned, if tariffs could not be reduced directly, the second-best strategy was to support appropriations that benefited their own constituents, thereby mitigating the perceived losses that had been imposed by protection. In this way, Democrats were able to salvage an otherwise unwinnable political situation.[7] Thus, while Republicans championed broad spending programs, Democrats concentrated on internal improvements, agriculture, and other constituency-sensitive items.

While tariff politics molded the substance of spending politics directly, tariff politics also molded budgetary politics indirectly. It was often argued that because the tariff was an indirect levy, it yielded revenues that were essentially "too high": the tariff fueled an expansion of government that citizens would have otherwise opposed if they had been required to pay for it through *direct* taxation.[8] Certainly the argument over the optimal level of taxing and spending is as much a normative as an empirical question, yet it does seem reasonable to assume that the low visibility of the tariff reduced citizen and legislative scrutiny of government spending, minimized perceived costs of government activity, and helped to produce a higher rate of spending than would have obtained under direct income taxation.

It should also be said that before the Sixteenth Amendment was ratified in 1913, internal taxes were barely more visible than the tariff. The chief

---

7 This situation has analogues in current spending politics, only with the role of the two parties reversed. Republicans as a general principal support lower spending than Democrats. However, Republicans also have learned that big government is a permanent feature of American life, thus they have been willing to advocate their own version of big government (preferring the expansion of the military aspects over the domestic) while participating in the "social pork barrel" for electoral gain. In both eras, the minority party has shown resiliency in maintaining its general ideological stances while making the best of a bad situation.

8 See Tawney (1910) and the speech by James Good in the *Congressional Record* (17 Oct. 1919, 7082). Tawney chaired the HAC between 1905 and 1911 and Good chaired it between 1919 and 1921.

source of internal revenue was excise taxes, primarily collected on alcohol and tobacco. Not only were these taxes less directly visible than an income tax, their status as "sin taxes" reduced the possibility that they would be reduced and actually facilitated periodic increases. Thus, throughout most of this period Congress maintained a taxation system that systematically helped to assign the political cost components of budgetary calculations an even lower weight than they are assigned today. The weight applied to costs increased when the income tax was instituted.

In the period after the Civil War, antiprotection Democrats typically favored replacing lost revenues with a new income tax (Seligman 1921; Ratner 1967). Thus, an income tax measure was attached to the Wilson-Gorman bill that cut the tariff in 1894; an income tax plan also accompanied the Underwood Tariff of 1913. It was the 1894 tax act that the Supreme Court held to be unconstitutional, overturning by a 5–4 vote the constitutional imprimatur that the court had earlier given to the Civil War income tax (Studenski and Krooss 1963, 222–224). The court's 1894 decision was reversed by the ratification of the Sixteenth Amendment. Income taxation in the United States began for good following the passage of an amendment to the Underwood Tariff.

The original 1913 income tax law directly affected a small percentage of citizens: only single people with $3,000 or more in income and married people who made over $4,000 a year. Still, in the first year this represented an infinite percentage increase to those who were directly taxed compared to their income tax liability in 1912. Consequently, a growing number of people began to have a somewhat more acute gauge of the actual cost of government, and many of them began to agitate in favor of retrenchment so that their taxes could be lowered.

Within just a few years, however, World War I required the expansion of the income tax base. Base broadening was accomplished by including all single people with incomes greater than $1,000 and married couples earning over $2,000. The issue of federal finance very quickly increased in salience as the composition of federal revenues changed (Figure 2.6). When this issue was coupled with the rapid inflation accompanying World War I, the stage was set for greater visibility of federal budgeting after the war, including greater visibility for structural reform proposals.

Federal spending

The other side of taxing was spending. Seen in broad terms, changes in the composition of the federal budget during this period were mostly driven by military policy and wars (Figure 2.7). The Civil War greatly increased military spending, of course, but in the long run its significance

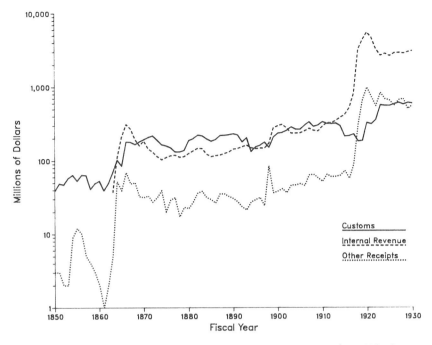

Figure 2.6. Composition of federal revenues, FY 1850–1930. Data from U.S. Census Bureau, *Historical Statistics of the United States* (Washington, D.C.: U.S. Government Printing Office, 1975), series Y352–6.

for spending had more to do with the vast sizes of debt and military pension payments required for the rest of the century. While a permanent "ratchet effect" of direct military spending was not associated with the Civil War, military spending did not return to lower prewar levels following the Spanish-American War and World War I.

Following the Civil War, veterans' pensions rose to take the place of dwindling interest payments. General spending on domestic projects grew secularly over time, but the changes were not as dramatic as those associated with interest, the military, and veterans benefits (Treasury Secretary 1922, Table K).

The domestic budget was dominated by the post office appropriations bill (10 percent of all spending in 1875, 18 percent in 1895, and 26 percent in 1915); the sundry civil bill (9, 7, and 9 percent) and the legislative, executive, and judicial appropriations bill (7, 4, and 3 percent). The rivers and harbors bill, typically the symbolic target of opponents of congressional extravagance, remained steady at approximately 2 percent of spending throughout the period.

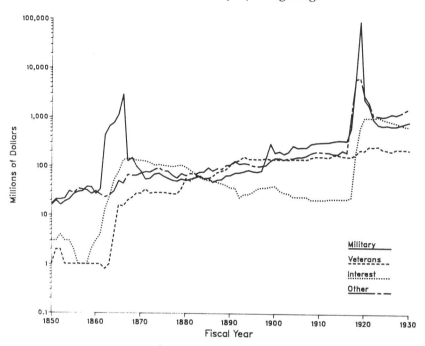

Figure 2.7. Composition of federal spending, FY 1850–1930. Data from U.S. Census Bureau, *Historical Statistics of the United States* (Washington, D.C.: U.S. Government Printing Office, 1975), series Y466–71.

The federal surplus and deficit

The confluence of taxing and spending was the deficit or surplus (Figure 2.8). The 1860s brought the previously unimagined difficulties associated with financing governmental debt that was a significant fraction of national wealth. The 1870s were a time of postwar retrenchment, when spending dropped even faster than revenues. The 1880s were marked by the persistence of embarrassingly large surpluses, which disappeared in the 1890s. In the period between the Spanish-American War and World War I, spending and revenues about kept pace with each other. Hence, after 1900, legislators found themselves constantly trying to balance the budget. Problems with budget balancing helped to prompt expansion of the Treasury secretary's financial reporting powers and administrative controls. The tremendous debt increase accompanying World War I matched that of the Civil War in relative terms, although it was handled more effectively than the Civil War's debt financing. By the end of the period under study, Congress was entering a wholly new age of federal finance, with levels of taxing, spending, and debt at new highs.

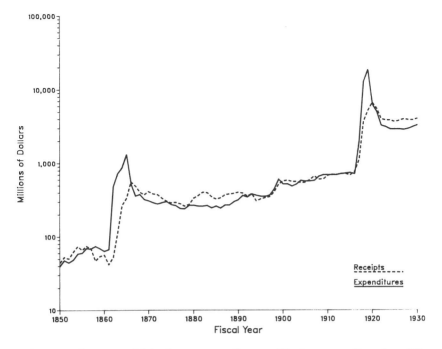

Figure 2.8. Summary of federal government finances, FY 1850–1930. Data from U.S. Census Bureau, *Historical Statistics of the United States* (Washington, D.C.: U.S. Government Printing Office, 1975), series Y335–6.

Reform movements

Finally, reform movements of various kinds made their marks on national politics during 1865–1921. The Civil War again had an important impact in influencing the emergence of reform movements that is often unacknowledged. Like the aftermath of most major wars, there was a pervasive desire to return to "normalcy" following the Civil War, indicated by the movement to retrench federal expenditures and to lessen the role of government in society. Like the normalcy period following World War I, the desire for a simpler political world in the 1860s and 1870s resulted in certain emerging reform movements being put on the back burner. The comedown from the war postponed action on various reform packages concerning issues such as naval and army reform, civil service, transportation regulation, and relations with Native American tribes. Political energy was instead focused on Reconstruction.

After the Compromise of 1877, the reform packages that had been put on hold for decades were once again debated. Coupled with the material changes occurring in the nation's economic and social systems, notably industrialization and urbanization, the reform movements that emerged have left their impacts to this day.

One of the best-known influences of reformism was the movement for a national executive budget. This movement gained special momentum through study commissions instituted by presidents Roosevelt (the Keep Commission) and Taft (the Taft Commission). When the Taft Commission went out of business in 1913, its members spawned a number of reform institutions, including the Institute for Governmental Research, now the Brookings Institution. These reformers were imbued with an ideology of centralization and executive leadership and a desire to structure the government on a "business basis."

In addition to the budget reform movement, reform movements addressing other internal governmental activities and social ills burgeoned after Reconstruction. Internal reform movements concentrated on issues such as Civil Service reform, education, military modernization, and general business efficiency. Social reform movements pushed the causes of Native Americans, labor reform, and health and safety regulation. Addressing any of these concerns would not come cheaply, even if handled efficiently. For instance, conversion of the navy from wind power to steam was an inherently expensive proposition. The convergence of these reform movements whose times had come inevitably made budgeting more conflictual and increased citizen attention to the services the federal government supplied. By 1921, the institutional reform movement had outlasted social reform. Yet, both had significant effects on budgetary politics and the politics of budgetary structure from Reconstruction to 1921.

THE DEVELOPMENT OF CONGRESSIONAL STRUCTURE AND EARLY BUDGETING

The development of the House budgetary structure proceeded as the House generally modernized and institutionalized. Polsby (1968) has argued that the marks of an institutionalized organization are three: boundedness, complexity, and universalism. On each score between 1865 and 1921, the House moved from being preinstitutionalized to being institutionalized almost to the extent that it is now.

In terms of boundedness, members became increasingly differentiated from other organizations, reelection to Congress became more common, and leaders were increasingly drawn from veteran members of the legislature. As for institutional complexity, functional differentiation within the House grew secularly. The number of standing committees, one measure of complexity, increased from thirty-eight in 1865 to forty-six in

1890 to sixty in 1920. Finally, the norms operating in the House became more universalistic, as the determination of committee membership and leadership began to follow set rules and procedures. After the revolt against Speaker Cannon, the norm of seniority became even more ingrained into the rules of House behavior.

The growth of institutionalization in the House interacted with the leadership styles of Speakers to influence the way budget reform politics was played out between 1865 and 1921. Before Thomas Reed was elected Speaker in 1889, that office had certain parliamentary powers, notably the power to appoint committee members and the power of recognition; but the low level of institutionalization caused floor activity to be relatively free-wheeling. One important method of floor control, the Rules Committee's "special orders," did not appear until 1883 (McConachie 1898; Galloway 1962; Robinson 1963; Bolling 1968, 44–47; Oleszek 1978, 88). Absent the widespread use of the "closed rule" and special orders, members freely attempted to amend legislation, using very loose definitions of germaneness. As we shall shortly see, loose floor control before the 1890s provided easy access to the floor for members most dissatisfied with budgetary politics, who frequently kept the House busy considering a string of reform proposals.

The Reed Rules, other institutionalization pressures, and the ability of Speakers Reed and Cannon to exercise firm control over legislative business drastically reduced the frequency with which the rank-and-file directly challenged the status quo between 1895 and 1911. Differences in the ease with which structural debates made it to the House floor meant that while reform politics in the 1870s and 1880s was highly visible, was fought out on the House floor, and was often brought to a vote, reform politics after 1890 was more controlled by leadership, was often hidden from public scrutiny, was fought out in party caucuses and other private meetings, and was rarely considered on the House floor itself. We should therefore be alert and not immediately conclude that because reform fights rarely reached the House floor after 1890, interest in budgetary structure necessarily dropped as precipitously as did public debate.

The Houses that finally accepted reconsolidation between 1919 and 1921 were institutionally quite different from either the free-for-all Houses before 1895 or the carefully controlled Houses between 1895 and 1911. The Houses that finally accepted change were ones in which strong central party control was on the way out, seniority was beginning to play a more significant role in guiding the actions of members, and individual members were growing to demand a more equal distribution of the chamber's resources.

71

Early budgeting in Congress

The earliest models of congressional style were drawn heavily from British parliamentary examples. Congress originally was content to allow the executive branch to develop detailed programs for its ratification. The House handled legislative proposals by resolving into Committee of the Whole for general discussion, thereby arriving at a sense of the body. Only after a definite direction had been chosen would a select committee be appointed to draw together the specifics (Ford 1898; Sullivan 1984; Sklandony 1985). In this arrangement, the executive-set agenda carried very heavy weight.

The partisan harmony that existed between the two branches in the early years of the nation combined with the simplicity of the scope of government to produce a bare-bones congressional budgetary structure and very simple appropriations acts. For instance, the first appropriation act provided lump sums for four general classes of expenditures: $216,000 for the Civil list, $137,000 for the War Department, $190,000 to discharge warrants issued by the former Board of Treasury, and $96,000 for pensions to disabled veterans. The entire statute itself was thirteen lines long (Fisher 1972, 110; 1 Stat. 95).

This exaggerated simplicity did not last. By 1794, Congress was considering two general appropriations acts each year: one for the support of the government and one to provide funds for the military. In 1799 a separate bill for the navy was passed, and seven other separate annual appropriations bills were created before the Civil War: fortifications (first passed in 1823), pensions (1826), rivers and harbors (1826), the military academy (1834), the Indian Department (1837), the post office (1844), and the legislative, executive, and judicial bill (1856).

Jurisdiction over spending and taxing remained with only one committee in each house, Ways and Means in the House and Finance in the Senate, but decisionmaking was divided into successively smaller and smaller units through the proliferation of annual appropriations bills. While there was tension in the House over the role of the Ways and Means Committee in deciding how much money would be spent for specific objects, efforts to strip Ways and Means of appropriations jurisdiction prior to the Civil War were unsuccessful, if they arose at all (Selko 1940, 84; Fenno 1966; Fisher 1972, 85–94, 1975, 19–20).

The Ways and Means Committee was not without its controversies, and reforms born out of dissatisfaction with policy outcomes were not totally unsuccessful. The first structural attack against the Ways and Means Committee came as a result of conflict over the use of the protective tariff. Legislators who favored protection and who were dissatisfied with Ways and Means' attitudes, which were not considered protectionist enough, managed to create the Committee on Manufacturers in 1819, to which Speaker Clay appointed only committed protectionists (Stanwood 1903, I:180). It was the Committee on Manufacturers, not Ways and Means, that favorably reported protective rates in 1824, 1827, 1830, 1832, and 1833, along with the 1828 "Tariff of Abominations."

This study is not about tariff reform, but we can see that by the early-nineteenth-century legislators were using structural change to remedy substantive conflict, and that the Ways and Means Committee was a center of controversy (Stanwood 1903, I:180–199; Selko 1940, 84). We can also note that the early challenges to Ways and Means, a committee whose members had developed a high level of institutional power based on their position early in the history of the House, focused only on one aspect of its work. It was long before dissatisfied members of the rank-and-file challenged Ways and Means on other issues that were not as highly valued as the protective tariff.

While Ways and Means had total jurisdiction over all taxing and appropriations bills before 1865, it would be misleading to state that it had total "control" over the budget. Ways and Means had a low level of control over the highly important pensions spending because pension *rates*, which determined pensions outlays, were not considered by the Ways and Means Committee but by other committees.

The handling of pensions for military service has long been a center of controversy, and the early nineteenth century was no exception (Orloff and Skocpol 1984). The practice of passing general pension laws and of providing for pensions to specific individuals through private bills began in the late eighteenth century. The first appropriations bill passed by Congress provided for revolutionary war pensions; and from the beginning of the Republic, Congress proved willing to circumvent general legislation and provide for pensions by private acts (Glasson 1918, 19). Passing pension legislation was very popular, and Congress had a difficult time resisting continued pressure to increase pension rates and expand coverage. Before 1865, Congress had passed legislation extending Revolutionary War pensions fourteen times, and the last pension from this war was not paid out until 1906 (Glasson 1918; Fisher 1975, 25).

The fact that an annual pension bill was reported by Ways and Means (the Appropriations Committee after 1865) could give one the initial impression that the committee had firm control over the amount spent for pensions in any given year. However, pensions were actually the first federal entitlement program since the annual appropriations bill merely replenished the fund out of which pensions had been paid the previous year and ensured that the fund would be sufficient the following year. It was the pension committees that had jurisdiction over pension rates and private pension bills. The job of Ways and Means was not really independent decisionmaking, but technical prediction of how much the pension bills would cost that year.

Therefore, even in this superficial overview of pre-1865 structural politics, we see the twin pulls of constituency and committee jurisdiction at work in determining where budgetary decisionmaking would be lodged. In the case of tariffs, a matter that competed for the place of most compelling issue before the Civil War, dissatisfied members were willing and able to seize control over a policy issue through shuffling jurisdictions. But Ways and Means remained able to retain most of its formal authority. In the area of pensions, the first federal program easily targetable to individuals, the House likewise enhanced control of pension rates by rank-and-file members and pensions committees. The difference between this and later fragmentation of spending authority was that Ways and Means, in considering the pension bill in the normal appropriations cycle, could at least adjust other spending bills in relation to pension spending demands before, rather than after, the fact.

The Civil War dramatically changed the complexity of federal government budgeting. The size of federal spending, taxing, and borrowing swelled to levels before unimagined. Before the Civil War, the most the federal government had ever spent in one year was $69.6 million (1856); receipts also peaked in 1856 at $75.1 million, while the record deficit stood at $30.8 million in 1847. The 1856 taxing and spending figures represented approximately 1.7 percent of gross national product (GNP) (Kendrick 1955, 100). In the first full year of the Civil War (1862), the federal government spent $474.8 million, 89 percent of which was deficit financed. By the last year of the War (1865), the federal government spent $1.3 billion, with a deficit of over $960 million; the accumulated debt from 1862 to 1865 was approximately $2.5 billion. This twentyfold increase in federal spending in such a short period of time created a management crisis in the federal government. Congress was almost unable to deal with a task of this magnitude, and by the time laws were passed to supply sufficient revenues, the war was winding down (Kimmel 1959, 61–65; Ratner 1967, 66–99). Thus, the modern development of the House's budgetary apparatus began to unfold at a time when the indirect costs of government budgetary action, mainly debt management, were at a historic high.

PART II

Spending reform and its consequences, 1865–1921

Introduction

For those overwhelmed with the dimensions of the federal budget in the 1980s, budgeting in the sixty years after the Civil War must seem idyllic. In these present days of deficits denominated in the hundreds of billions of dollars; myriad committees with various powers over budget authority, outlays, and entitlement authorization; and great debates over the mix of fiscal policy instruments, the nineteenth century seems like placid waters. In the late-nineteenth and early-twentieth centuries deficits were denominated in the hundreds of thousands of dollars, with $100 million surpluses common. Before the Civil War, jurisdiction over both spending and taxing was consolidated in only one committee in each chamber. Even when appropriations jurisdictions were parceled out among seven House committees after 1885, the numerous centers of budgetary power were at least well-identified and were controllable by party leaders. And in a pre-Keynesian world, government just did not worry about fiscal policy, only about budget policy (Kimmel 1959).

Yet to paint a picture of utter serenity would be grossly misleading. By today's standards budgeting between 1865 and 1921 was simple and manageable, but seen at its own scale, and examined at a closer level, budgeting was quite contentious. For, no less than today, the federal budget stood as the best symbol delineating who were the government's winners and losers. By modern comparison the size of federal spending was small; but what little there was, was fought over fiercely. Federal governmental budgeting created strong undercurrents felt throughout the society: Fledgling industries were protected by tariffs; peace with Native American tribes was bought for white western settlers; and veterans (or those who claimed to be such) and their families lived off federal largess following the end of hostilities. In short, although the great administrative state that we know today was only embryonic, what the federal government had to distribute during this era – land, pensions, post offices, rights of eminent domain – defined a range of issues and a style of politics that is not fundamentally foreign to the present.

In Part II, I examine the growing institutional complexity of the budget system in the House. The period begins in 1865 with utter structural simplicity. It ends with the institution of the epitome of classic progressive reforms. The middle, some have argued, was chaos. During the battles over levels and loci of budgetary controls there was a rich competition among House members over how to structure budgeting. Changes that we now regard as historically important usually did not seem inevitable then, and as we shall see, structural changes were taken with a number of false starts, a good deal of ineptitude, and varying degrees of success.

Between 1865 and 1921 there were over thirty attempts of varying range, scope, intensity, and success to alter budgetary structure made in the House. A catalog of those attempts is given in the Appendix. What follows is a full exploration of these cases. Chapter 3 describes the cases of budget reform success and failure up to 1885; Chapter 4 analyzes the changes in spending decisions under the regime of 1885; and Chapter 5 carries the case development to 1921.

3

The politics of budgetary structure, 1865–1885

The time between the House Appropriations Committee's (HAC) creation in 1865 and its wholesale loss of institutional power in 1885 was one of nearly continual debate over the proper way to structure the appropriations process in the House. The debate started slowly, but by the late 1870s its intensity had increased substantially.

As we shall see, the debate was guided by the theoretical dynamics identified in Chapter 1, which informed the structural preferences of members and helped to determine their reform tactics. Of the dynamics identified as key to understanding structural politics, two especially stood out during the period covered in this chapter, giving rise to the most important reform attempts and ultimately shaping the form of the new appropriations process that was in place by 1885. The first key dynamic was the tension between leadership and rank-and-file preferences. With only a couple of important exceptions, the structural debate after 1865 was prompted by the dissatisfaction of the rank-and-file with the status quo; the rank-and-file frequently opposed the formal structures of centralized spending control, which leadership usually defended vigorously. The split between leaders and backbenchers was greatest among Democrats, whose southern members occasionally found themselves in direct conflict with the preferences of northern Democratic Speakers.

Because they lacked firm control over the rewards and punishments that later Speakers (from Reed to Cannon) would wield, and because they lacked the greater partisan homogeneity that allowed later Speakers to wield such control, Democratic Speakers frequently found themselves at the losing end of structural fights in the 1870s and 1880s. Samuel Randall, the Speaker most often pummeled on the House floor by his copartisans, was eventually deposed from his leadership position, not only (or even primarily) because of his incongruence on structural issues, but also because of the incongruence between him and the rest of his party on other major issues of the day, principally the tariff. Randall's successor, John Carlisle, learning from Randall's mistakes, decided not to oppose the obvious structural preferences of his followers, and instead led the fight himself to strip the HAC of most of its authority.

The second key dynamic was the differences among members who were most committed to expanding internal improvements. While it is common to paint all supporters of the pork barrel with the same brush, there was real disagreement among them during this time over the best way to provide a continuing, satisfactory level of internal improvements spending. So pork barrel supporters stood in opposition to nonsupporters; but they could also be divided among themselves, between those favoring the centralization of pork barrel spending in one committee (and thus favoring the crafting of project omnibuses) and those favoring the fragmentation of pork barrel oversight. Once supporters had succeeded in removing the rivers and harbors bill from the HAC in 1877, they drew up sides against each other in fights over the degree of future fragmentation. These structural battles among supporters of the pork barrel produced a number of interesting instances in which the principals analyzed in detail the theoretical issue of whether centralization or dispersion would maximize spending.

The precarious position of party leaders and the uncertainties among high-demand members were the two most common motive forces in driving reform politics during this twenty-year period. In this chapter we shall see that the other factors identified in Chapter 1 also came into play. The vagaries of the economy, for instance, provided the backdrop against which many of the structural battles were waged: Initial scarcity following the Civil War provoked initial support for control efforts, the desire to rebuild the South following Reconstruction and the recession of the 1870s spurred on attempts to relax the oversight of internal improvements, and renewed economic health in the 1880s made spending expansion and structural dispersion easier to accomplish.

When we look back a century ago, the particular turns that reform politics took between 1865 and 1885 seem inevitable. In fact, many of those turns *were* inevitable in a way since there is something almost inherent about committees wanting to expand their jurisdictions, members of Congress trying to gain monopoly control over spending dear to their constituents, and elected politicians taking advantage of abundance to reward their supporters out of the general till. But *at the time*, the turns did not seem so inevitable. It is to that time, and to the details of the era, that we now turn.

The politics of budgetary structure

In the midst of the tremendous strain on governmental capacity brought on by the Civil War came the first lasting reform of the congressional budgetary process since the creation of the Ways and Means Committee: The House created the Appropriations Committee in 1865. (The Senate followed suit in 1867.) The Appropriations Committee was created by dividing the Ways and Means Committee into three parts. The first two parts were the committee's spending and taxing functions; the latter remained with Ways and Means and the former moved to Appropriations. The third function, which does not concern us directly, was oversight of the banking system, which was transferred to a new Banking and Currency Committee.

The division of the Ways and Means Committee was a major change produced with surprisingly little fanfare or public rancor. The Appropriations Committee's creation may have produced behind-the-scenes conflict, but it was not reported by the press, and the whole episode was not controversial enough for the principals, Thaddeus Stevens and Samuel Cox, to comment on in memoirs or letters. The common conclusion, expressed in contemporary newspaper accounts, was that the Appropriations Committee was created because Ways and Means was overworked, not because House leaders wanted to discredit Ways and Means or because House members were dissatisfied with the substantive direction that the committee *wanted* to take.

House members who debated the split of the Ways and Means Committee on 2 March 1865 were aware that the formal separation of budgetary questions could result in a decrease in coordination between spending and taxing, and could ultimately produce increased spending. Yet remedying the confusion wrought by the growth in the Ways and Means Committee's work load was of more immediate concern than long-run coordination issues. Cox, who chaired the committee that reported the creation of the Appropriations Committee, took pains to address this point when he reported to the House:

I need not dilate upon the importance of having hereafter one committee to investigate with nicest heed all matters connected with economy. The tendency of the time is to extravagance in private and in public. We require of this new committee their whole labor in the restraint of extravagant and illegal appropriations....

Each member of the Ways and Means has his specialty – each Olympian.... And yet, sir, powerful as the committee is constituted, even their powers of endurance, physical and mental, are not adequate to the great duty which has been imposed by the emergencies of this historic time. (CG, 38-2, 2 Mar. 1865, 1312)

After discoursing about the numerous details and vast size of the various appropriations, tariff, and revenue acts that Ways and Means had handled in recent years, Cox went on to ask: "Is it not wise to divide such labors as have been described? Who wishes to overwork any set of gentlemen in this or any future Congress?" (CG, 38-2, 2 Mar. 1865, 1313).

The debate that followed also showed that members of Congress (MCs) recognized long-run perils involved in separating spending from taxing oversight, but concern about Ways and Means' immediate work load seemed more compelling. Even Thaddeus Stevens, who chaired Ways and Means, was somewhat indifferent about the matter, even as he raised some questions about the ability of Congress to minimize spending and deficits under the proposed new regime:

[The change] will affect the next Congress, and I have no doubt that whoever is Speaker then will make a proper selection of members of the committees. I do not feel any interest in the matter at all. I do not know whether my colleagues on the committee do....

The only doubt I have in regard to it is the proposition to separate the duties of finance from those of appropriations. I have some doubts as to the propriety of that. I have no desire myself to have it one way or the other. Certainly the labors of the committee would be very much lessened by it. But the two subjects seem to be very properly connected; and I have some doubts as to the propriety of separating them; ... yet I think the gentleman from Ohio [Mr. Cox] is sincere when he says that this matter has not been prompted by any action of the present committee. (CG, 38-2, 2 Mar. 1865, 1315)

The reform created so little controversy that debate was disposed of in seven pages of the *Congressional Globe*, and the rules change was passed by voice vote (CG, 38-2, 2 Mar. 1865, 1517).

This shift from unified budgetary oversight to considering spending and taxing in separate committees is the first case of many in which the House decentralized in order to effect greater control of overall budgetary policy. There are strong theoretical arguments to be made for using a division of labor in these situations. At a certain level of division of labor, before monitoring costs become prohibitive, organizations can often handle large, complex problems more effectively when the task is divided and selected individuals concentrate their efforts in one direction to the exclusion of others.

Yet there were options available to MCs in 1865 other than division and fragmentation, and there were many ways in which they could have implemented a division of labor. For instance, leadership could have proposed expanding the Ways and Means Committee. (In fact, this was a tack frequently taken by the House after 1865 as societal and political pressures increased on its committees.) And the expansion of Ways and Means could have been coupled with the further development of the nascent subcommittee system, allowing detailed scrutiny of spending and taxing bills while still vesting coordination with the full committee and its powerful chair.

Therefore, the House leadership did not randomly choose to divvy up the Ways and Means Committee's jurisdiction. Rather, the choice of the reform that was suggested by the leadership was significantly influenced by the strategic situation. Other options were precluded from the start. For instance, the prospect of expanding the size of Ways and Means undoubtedly proved unsavory to both rank-and-file House members and to party leaders. An expanded Ways and Means Committee, overseeing a vastly expanded state apparatus, would have significantly increased the institutional resources of its chair and members. Increasing the power of the committee and its chair would in turn have provided a more potent challenge to the independent spending preferences of nonmembers of Ways and Means, and would have created a strong rival to the power of the Speaker.[1]

In short, the creation of the Appropriations Committee embodied a balance between the perceived need for greater fiscal control and the aversion to concentrating institutional resources among a limited set of individuals. The *technical* problem of overwork was solved by bringing more people to the task; the *political* problem of institutional power was solved by dividing budgetary responsibility among two power centers. Leadership retained much of its institutional power since it was in the position to mediate disputes between the two committees.

In the short term, members of the House seemed to be satisfied with the new budgetary regime and did not seek any further formal spending controls for another decade. Thaddeus Stevens was named the first chair of the Appropriations Committee in the next Congress. The active collaboration between the Ways and Means and Appropriations committees, which had been predicted when the rules change was passed, actually occurred. There was a national consensus, reflected in Congress, that Civil War spending had indeed been extravagant, that waste had been widespread, that war profiteering had been rampant, and that Congress had to get a handle on the situation. Coupled with the overwhelming Republican majorities from 1865 to 1875 and the focus on reconstructing the South to the detriment of addressing other domestic issues, HAC initially drew widespread support for its efforts to chart a retrenching course.

---

1 In fact, Ways and Means and Appropriations *did* become rival power centers in later decades with, for instance, the ranking Democrat on the Ways and Means Committee eventually being recognized as either the floor leader of the Democratic party or as the leader of the second-largest major faction of Democrats in the House.

CONTROL WITH A DASH OF PARTISANSHIP:
THE HOLMAN RULE

The regime that began in 1865 was safe from attack in its early years. The earliest skirmishes over appropriations structure after 1865 were minor. The first of these occurred between 14 and 16 December 1874 (43rd Cong., 2nd sess.) during the consideration of the legislative, executive, and judicial appropriations bill.[2] The structural issue raised in 1874 involved the relatively inconsequential Army Asylum for disabled soldiers and what we would now recognize as "off-budget" spending.

The asylum had been funded off budget throughout its existence, with funds coming from the forfeited pensions of soldiers who were declared deserters. Declaring a veteran to have been a deserter was not a self-executing task, and the asylum employed a staff of clerks whose job it was to declare as many veterans as possible to be deserters. This state of affairs changed when William Wheeler moved to place the asylum on budget, abolish the clerks' positions, and as a consequence make the asylum's budget more secure while at the same time increasing the financial security of soldiers who had borderline service records (in addition to protecting those who had been slow to claim their legally entitled benefits) (CR, 43-2, 14 Dec. 1874, 74; 16 Dec. 1874, 105).[3] While this was not a major landmark in the history of structural politics, it does highlight some persistent themes in House structural politics, primarily the structural protection of popular programs, which the asylum's off-budget status provided before 1874, and the protection of important constituency groups, which was the political effect of Wheeler's motion.[4]

In the conventional history of budget reform between 1865 and 1921 the next significant move after the creation of the HAC in 1865 was the passage in 1876 of what has been called the Holman Rule. This rule – named after its staunchest supporter, John Holman (D-IN) – made substantive riders to appropriations bills in order, so long as they purported to retrench spending. While recent budgetary scholars have focused on the *retrenching* side of the rule, suggesting that its purpose was simply policy-neutral frugality, the events surrounding its passage and imple-

---

2 The legislative, executive, and judicial bill provided appropriations for the various Washington-based operations of the federal bureaucracy.

3 Many deserters, so called, were declared such without ever being notified. Also, many of the declared deserters had merely never picked up their pension checks: This was the only way that the asylum could claim those dormant funds.

4 Since Wheeler was also a national political figure (he was elected vice president under Hayes in 1876), his motion was probably most significant for the symbolic uses to which it could be put, rather than for the magnitude of the policy change that resulted.

mentation suggest a clear and strong partisan bias to its politics (Fisher 1975; Schick 1984).

Between 1837 and 1876, House Rule 120 had governed the consideration of floor amendments to appropriations bills. It read:

No appropriation shall be reported in such general appropriation bills, or be in order as an amendment thereto, for any expenditure not previously authorized by law, unless in continuation of appropriations for such public works and objects as are already in progress, and for the contingencies for carrying on the general departments of the Government.

While the first half of the rule reads as a restrictive measure, the second half was quite permissive. In fact, the *Digest* of the House Rules reported that the latter half of Rule 120 not only allowed for amendments to increase expenditures, especially salaries, but that "it was framed for that very purpose" (Barclay, 1874, 16; CR, 44-1, 17 Jan. 1876, 445). Being able to extend appropriations for public works and to increase the salaries of federal workers was of great importance during this period of party rule linked by patronage. In fact, Rule 120 had been frequently used by Republicans after the Civil War to quietly raise the salaries of patronage appointees even beyond that allowed by law.

As reported to the 44th House, the Holman Rule, which replaced Rule 120, read:

No appropriation shall be reported in such general appropriation bills, or be in order as an amendment thereto, for any expenditure not previously authorized by law, unless in continuation of appropriations for such public works and objects as are already in progress. *Nor shall any provision in any such bill or amendment thereto, changing existing law, be in order except such as, being germane to the subject-matter of the bill, shall retrench expenditures.* (CR 44-1, 17 Jan. 1867, 445; emphasis indicates the new part of Rule 120 proposed by the committee)

The very brief debate that preceded the Holman Rule's passage revealed some of the partisanship that underlay its politics. Democrats emphasized the retrenching aspects of the rule. Republicans focused on the part of the rule that allowed the HAC or the House floor to add legislative provisions (riders) to appropriations bills, and thus to change law through the appropriations process. Republicans perceived the rule as a Democratic attempt to centralize policymaking within the HAC, and by implication, to loosen the controls that the far-flung legislative committees had had on federal agencies. As James Garfield argued: "To give this Appropriation Committee such a general sweeping power now is substantially to render obsolete the power of all the other committees of the House" (CR, 41-1, 17 Jan. 1876, 445).

The Republican fears were quite plausible. Democrats had been out of power in the House for nearly two decades and were searching for ways to gain leverage over the Republican-dominated executive (White 1958, 49–50, 60–66). Given a Republican presidency and Senate in 1876, Democratic prospects for legislative success were slim. The best hope they had for gaining movement on strongly divisive measures – such as army regulation, the status of the South, and administrative reform – was by insisting on adding substantive legislation to appropriations bills.[5] While this practice has become commonplace today, its initiation in 1876 marked a bold gamble on the part of House Democrats that they could win in the game of appropriations brinkmanship.

Voting on the Holman Rule also betrayed the partisan frame into which members put the issue. Almost no Democrats shared Garfield's objection to enhancing the HAC's power; the partisan split was reflected in the roll call on this particular rule in which Democrats favored adopting it 151 to 6 and Republicans opposed it 4 to 94.

Finally, the roll call was not the only indicator of the Holman Rule's partisanship. Another indicator, which revealed itself across the next four decades, was the pattern of the rule's periodic enactment and repeal. Simply put, the chances of the rule being enacted increased substantially when a Democratic House faced a Republican president; the rule was typically repealed when the two institutions were controlled by the same party.

To see this partisan pattern of passage and repeal better, we need to go back one Congress, to the 43rd in 1874. Holman first proposed his rule on the House floor during that Republican-controlled House, only to have it fall on deaf ears (*House Journal*, 43-2, 10 Dec. 1874, 46). When he proposed his rule in 1876 and got it passed, the main thing that had changed in the intervening two years was party control of the chamber: The 44th House was the first after the Civil War to be controlled by Democrats.

The Holman Rule's enactment from Congress to Congress continued

---

5 The classic example of the Democrats' use of legislation on appropriations bills was the repeal of the Reconstruction-era act that authorized federal troops to "ensure the peace" at polling places in the South. Especially in the aftermath of the disputed 1876 election in which the role of federal forces in South Carolina and Louisiana was wrapped up in the confusion surrounding those states' electoral outcomes, Democrats viewed this use of the army as part of a Republican power grab. House Democrats were barred from repealing this legislation outright in the 45th Congress (1877–1879) because Republicans controlled both the Senate and the White House; Democrats gained control of the 46th Senate, but the Republican Hayes still was president.

The army's electoral role in the South was repealed through a proviso attached to the FY 1880 army appropriation bill. Hayes returned the bill without his approval, citing solely this provision in his veto message. The veto was sustained; but with no money appropriated for the army barely a week before the start of the fiscal year, Hayes finally relented, and "army interference at the polls" was ended.

to depend on the partisan composition of the federal government over the following decades (Figure 3.1). The Democratic House first passed it in 1876 when there was a Republican president (Grant). Republicans gained control of the House in the 47th Congress and did not repeal the rule. When the Democrats returned to the 48th House, they, too, retained the rule. The rule was repealed in the 49th House, the first time that the term of a Democratic president coincided with a Democratic House after the Civil War. The next time the rule was enacted was the 52nd Congress, which was the next time a Democratic House faced a Republican president.

The Holman Rule was not repealed when Cleveland returned to the White House during the Democratically controlled 53rd House, but it was repealed in the 54th Congress, when Republicans regained control of the House. During the 1897–1911 period, which was marked by unbroken Republican control of the entire federal government, the Holman rule was never enacted. But, the Democratic 62nd House, which broke the Republican winning streak, did reenact the Holman Rule in 1911 to use against President Taft (see Chapter 5).

While the association between partisan composition of the House and Holman Rule enactment before 1921 is not 100 percent predictive, it is clear that the Holman Rule was generally seen by both parties as a Democratic weapon for use against Republican presidents. The Democratic rank-and-file was willing to give up some strategic leverage over appropriations bills through this device, putting the Appropriations Committee in a better position to oversee and control Republican administration officials. After the devolution of 1885, of course, this leverage would also extend to the legislative committees directly. Then, Democrats would have two avenues, the appropriations and legislative processes, to get legislation to the floor and to raise the likelihood of circumventing a presidential veto.

The rule's usage in years to come also reveals its partisanship. For instance, it was via the Holman Rule that most Reconstruction legislation was repealed: Repeal had been impossible through the normal legislative route because of the control of the Senate and White House by Republicans. Also, structural reorganizations were attempted by Democrats under the protection of the rule, as in 1879 when a motion was made to transfer the Indian Bureau from the Interior Department to the War Department under the guise of economy. The baroque twists that the rule's implementation took, as all manner of substantive amendments were admitted under the guise of retrenchment, require over eight chapters in Hind's and Cannon's *Precedents* (Hinds 1907, vol. 4, chaps. 95, 97, 98; Cannon 1935, sec. 1125, chaps. 223–227).

Certainly, it is reasonable to assume that the rule's implementation

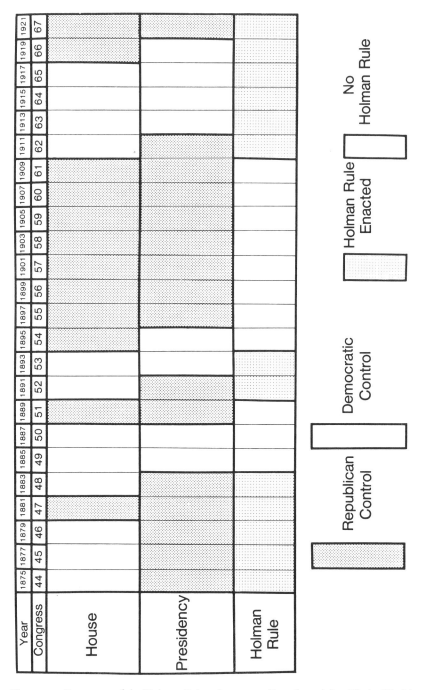

Figure 3.1. Enactment of the Holman Rule, 1875–1921. Data from Asher Hinds, *Hinds' Precedents of the House of Representatives* (Washington, D.C.: U.S. Government Printing Office, 1907), vol. 4, chaps. 95, 97, 98; Clarence Cannon, *Cannon's Precedents of the House of Representatives* (Washington, D.C.: U.S. Government Printing Office, 1935), sec. 1125, chaps. 223–227.

would, over the long run, ruffle the feathers of both Republicans *and* Democrats whose committees lost effective control over legislation and the legislative agenda (Garfield 1879). But it is also evident that the Democrats' *initial enthusiasm* for the Holman Rule stemmed as much from a desire to develop a tool with which to battle Republicans as a desire to tighten spending control as a general principle.

STRUCTURAL QUESTIONS HEAT UP: WATER PROJECTS

As Congress's attention increasingly turned away from reconstructing the South to more general national issues, the politics of budgetary structure intensified, and the House began to consider structural issues that were more lastingly consequential than those raised by Wheeler or even Holman. Starting in the middle 1870s, the House considered a series of proposals that were aimed toward granting the legislative committees greater autonomy in setting spending priorities. Some of these proposals succeeded in their quest to force the sharing of spending decisionmaking; most failed. The first of these proposals, and the type that recurred most frequently in the 1870s and 1880s, were those that dealt with the control of the pork barrel and water projects.

Questions about the scope and distribution of the internal improvements program intensified as the nation resumed the economic expansion interrupted by the Civil War and the Panic of 1873, and as the southern members who reentered Congress began to demand more southern water projects (Woodward 1966, 1971; Seip 1983). Not only did legislators compete over the location of projects, but a significant number questioned the legitimacy of the pork barrel entirely. These latter legislators questioned whether any but the most obviously national of water projects – even those that would have benefited their constituents directly – should be built at all.

Try as they might, pork barrel opponents were unsuccessful in abolishing the pork barrel, and by the 1870s they had altered their tactics to reflect that reality. Opponents of the national pork barrel had resigned themselves to its practical reality by supporting procedures designed to reduce internal improvements spending as much as possible. As far as these pork barrel opponents were concerned, if there had to be internal improvements at all, maximum power should be given to the Appropriations Committee in setting spending levels.

Strict centralization in the consideration of rivers and harbors spending had existed before the Civil War, as the Ways and Means Committee alone reported the annual rivers and harbors bill. Pressure to expand rivers and harbors decisionmaking eventually led to a compromise, sometime after the Civil War, between those favoring strict control and those preferring spending expansion. The compromise consisted of serial referral, in which the Commerce Committee would report out a rivers and harbors bill, which would then be referred to the Appropriations Committee before it could be considered on the floor. Through this procedure, proponents of spending got the ability to determine the general geographic distribution of projects, while the HAC got the ability to reduce the bill's aggregate level.

The 45th Congress (1877–79) began the disintegration of the pork barrel comity that had prevailed for a decade. During this Congress, two ongoing, parallel challenges to the institutional status quo were launched. The first challenge was to the Appropriations Committee and its authority to regulate the level of appropriations found in the rivers and harbors bill. The ultimate victor in this set of challenges was the Commerce Committee, which eventually asserted sole domination over this bill. The second challenge was to the Commerce Committee itself, as other legislative committees that also had some authority in the internal improvements area sought a share of agenda control in this issue. An institutional equilibrium was eventually reestablished, but not without considerable attention to the matter on the floor of the House.

On 5 November 1877, less than a month after the organization of the 45th Congress, John Reagan (D-TX) of the Commerce Committee introduced a resolution directing the Select Rules Committee to study the question of the jurisdiction of rivers and harbors legislation in the House. A month later (4 December 1877) Gustavus Schleicher, the chair of the Committee on Railways and Canals, entered the fray by presenting a report from his committee challenging the right of the Commerce Committee to examine the rivers and harbors bill at all.[6] Schleicher's argument rested on the Railways Committee's reading of House Rule 94, which stated that the duty of the Railways and Canals Committee was "to take into consideration all such petitions and matters or things relating to roads and canals and the improvement of the navigation of rivers as shall be presented or may come in question and be referred to them by the House."

Speaker Samuel Randall was annoyed by the Railways Committee's impertinence in claiming jurisdiction over a bill that had *historically* belonged to another committee and ruled that their attempt to claim all water project legislation to themselves was out of order. However, many

6 Fisher (1975, 22, fn. 33) identifies this action as the first instance in which the Commerce Committee wrested control of rivers and harbors appropriations from the HAC. This is clearly not the case. The event to which Fisher refers occurred five months later and is discussed below.

legislators expressed interest in the matter, so debate on the issue ensued by unanimous consent (CR 45-2, 4 Dec. 1877, 18-26).

The debate, which lasted two full days, is reminiscent of the old adage, "if the facts are against you, argue the law; if the law is against you, argue the facts." Schleicher and others who favored his Railways Committee's stance reasoned that the House rules were clear. Defenders of the Commerce Committee argued that House precedent was controlling in this situation, regardless of what the rules said.

As debate unfolded, it became clear that the Railways and Canals Committee stood alone in its assertion of jurisdictional dissatisfaction. Only members of the Railways Committee defended this jurisdictional raid, while defenders of the Commerce Committee came from around the chamber, including not only members of the Commerce Committee itself, but also Speaker Randall and James Garfield, the most influential Republican member of Ways and Means.

Some Railways and Canals Committee members unsuccessfully tried to dispel the belief that their action was a brute power grab. John Mitchell (R-PA) claimed: "I desire to say that there is no interest at all involved affecting myself or the locality which I have the honor in representing in this House." But others on the Railways Committee defended their action more forthrightly, such as Thomas Crittenden (D-MO) who said: "There is a laudable ambition . . . that I think should prompt every committee of this House to seek the business that legitimately belongs to it" (CR, 45-2, 4 Dec. 1877, 24; 5 Dec. 1877, 28).

While members of the Railways and Canals Committee were busy arguing the rules of the House, those on Commerce's side repeatedly cited custom and precedent. John Reagan argued:

The Committee on Commerce having been constituted with reference to the rules and practice of the House, to take away from them at this time their accustomed jurisdiction and transfer it to a committee that never before had it would be a direct reflection either upon the capacity or the integrity of the Committee on Commerce. (CR, 45-2, 4 Dec. 1877, 23; also note Rhea's comments, CR, 45-2, 4 Dec. 1877, 34–35)

Along with the long speech defending his committee, Reagan produced a table documenting that, regardless of the written rules, only the Commerce and Ways and Means/Appropriations committees had reported any rivers and harbors bill since 1816. Of 1,441 total bills that passed the House concerning rivers and harbors from 1831 to 1877, only 5 had been referred to Railways, while 1,436 had been referred to the others (CR 45-2, 4 Dec. 1877, 21). Despite what the rules said, Reagan argued, practice dictated that the Rivers and Harbors bill belonged with Commerce.

Unfortunately for our purposes, no vote was ever taken on this issue.

The resolution from the Railways and Canals Committee was referred to the Select Committee on the Rules at the end of the second day of debate, and the resolution was not discussed on the floor for the rest of that Congress.

Although members of the Railways and Canals Committee made a strong case for its sole oversight of all water project legislation, based on a reading of the rules, its case was doomed to failure from the beginning. Rank-and-file members had to be convinced that a jurisdictional reshuffling would not only bring the rules and legislative practice closer into line, but would also improve substantive outcomes significantly enough to overcome the institutional costs that would have been incurred through taking power from the Commerce Committee. In casting the debate in pure legalisms and not focusing on substantive gains to be had from the change, Railways did not make it clear how rank-and-file members would have benefited by supporting this jurisdictional raid.

In fact, it is fairly clear that a shift from Commerce to Railways would not have altered the *geographic* basis of allocating water projects. For instance, in both the 44th and 45th Congresses each committee had members from districts bordering on the great national rivers, and the regional balance of the two was very close.[7] The only real geographic difference in memberships was that Railways had a slight midwestern tilt.[8] The regional similarities between Commerce and Railways is also revealed when we consider the specific locations of the twenty-two districts from which members of the two committees came during the 44th and 45th Congresses. Of those twenty-two districts, fourteen were adjoining.[9] Thus, it is not at all clear what most proponents of rivers and harbors spending would have gained substantively from taking water projects from one committee and giving them to another.

Not only were the substantive gains to be had from shifting jurisdictions nonexistent, but Commerce was able to defend its institutional

7 Remarks concerning the location of districts are based on maps contained in Martis (1982).
8 The regional composition of Railways and Commerce should also be contrasted to that of the Appropriations Committee. At this time the HAC had no members from west of the Mississippi – prime pork barrel territory. Shifting power away from the Appropriations Committee had clear regional implications. Shifting power between Railways and Commerce did not have clear regional implications.
9 For instance, in the 44th Congress, Edward Kehr of Missouri's 1st district and William Stone of Missouri's 3rd district were on the Commerce and Railways committees, respectively. The 1st and 3rd districts of Missouri were both in St. Louis. Other examples of adjoining districts among members of both committees were as follows (Commerce Committee members listed first in each pair): *44th Congress*: Indiana 8 and 7; Pennsylvania 16 and 20. In the *45th Congress*: Minnesota 1 and Wisconsin 3; Pennsylvania 15 and 16; New Jersey 3 and 5; New York 4 and 5.

position, in part, by relying on the resources of party leaders. Leadership from both parties rose to support the Commerce Committee in this instance. As we shall see, when the gains to be had from opposing party leaders were substantial, the rank-and-file might abandon their leaders. With the probable gains close to zero in this instance, however, the safe strategy was to support leadership and oppose Railways and Canals.

Dissent over rivers and harbors legislation continued throughout the 45th Congress. The second major incident concerned the Commerce Committee, the Appropriations Committee, and the rivers and harbors bill. When this episode was over, the Commerce Committee had made the first substantial move in asserting for itself sole jurisdiction over water project appropriations.

This conflict began as John Reagan rose on 22 April 1878 and moved that the rules be suspended and that the rivers and harbors bill be passed (CR, 45-2, 22 Apr. 1878, 2713).[10] The point of this motion was to bypass the HAC, and thus to short-circuit serial referral. The effect of the suspension motion was also to avoid the provisions of rule 121, which allowed for individual items on public works bills to be voted on separately.

Opponents of Reagan's motion immediately sprang into action. Samuel Cox (D-NY) objected to the proceedings, arguing that Article I, section 8 of the Constitution gave Congress the right to regulate commerce with foreign nations and between states but "it never intended to pay money by the million [sic] for local improvements to inconsiderable rivers and creeks." He continued by saying that "the shrieks of locality may be loud; for one I will not heed them by making precedents whose effect is to destroy constitutional limitations and beget a log-rolling system utterly subversive of fair legislation" (CR, 45-2, 22 Apr. 1878, 2713).

Reagan's opponents tried to stall action on the floor by forcing a series of roll call and teller votes, but Reagan's motion eventually received a favorable vote of 167–66. If this motion was aimed at effecting both a short-term substantive victory for water project spending and a long-term structural victory for the Commerce Committee and others interested in enhancing the nation's internal improvements program, then this roll call should have been structured in predictable ways. Since the substantive issue typically reflected regional interests, we should expect the less-developed regions (the South and states west of the Mississippi) to have been Reagan's strongest supporters[11] (Table 3.1). Because the issue

---

10 Wander (1982a, 50) states that Reagan tried this tactic in the first session of the 45th Congress, but a diligent search for that episode proved fruitless.
11 I lump together members from west of the Mississippi (excluding the old Confederacy) in the data analysis done in this chapter because there were so few of

Table 3.1. *Regional definitions in roll call analyses*

New England
Maine, New Hampshire, Vermont, Massachusetts, Rhode Island, Connecticut
East
New York, New Jersey, Delaware, Maryland, West Virginia, Pennsylvania
Confederacy
Virginia, North Carolina, South Carolina, Georgia, Alabama, Florida, Mississippi, Tennessee, Louisiana, Arkansas, Texas
Midwest
Ohio, Kentucky, Indiana, Michigan, Illinois, Wisconsin
West[a]
Minnesota, Iowa, Missouri, Kansas, Nebraska, Colorado, Nevada, Oregon, California
Prairie[b]
Minnesota, Iowa, Missouri, North Dakota, South Dakota, Nebraska, Kansas, Oklahoma
Mountain/West[b]
Montana, Wyoming, Colorado, New Mexico, Idaho, Utah, Arizona, Nevada, Washington, Oregon, California

[a]Analysis in Chapter 3.
[b]Analysis in Chapter 5.

had long-term formal implications for the jurisdictions of committees, we should also expect members of the HAC to have voted no and members of Commerce to have voted yes. And, since the majority party leadership should have tried to exert added pressure on its followers to support the structural status quo, we should expect Democrats, ceteris paribus, to have voted no.

The logistic regression analysis of this vote reveals these patterns, although the party effect is both statistically and substantively weak (Table 3.2).[12] Southerners and westerners were clearly the most likely to support

them in the House at the time, especially members from the far west, not because western issues could not be further differentiated. For instance, in the vote analyzed in Table 3.2, only five members from west of Nebraska voted.

12 Table 3.2 and all subsequent tables reporting multivariate roll call analysis report values based on logistic regressions. Logistic regression varies from standard ordinary least squares (OLS) regression in that OLS is linear in the parameters while logistic regression is not. The other way of expressing this difference is that OLS fits a straight line to the data, while logistic regression fits an S-shaped curve, allowing for the fact that voting data, which is analyzed here, is bound by values of 0 and 1. In OLS, the impact that an independent variable has on values of the dependent variable is independent of the values of the other independent variables. However, in logistic regression, the impact that an independent variable has on values of the dependent variable varies according to the values of the other independent variables. (*Continued on p. 96.*)

Table 3.2. *Effect of party, region, and committee membership on vote to suspend the rules to pass the rivers and harbors appropriations bill, 45th Congress, 1878 (logistic regression)*

Effect	Estimate[a]
Intercept	0.436
Party (Democrats)	−0.223
Regions (excluded = East)	
New England	1.363
Confederacy	1.753***
Midwest	0.295
West	2.279***
Committees	−1.767***

N = 225
Proportion voting yes = 73.7
Percent correctly predicted = 75.0

Estimated probabilities that types of members would vote yes:

1. By region and party[b]

Region	Republicans	Democrats
New England	0.858	0.829
East	0.607	0.553
Confederacy	0.899	0.877
Midwest	0.675	0.624
West	0.938	0.924

2. By committee membership[c]

Appropriations Committee: 0.364
Commerce Committee: 0.951
Neither committee: 0.770

Note: Estimates were produced using only members who were either Republicans or Democrats. The Committee variable was defined such that it equaled 1 if the member was on the Appropriations Committee, −1 if the member was on the Commerce Committee, 0 otherwise. For regional definitions, see Table 3.1.
[a]Statistical significance: ***, $p \leq$ .01. Other coefficients insignificant at $p <$ .10.
[b]Assuming the members served on neither the Appropriations nor the Commerce Committee.
[c]Setting regional and party variables to their means.

Reagan, controlling for party and committee membership, reflecting the greater vigor with which these members sought water projects.[13] HAC members were more likely to be opponents, while members of the Commerce Committee were highly likely to support their chair.[14]

Reagan's victory was not taken lying down by members of the Appropriations Committee and by the others in the House who were opponents of water project spending. As the vote on passage of the bill was being taken, a petition was circulated around the House floor protesting the vote under way. Immediately upon passage of the rivers and harbors bill, Cox tried to get the floor so that he could read the petition into the record as a question of privilege.[15] While members wrangled over whether

The interpretation of logistic regression coefficients is not as straightforward as the interpretation of OLS coefficients, yet the interpretation is not all that difficult. If we represent a yes vote by setting the dependent variable to 1 and let a no vote be represented by 0, then the probability that a particular type of MC would vote yes can be predicted from the logit coefficients by the use of the following formula:

$$\text{Prob Yes} = \frac{1}{1 + \exp[-(B_0 + B_1 X_1 + \cdots + B_n X_n)]}$$

For example, using the data from Table 3.2 we can predict the probability that a midwestern Republican on the Commerce Committee would vote yes by doing the following substitution (Party = 0; Midwest = 1; Committees = −1):

$$\text{Prob Yes} = \frac{1}{1 + \exp\{-[0.436 - 0.223(0) + 0.295(1) - 1.767(-1)]\}}$$

If the imaginary member were a Democrat (Party = 1), then the probability of him voting yes would be lowered from 0.924 to 0.907.

13 Brady and Morgan (1983, Table 3) report that between 1870 and 1880 the amount spent in the South on water projects increased about 730%, the border states increased about 710%, western states increased about 1200%, while the Midwest increased only 25%, and the East, 100%. Brady and Morgan's regional divisions are different from those used in this study, but the results are generally comparable. Also see Brady and Morgan (1987, 223–224).

14 The committee variable in Table 3–2 takes on a value of 1 for HAC members, −1 for Commerce Committee members, and 0 for all other MCs. I used a single variable for the two committees in this case because the small number of members from each committee voting on the issue (eleven from Appropriations and six from Commerce) caused each standard error to balloon. In other roll call analyses in this book, where we do not have this problem of "sparse cells," separate variables for each committee are used.

15 House Rule 9 defined a question of privilege as follows: "Questions of privilege shall be, first, those affecting the rights of the House collectively, its safety, dignity, and the integrity of its proceedings; second, the rights, reputation, and conduct of Members individually in their representative capacity only; and shall have precedence of all other questions, except motions to adjourn." Allowing Cox to proceed would not have undone the previous vote, but it would have tainted the precedent Reagan was trying to set.

Table 3.3. *Voting for passage of the rivers and harbors bill under suspension by voting to uphold the question of privilege, 45th Congress, 1878*

		Question of Privilege			
	Vote	Yes	No	NV[a]	Total
Passage of rivers and harbors	Yes	8	121	38	167
bill	No	31	30	5	66
	NV[a]	13	29	16	58
	Total	52	180	59	291

[a] Not voting.

doing so was in order, Reagan's supporters managed to adjourn the House (CR, 45-2, 22 Apr. 1878, 2717–2718).

The House took up Cox's protest the next day in a proceeding that was about as rancorous as House debate can get. Opponents and supporters of internal improvements argued interminably over whether reading the Cox protest was allowable under the House rules.[16] In the process of reading the protest, Rep. Omar Conger (R-MI) even demanded that language contained in it be "taken down" as an "insult to the House."[17] After long and protracted debate over whether the protest indeed involved a question of privilege, the House ultimately turned down the request of the protesters by a vote of 59–180. Almost everyone who originally voted to pass the bill also voted against certifying the Cox protest a question of privilege (Table 3.3). On the other hand, those who had originally voted against the bill split almost evenly.

The outcome of the Cox protest is interesting because of the institutional issues involved. On one level, the protest involved a question of parliamentary hair splitting because even certifying the protest to be a question of privilege would not have undone the previous vote passing the rivers and harbors bill. The more significant level of the protest involved the weight of precedent to be given Reagan's successful motion. In bringing the protest, the Cox group recognized that once a procedure had been successfully attempted on the House floor, that attempt was entered into the precedents of the House and made easier to repeat. They

16 The proceedings of 23 April 1878 begin at CR, 45-2, 23 Apr. 1878, 2737.
17 The offending words accused House members of combining for "general spoliation upon the Treasury." Cox withdrew the word "spoliation" in favor of "exhaustion;" even then, the substitution of words was not accomplished without protracted argument.

were hoping to cut their losses by making it more difficult for Reagan to bypass Appropriations in the future.

Reagan's supporters also realized the importance of the precedent being set. By voting almost unanimously to deny that the issue was a question of privilege, Reagan's supporters indicated that they not only favored the passage of that particular bill, but that they approved of the way in which the bill was passed and suggested that they would favor the use of suspension in the future. As it turned out, therefore, Cox's attempt at protest backfired, and Reagan's ad hoc tactic became even more ingrained in House procedures.

As we shall soon see, this was by no means the final word on how the rivers and harbors bill would be overseen in the near future. Yet it did set a pattern for the decade to come: Members of the House who were otherwise influential were no match for the Commerce Committee and its supporters.

AN ESCALATION OF STRUCTURAL DISCORD: COMMERCE IS REINFORCED AND AGRICULTURE BREAKS AWAY

The 45th Congress was just the beginning for the Commerce Committee and its quest to assert monopoly agenda control over water project spending. Within the next eight years, at least seven proposed rules changes aimed directly at the subject of internal improvements reached the House floor. Most of these represented a challenge to the Commerce Committee in one way or another.

The water project debate heated up in the 46th Congress (1879–81). But, once the 46th Congress was in progress, structural debates became expanded beyond internal improvements, raising the issue of how the entire federal budget would be overseen.

Rules changes were in the air as the 46th Congress convened on 18 March 1879. The House rules had come under increasing attack in recent years for being clumsy and confusing: A total of 169 rules had accumulated since the previous revision in 1860, and the orderly functioning of the House floor had become impaired. The Democrats had been returned to control of the House for the third consecutive Congress, and because the current rules had evolved during a period of Republican domination, there was some feeling among the majority that the rules should reflect more of a Democratic cast (Alexander 1916, 193–196; Galloway 1976, 53–54). Democratic House members proved very eager to begin the rules revision.

Even before Speaker Randall could appoint a Rules Committee, interest in altering appropriations structure was shown when five proposals were put forward affecting appropriations: James Garfield proposed deleting

Table 3.4. *Proposals for restructuring appropriations jurisdictions,*
46th Congress, 1879–1881

	Resolution author			
Bill	Springer	Hooker	Muldrow	Shallenberger
Consular and Diplomatic	X	X	X	X
Army	X	X	X	X
Military Academy				
(to Military Affairs Comm.)	X	X	X	X
Indian Affairs	X	X	X	X
Post Office	X	X	X	X
Naval Affairs	X	X	X	X
Pensions	X	X	X	X
Agriculture	X		X	
Rivers and Harbors				
(to Commerce Committee)		X	X	X
Public Buildings		X	X	X
District of Columbia		X		X
Mississippi River		X		X
Patents			X	

the Holman Rule and four members [William Springer (D-IL), Charles Hooker (D-MS), Henry Muldrow (D-MS), and William Shallenberger (R-PA)] proposed different variations on one theme: the removal of substantial appropriations power from the Appropriations Committee and its transfer to the legislative committees (Table 3.4).

The next day Randall appointed a Rules Committee consisting of himself, two other Democrats – Alexander Stephens (GA, chair of the Coinage, Weights, and Measures Committee) and Joseph Blackburn (KY, HAC member) – as well as two Republicans – William Frey (ME, Ways and Means) and James Garfield (OH, HAC). In addition to being influential members of their respective parties, each Rules Committee member was noted for his position in favor of strong centralized control over appropriations and resistance to increased federal spending. As well, three of the four Randall appointees had a position on one of the two powerful finance committees. Thus, the ground was set for conflict between the more control-oriented leadership and rank-and-file House members over how appropriations would be handled.

Within a month, the Rules Committee returned with the first of its proposals to restrain spending by proposing to increase the majority needed to pass an appropriations bill under suspension of the rules from two-thirds to three-fourths (CR 46-1, 9 Apr. 1879, 328). The principal target of this move was the rivers and harbors bill.

Table 3.5. *Votes to pass the rivers and harbors bill in the House,
45th–49th Congresses, 1878–1887*

Congress–session	Year	Vote	% Yes
45–2	1878	166–66[a]	71
45–3	1879	186–67[a]	74
46–2	1880	179–48[a]	74
46–3	1881	163–84	66
47–1	1882	120–47	72
47–1	1882	122–59[c]	67
47–2	1883	112–91	55
48–1	1884	156–104	60
48–2	1885	192–88[a]	69
49–1	1886	142–102	58
49–1	1886	102–135[b]	43
49–2	1887	178–89[b]	67

[a] Vote to suspend the rules and pass the bill.
[b] Vote to approve conference report.
[c] Vote to override presidential veto.

The Rules Committee's proposal was received in light of the Commerce Committee's emerging practice of passing rivers and harbors bills under suspension of the rules (NYT 10 April 1879, 6). The practice of bringing the rivers and harbors bill up under suspension was certainly a strategy with both perils and benefits for Commerce. Its positive aspect was that suspension guarded the bill against amendment; opponents could not whittle down the bill, nor could overzealous local supporters upset the water cart by adding even more projects to the list. In this regard it served the same purpose as the closed rule for the Ways and Means Committee in the 1950s and 1960s. The negative aspect of suspension was that it required a two-thirds vote rather than a simple majority. This latter condition presented a real threat to continued rivers and harbors spending since majorities voting for final passage of the rivers and harbors bill continued to hover around two-thirds (Table 3.5). Raising the required majority from 67 to 75 percent would have made Commerce's use of suspension riskier and perhaps would have required the committee to accommodate the HAC or other low-demand centers in the House in order to pass water project legislation in the future.

Because suspension was a strategy that could have either retarded or advanced continued spending on internal improvements, Commerce would have clearly preferred to be able to *choose* its use of suspension rather than having the avenue forced on it. But one other strategic factor virtually dictated the use of suspension by Commerce to pass the bill after its coup against the Appropriations Committee the previous year – Commerce lacked the authority to bring its legislation to the House floor as privileged business. Most committees, Commerce included, had to wait their turn on the House calendar before their legislation could be brought to the floor.[18] Appropriations and Ways and Means did not have to wait since they were granted the privilege to report their legislation at any time. The HAC was reputed to hold onto its finished bills and then to bring them up when it looked as if a piece of unwanted legislation was about to be considered. Thus, Commerce could be bumped off the floor by the Appropriations Committee, which was willing to use its privileged reporting status as a strategy to thwart legislation of which its members disapproved – a class into which the rivers and harbors bill fell (Brady and Morgan 1987, 214).

In arguing for raising the majority needed to pass an appropriations bill under suspension, Joseph Blackburn tried to convince House members that it was not directed at the Commerce Committee, and he noted that both the sundry civil bill (reported by the HAC) and the rivers and harbors bill (reported by Commerce) had recently been passed under suspension of the rules with very little prior notice. During the second session of the 45th Congress, the sundry civil appropriations bill, which contained $20 million (16 percent of all the annual bills that year) passed under suspension, the bill having been printed on the day of its passage. Increasing the majority needed to pass a money bill under suspension, Blackburn argued, would encourage both the Appropriations *and* Commerce committees to allow more time for consideration of their bills.

Taking Blackburn at his word that the real culprit was the Appropriations Committee, John Kenna (D-KY), a member of the Commerce Committee, rose to amend the proposed change, making it applicable only to bills reported by the Appropriations Committee (CR, 46-1, 9 Apr. 1879, 328). He argued that Commerce had to operate under suspension because of the Appropriations Committee's chronic tardiness and if anyone was to be punished, it should be Appropriations, not Commerce.

The ensuing debate over Kenna's amendment touched on all areas of committee jurisdiction, resulting in an acrimonious exchange between members of the Commerce and Appropriations committees. Commerce Committee members accused the HAC of abusing its privilege to bring legislation to the floor at any time, monopolizing the floor late in the session. Commerce defended its use of suspension by arguing that the Appropriations Committee's actions left them no choice.

---

18 The practice of bringing up legislation under special orders, or "rules," did not begin until 1883 (Robinson, 1963, 59).

Of the five major speeches made in defense of the Commerce Committee, all were made by Democrats, and three were by members of the Commerce Committee; of the four who supported the Rules Committee's position, three were on the Appropriations Committee (Blackburn, Sparks, and Garfield), and the fourth was Speaker Randall. The issue, therefore, became transformed on the floor from one about the fate of internal improvements and committee jurisdiction into one of leadership loyalty. As debate was ending, John Reagan rose and moved that the following be substituted for the Rules Committee's recommendation:

> That hereafter the Committee on Commerce shall have the same privilege to report a bill making appropriations for the improvement of rivers and harbors that is accorded to the Committee on Appropriations in reporting general appropriations bills. (CR, 46-1, 9 Apr. 1879, 332)

When the vote was finally taken, Reagan had won 100 to 88 on a division vote and by an even larger 146 to 97 roll call vote (CR, 46-1, 9 Apr. 1879, 332).

Reagan's triumph over leadership in this situation initially brings to mind Woodrow Wilson's comments about the Speaker's powers, published five years later:

> The Speaker of the House of Representatives stands as near to leadership as any one; but his will does not run as a formative and imperative power in legislation much beyond the appointment of the committees who are to lead the House and do its work for it. . . . He is a great party chief, but the hedging circumstances of his official position as presiding office prevent his performing the part of active leadership. He appoints the leaders of the House, but he is not himself its leader. (Wilson 1956, 58)

Yet, closer analysis of the vote reveals that leadership was more influential in this vote than the fact of Speaker Randall's defeat would indicate. Because the substantive and structural issues here are substantially the same as those involved in the roll call taken in the 45th Congress (Table 3.2), we can statistically model this present vote in the same way. That is, the vote should have been structured along regional, committee, and party lines. The regional effects should tap differing preferences for water project spending; the committee effects should tap the conflict between the Appropriations and Commerce committees; while the party effect should tap the extent to which the Democratic leadership, which was being directly challenged by this motion, could mobilize its followers.

And in fact, southerners and westerners were once again the strongest regional supporters of Reagan, once we control for party and committee membership (Table 3.6). Also, as with the previous vote, members of the Appropriations Committee favored limiting the Commerce Committee's

Table 3.6. *Effect of party, region, and committee on vote to give the Commerce Committee privileged position to report the rivers and harbors bill, 46th Congress, 1879 (logistic regression)*

Effect	Estimate[a]
Intercept	0.033
Party (Democrats)	−0.718***
Regions (excluded = East)	
New England	−0.127
Confederacy	1.712***
Midwest	0.448
West	2.060***
Committees	
Appropriations	−1.818***
Commerce	2.606***

$N = 239$
Proportion voting yes = 64.7
Percent correctly predicted = 66.5

Estimated probabilities that types of members would vote yes:

1. By region and party[b]

Region	Republicans	Democrats
New England	0.477	0.308
East	0.508	0.335
Confederacy	0.851	0.736
Midwest	0.618	0.441
West	0.890	0.798

2. By committee membership[c]

Appropriations Committee: 0.952
Commerce Committee: 0.192
Neither committee: 0.594

Note: Estimates were produced using only members who were either Republicans or Democrats. For regional definitions, see Table 3.1.
[a]Statistical significance: ***, $p < .01$. All other coefficients insignificant at $p < .10$.
[b]Assuming the members served on neither the Appropriations nor the Commerce Committee.
[c]Setting regional and party variables to their means.

latitude while members of the Commerce Committee favored their own power accretion.[19]

The biggest changes over the previous roll call vote appear in party votes. Party shows a much stronger effect in the 1879 vote, reflecting greater leadership mobilization on a clear leadership issue. In fact, the effects of party were so strong that the only regions where a majority of Democrats opposed their leaders were the South and West.[20] Interest in internal improvements among western and southern constituents was so intense that their representatives were more afraid of constituent sanctions, should they oppose Reagan, than of incurring the disloyalty costs that party leaders were sure to extract because of this defection.

The outcome of this brief fight over the relative advantages the rules would afford water project legislation provides some insights into understanding the limits to structural centralization and decentralization in the House, as well as revealing the relative weights members put on leadership, committee, and region in making their structural decisions. In this case, presented with the clear alternative between shortening or extending the leash of the Commerce Committee, the House chose looser control. But Democrats, experiencing competing pressures from both constituents and party leaders, found themselves divided on the vote. Only those Democrats whose regions had a tremendous stake in water projects overwhelmingly opposed leadership, indicating that for them, the potential for electoral punishments should they vote no outweighed the institutional loss due to leadership punishment should they vote yes.

Although the Rules Committee was set back in its efforts to impose greater control over water project spending during the first session of the 46th Congress, it continued its crusade to impose greater spending control during the second session. The difference in the second session, however, was that the relatively narrow issue of suspension of the rules gave way to broader questions about the appropriations process. The vehicle for this wide-ranging debate was the long-awaited comprehensive proposal to overhaul the House rules.

No area of the rules was left untouched in the Rules Committee's reform recommendations, as the old rules were grouped by subject into 44 main new rules. Thirty-two old rules were judged unnecessary and

19 Separate variables for each committee are included in this analysis because we have sufficient members of each committee (thirteen apiece) to avoid the sparse cell problems we had in Table 3.2.
20 Moving away from the simulated results reported in Table 3.6 and looking at the empirical probabilities, we see that Democratic southerners voted 43–17 (72%) with Reagan, the west voted 10–2 (83%) on Reagan's side, while all other Democrats opposed Reagan 24–34 (41%).

dropped; 12 were untouched; and 145 others were consolidated into 32 rules (CR, 46-2, 6 Jan. 1880, 198–207). Debate on the changes consumed fourteen days over a two-month period. Six of the fourteen days of debate were given over to the appropriations process, indicating the importance of spending in the minds of House members.

Although the Commerce Committee had already won one battle over the rules during this Congress, the Rules Committee continued to try to circumscribe its strategic options. The way the Rules Committee tried to accomplish this circumscription was by proposing a reinstitution of the old serial referral mechanism for the rivers and harbors omnibus spending bill.

The analysis by the Rules Committee supporting serial referral addressed the question of central spending control directly. They argued that the emerging practice of allowing water project spending to bypass the Appropriations Committee served to insulate internal improvements policy from other spending decisions. The purpose of the Rules Committee's recommendation was to reenter rivers and harbors appropriations into the budgeting mainstream and to make it easier to constrain internal improvements decisions by other fiscal factors:

[The Appropriations Committee] should have entire charge of *all* those [appropriations] bills, in order that they might the more fairly and fully control the entire question of appropriation of revenue for carrying on the several departments of the Government. It follows as a logical sequence that, if any other committee is to take charge of *one* of the general appropriations bills, the interests therein involved and considered will stand separate and apart from the interests involved and considered in the other bills, and as a further result any scheme of reduction of expenditures made necessary by a deficit of revenue for that fiscal year must be executed by the Committee on Appropriations without respect to the interests involved in the bill so taken from them, thereby leaving that particular interest to stand independent of and without any relation whatever to the other interests for which appropriations are annually made. (CR, 46-2, 6 Jan. 1880, 200)

When general debate opened on the new rules, the exchanges concerning the rivers and harbors bill's independence from the Appropriations Committee "created considerable merriment" in the House (NYT 9 Jan. 1880, 1). Not surprisingly, John Reagan was quick to attack the proposal. He asserted that it would, first, undermine the authority of the Commerce Committee since the Appropriations Committee would become an appeals court for those dissatisfied with the decisions of Commerce.[21] Second, he argued, Appropriations did not have the personnel or expertise with which to make a detailed investigation into the rivers

---

21 This first argument was a bit disingenuous since the HAC had by then established a reputation as being a firm budget cutter, not an expansionary "appeals board."

and harbors bill anyway. Thus, he concluded that the HAC would grow to rely on Commerce's work in crafting the final rivers and harbors bill, transforming the Commerce Committee into a collection of clerks working for the Appropriations Committee. John Reagan was not about to be anyone's clerk.

Once debate turned to perfecting the rules on the floor, the proceedings were protracted, tedious, and acrimonious. The proceedings are summarized here in a way that emphasizes the chronological development of floor action, but in fact, consideration frequently jumped randomly from rule to rule. This means that floor consideration was often anarchic, and the same issues were frequently brought up numerous times during the two months as if they were new concerns.

Reagan's specific objections to the Rules Committee's recommendations were dealt with expeditiously. Early in the proceedings, he moved that the objectionable serial referral proposal be deleted from the rules altogether. Reagan succeeded in the vote in Committee of the Whole by 110–40 (CR, 46-2, 2 Feb. 1880, 663). The following day, four members tried to limit Commerce's strategic discretion by prohibiting the rivers and harbors bill from being considered under suspension. Each of these motions failed, one by a voice vote and the other three by teller votes of 43–87, 50–84, and 40–71 (CR, 46-2, 3 Feb. 1880, 684).

Yet, at the same time that rank-and-file members were showing support for an independent rivers and harbors bill, they were also reluctant to expand the spending latitude of committees other than Commerce. Several representatives tried to further weaken the Appropriations Committee by requiring it to share spending oversight with all the legislative committees. But, when the four general decentralization proposals sponsored by Springer, Hooker, Muldrow, and Shallenberger (Table 3.3) were brought up, each was killed by a voice vote. And, when Shallenberger later moved to require the Appropriations Committee to refer appropriations bills serially to the relevant legislative committees, he lost on a 61–122 vote (CR, 46-2, 11 Feb. 1880, 827).

Failing the wholesale approach to loosening the Appropriations Committee's hold over spending decisions, many representatives switched to the retail approach, by moving to redistribute pieces of the HAC's jurisdiction. Retailing decentralization proved only slightly more successful than wholesaling.

D. Wyatt Aiken (D-SC), a member of the Agriculture Committee, moved that his committee be given jurisdiction over funding the Agriculture Department. This passed by a vote of 93–64 (CR, 46-2, 3 Feb. 1880, 684–686). Then, Thomas Browne (R-NY) of the Military Affairs Committee moved that the army appropriations bill be transferred to the

Military Affairs Committee. This was met with protests by Joseph Blackburn:

I know very well it is proper and right that each Department of the Government should have its own especial friends upon this floor. The Committee on Naval Affairs is selected by the Speaker with the view of getting together men who are friendly to that department. . . . That is the theory of the construction of the committees of this House; and it is a proper theory.

The Committee on Appropriations stands in a very different attitude. . . . [It is] selected as a fair and impartial arbiter. (CR, 46-2, 3 Feb. 1880, 687)

Washington Whitthorne (D-TN) joined Blackburn's protest by noting that when he (Whitthorne) chaired the Naval Affairs Committee, he and the Appropriations Committee chair often consulted about cuts to the naval appropriations bills. Whitthorne did not think that this arrangement had harmed the navy in any way, implying that the army was not harmed by the present arrangement either. Browne's motion failed by a vote of 93–107 (CR, 46-2, 3 Feb. 1880, 687–688, 690).

But, the onslaught continued. Next, William Shallenberger (R-PA, Public Buildings Committee) moved that the appropriations for public buildings be removed from the Appropriations Committee and be lodged with the Committee on Public Buildings. Shallenberger's amendment elicited little debate, except for that of Hiesler Clymer (D-PA), a member of the Appropriations Committee:

Belonging to that unfortunate body of gentlemen in this House called the Committee on Appropriations, possibly I should say nothing, because they do not seem to have any rights that any one here is bound to respect. [Laughter] Yet, sir, I cannot but feel that this committee gradually, day by day, is coming to see more clearly that the necessities of legislation, of good government, of economic government, require that the public expenditures should be reported from some one common source. (CR, 46-2, 5 Feb. 1880, 729)

The hostility that Clymer sensed as being directed toward the Appropriations Committee was apparent in voting on Shallenberger's motion, as the House passed it by a vote of 100–81 (CR, 46-2, 5 Feb. 1880, 731).

Finally, Robert Vance (D-NC), chair of the Patent Committee, joined in the spirit of the occasion by moving to remove the Patent Office appropriations from the Appropriations Committee and to give it to his committee. Vance explained:

[If] the Committee on Agriculture, the Committee on Public Buildings and Grounds, and the Committee on Commerce shall have control of the appropriations bills for all matters pertaining to those different departments I think . . . the Committee on Patents should have control of, and report, appropriations bills for the support of the United States Patent Office. (CR, 46-2, 11 Feb. 1880, 824)

Vance's plea of "me too" went unheeded, as his appeal lost on a 39–83 vote (CR, 46-2, 11 Feb. 1880, 824).

As the jurisdiction of the HAC was being debated in the Committee of the Whole, the Commerce Committee's prerogatives also began to come under attack by other decentralizers. George Caball (D-VA), a member of the Railways and Canals Committee, moved to shift the entire rivers and harbors bill from Commerce to his committee, a proposal that was defeated 63–88 (CR, 46-2, 5 Feb. 1880, 726–728).

Caball was followed by J. R. Chalmers (D-MS), a member of the Mississippi River Committee, who proposed that legislation funding improvements to the Mississippi River and its tributaries be lodged with his, not Reagan's, committee. Chalmers' justification for this motion was forthrightly stated:

[The Commerce Committee] have spent millions and millions of dollars upon other rivers and other harbors, while these great navigable waters...have been comparatively neglected. We ask you to place this great interest in the hands of a committee friendly to it, that we may be enabled to improve those waters as they demand and desire to be improved. (CR, 46-2, 5 Feb. 1880, 732)

While proponents of the division of water project oversight into two committees argued that the Commerce Committee had neglected the Mississippi, supporters of the Commerce Committee replied that the proposed transfer of jurisdiction would allow water project opponents to "divide and conquer."[22] Division of water project legislation, it was argued, would allow opponents of any such spending to play the supporters off against each other, leading to decreased spending in the long run.

In the end, those who believed the Mississippi River could best be protected by the Commerce Committee prevailed on a 93–46 vote to keep jurisdictional lines unchanged. This would be only the first time, however, that Commerce found itself structurally vulnerable to attack from the pro-Mississippi side of the House. When the dust had settled and the consideration of the rules by the Committee of the Whole was complete, neither leadership nor proponents of more liberal spending had won full victories. Jurisdiction over the rivers and harbors bill remained lodged in the Commerce Committee, where it had been since the 45th Congress, representing a loss to would-be retrenchers. But would-be expanders of the pork barrel were also denied even greater spending autonomy. And, given the opportunity to diminish the jurisdiction of the

22 Remarks of Eliza Phister in CR, 46-2, 11 Feb. 1880, 822; see also Reagan's remarks, CR, 46-2, 5 Feb. 1880, 732.

Appropriations Committee radically, the House demurred and nibbled off discrete portions.

Of course, consideration of the rules changes in the Committee of the Whole did not close this chapter of structural reform by any means. That is because the House rules, then as now, required that amendments adopted in the Committee of the Whole (and *only* the amendments adopted by the Committee of the Whole) had to be considered again formally by the entire House. In this final consideration by the whole body, some of the fragmentation approved by the Committee of the Whole was further reduced.

Three deviations from the Rules Committee report that concern us were approved by the Committee on the Whole and thus were considered by the entire House: (1) oversight of the rivers and harbors bill solely by the Commerce Committee, (2) oversight of agricultural spending by the Agriculture Committee, and (3) oversight of public buildings spending by the Public Buildings and Grounds Committee. Lodging the rivers and harbors bill with the Commerce Committee was accepted by a voice vote. Decentralizing the Agriculture Department appropriation initially lost on a teller vote of 63–99, but supporters of the department were able to more than double their numbers in a roll call vote in favor of decentralization, 133–102. And, finally, giving the public buildings appropriations to that committee lost by a roll call vote of 101–136 (CR, 46-2, 2 Mar. 1880, 1260–1262).

Why did a majority of the House choose to take agricultural spending from the Appropriations Committee, but not public buildings spending? An analysis of the two roll calls suggests the answer. The first roll call was on agricultural appropriations. That vote has been analyzed here, first, as a function of party, region, and committee membership, so that it can be compared with the other roll calls to be studied in this volume (Table 3.7). We find in this analysis that the Democratic majority leadership was unable to hold together its party on the vote, as Democrats voted no differently than Republicans.

Why were the Democratic leaders unable to hold together their followers? The findings reported in Table 3.7 suggest that regional factors may have contributed to the voting patterns, but the regional variables in that analysis are too blunt to measure well the important regional variations. Thus, I reanalyzed the same vote, this time substituting for the regional variables a single variable that measures the percentage of urban population living in the state of each representative.[23] This reoperationalization of local interest shows the strong pull of constituency, as

23 It would be preferable to measure urban/rural interest at the district level. Unfortunately, such district-level measures do not readily exist for this time period.

Table 3.7. *Effect of committee membership, region, urban character of state, and party on vote to remove the Agriculture Department appropriation from the Appropriations Committee, 46th Congress, 1880 (logistic regression)*

Effect	Estimates[a]	
Intercept	−0.071	1.058***
Party (Democrats)	−0.010	−0.184
Regions (excluded = East)		
New England	−0.015	—
Confederacy	0.538	—
Midwest	0.724*	—
West	0.590	—
Percent urban in state	—	−2.254***
Committees		
Appropriations	−3.132***	−3.047***
Agriculture	0.845	0.754
N	221	221
Proportion voting yes	55.7	55.7
Percent correctly predicted	62.0	66.1

Estimated probabilities that types of members would vote yes:

1. By region and party[b]

Region	Republicans	Democrats
New England	0.479	0.476
East	0.482	0.480
Confederacy	0.615	0.612
Midwest	0.658	0.655
West	0.627	0.624

2. By committee membership[c]

Appropriations Committee: 0.058
Agriculture Committee: 0.767
Neither committee: 0.585

3. By urban character of state[d]

Urban character	Democrat	Republican
Most urban state (Rhode Island, % urban = 81.9)	0.274	0.313
Least urban state (Mississippi, % urban = 3.1)	0.691	0.729

Note: Estimates were produced using only members who were either Republicans or Democrats. For regional definitions, see Table 3.1.
[a]Statistical significance: ***, $p < .01$; *, $p < .10$.
[b]Assuming the members served on neither the Appropriations nor the Agriculture Committee.
[c]Based on estimates in first column of table, setting regional and party variables to their means.
[d]Based on estimates in the second column, setting committee variables to zero.

those members from the most rural states were significantly more likely to vote for independent agricultural spending than were members from the more urban states. If we were able to measure the level of urban population on a *district* level, rather than having to rely on state-level data, the relationship would undoubtedly be even stronger.

Thus, the pattern of voting suggests that on the issue of agricultural spending, the Democratic rank-and-file believed that whatever retribution the leadership would have extracted on account of their disloyalty could not have matched the opposition they would have felt back home had they voted against agriculture. At this time, the Democratic party was more rooted in agricultural states than were the Republicans, and thus the rank-and-file leaped at the chance to aid agriculture in a highly visible way.[24]

Further evidence that the special constituency appeal of agriculture lured Democrats away from leadership in this first vote is provided by the vote on public buildings spending, which was taken directly after voting on agriculture. First, almost half of the Democrats who had opposed leadership on the agriculture vote (32 of 70) returned to the fold in the vote on public buildings (Table 3.8), while only a fifth of the Republicans who had previously voted to remove agricultural spending from the Appropriations Committee (11 of 50) changed their position. The ability of the Democratic leadership to regain the support of half of its heretofore disloyal flock returned the vote on public buildings to previously established patterns (Table 3.9). In this second vote, the Democratic rank-and-file voted more solidly with leadership, though clearly without unanimity. In fact, the old Confederacy, which was almost entirely Democratic, did exhibit a greater tendency to support the decentralization of public building spending, again reflecting the interest the South showed in using federal largess to help rebuild its economy. Still, the degree of Democratic defection in the vote on public buildings far from approached that on the agriculture vote.

Thus, the pattern of votes on the decentralization of these two items reveals the extent to which constituency sentiment can overcome leadership entreaties, and vice versa. When the issue was agriculture, the economic center of the nation in 1885 and the constituency center of the Democratic party, Democrats were more willing to follow their constit-

---

24 One measure of the relative rural character of the two parties in the 46th Congress is that, on average, Republicans came from states in which the average urban population was 37.2 percent, while the average urban population of the states from which Democrats came was 20.4 percent. The average urban population of minor party members was an even more impressive 2.2 percent. The data on urban and rural populations was drawn from Census Bureau (1976) (also see Brady 1978).

Table 3.8. *Vote to give agricultural appropriations to the Agriculture Committee by vote to give public buildings appropriations to the Public Building Committee and party, 46th Congress, 1880*

		Public buildings		
		Yes	No	Total
Democrats				
Agriculture	Yes	38 (54.3%)	32 (45.7%)	70
	No	5 (10.0%)	45 (90.0%)	50
	Total	43	77	120
Republicans				
Agriculture	Yes	39 (78.0%)	11 (22.0%)	50
	No	6 (15.4%)	33 (84.6%)	39
	Total	45	44	89

uents and oppose their leaders. When the issue was public buildings, a fertile field for the pork barrel but not central to many local economies, leadership was better able to control its followers, and thus repel this attack on the rules.

Therefore, through rank-and-file Democratic disloyalty grounded in constituency interest, agricultural spending was relocated to the Agriculture Committee. Through a reawakening of party loyalty, the Appropriations Committee's bloodletting was kept to a minimum. Party loyalty was also clear at the end of the entire debate, when after almost two calendar months of arguing about the rules, the House finally adopted them by a 122–88 party line vote (CR, 46-2, 2 Mar. 1880, 1266; WP, 3 Mar. 1880, 1).

ESCALATION YET AGAIN: WATER PROJECTS AND GENERAL FRAGMENTATION

Following the major struggle over the rules, jurisdictional squabbles receded for the remainder of the 46th Congress. The election of 1880 sent James Garfield to the White House and elected the first Republican House majority since 1872. The Republican leadership in the 47th Congress showed no desire to undo the decentralization that had occurred in the previous Congress or to repeal the Holman Rule. The Rules Committee report at the beginning of the 47th Congress merely proposed enlarging

Table 3.9. *Effect of committee membership, region, and party on vote to remove the public buildings appropriation from the Appropriations Committee, 46th Congress, 1880 (logistic regression)*

Effect	Estimate[a]
Intercept	−0.108
Party (Democrats)	−0.919***
Regions (excluded = East)	
New England	0.073
Confederacy	0.767*
Midwest	0.154
West	0.188
Committees	
Appropriations	−2.371**
Public Buildings	2.478**

$N = 226$
Proportion voting yes = 41.3
Percent correctly predicted = 62.8

Estimated probabilities that types of members would vote yes:

1. By region and party[b]

Region	Republicans	Democrats
New England	0.491	0.278
East	0.473	0.264
Confederacy	0.659	0.435
Midwest	0.511	0.294
West	0.520	0.302

2. By committee membership[c]

  Appropriations Committee: 0.062
  Public Buildings Committee: 0.894
  Neither committee: 0.414

Note: Estimates were produced using only members who were either Republicans or Democrats. For regional definitions, see Table 3.1.
[a] Statistical significance: *, $p < .10$; **, $p < .05$; ***, $p < .01$.
[b] Assuming the members served on neither the Appropriations nor the Public Buildings Committee.
[c] Setting regional and party variables to their means.

most committees. Nevertheless, while the leadership showed no willingness to upset existing liberal arrangements concerning water projects and the Agriculture Department, members of the rank-and-file continued in their efforts to upset the water cart.

When the rules were being considered, J. Floyd King (D-LA), a member of the Mississippi River Committee, moved that his committee be given jurisdiction over spending for improvements on the Mississippi. As far as King was concerned, Commerce's stingy attitude toward the Mississippi forcefully argued for further fragmentation:

There is a timidity experienced by committees who have large subjects to handle, a timidity that is not warranted by the boldness and onward spirit of the American people.... [Last year] the Committee on Levees and Improvements reported ... an appropriation of six millions to carry out the plans laid down by the Mississippi River commission for the improvement of that stream. The Committee on Commerce cut down the grant to one million. (CR, 47-1, 18 Jan. 1882, 493)[25]

As in the past, debate over altering spending jurisdictions directly addressed the matters of spending levels. For instance, in supporting King, Poindexter Dunn (D-AR) reiterated King's complaint about the previous year's slash in Mississippi River appropriations. John Thomas (R-IL), the chair of the Mississippi River Committee, stated that the Commerce Committee neglected the truly navigable streams in response to improving "cat fish slough and trout-brooks" (CR, 47-1, 18 Jan. 1882, 494). Oscar Turner (D-KY) also supported King's motion, revealing a feeling of political betrayal in the process:

I believe that we would have carried this proposition at the second session of the 46th Congress, but gentlemen were induced to believe that they would get larger appropriations from the Committee on Commerce. But, their hopes were in vain – they were deceived. (CR, 47-1, 18 Jan. 1882, 496)

Immediately following the attack by four consecutive speakers, supporters of the Commerce Committee responded. Vocal defenders of the Commerce Committee were more geographically dispersed than were supporters of the Mississippi River Committee, coming from four states

25 The Mississippi River *Commission* to which King referred was created by Congress in 1879 (Act of 28 June 1879) to supervise the reconstruction of the levees along the Mississippi River, most of which had been destroyed during the Civil War. Along with the creation of this commission, a convention of representatives from concerned states met in 1879 to develop a general plan of action to improve the river (NYT, 4 Dec. 1879, 5; 18 Oct. 1879, 2). The Mississippi River *Commission's* recommended price tag was in excess of five million dollars for initial work on the Mississippi (U.S. Congress 1880). In addition to the dispute in the House over money, there was debate over methods: The Commerce Committee favored dredging channels and building harbors on the river, while the Mississippi River Committee favored money for flood control and the construction of levees (Frank 1930).

far removed from the river (Michigan, Texas, Colorado, and Maryland) and from four states that bordered on it (Louisiana, Minnesota, Illinois, and Kentucky).

One of the greatest surprises in the debate was when Rep. Mark Dunnell (R-MN), who had chaired the Convention on the Improvement of the Mississippi River, sided with the Commerce Committee. Dunnell was not convinced that giving this part of the rivers and harbors bill over to a more narrowly based committee would do the Mississippi River much good. He argued that taking appropriations to improve the Mississippi River from the Commerce Committee would take from the internal improvements bill "much of its strength, and to a certain extent a great element that must enter into a river and harbor appropriation bill" (CR, 47-1, 19 Jan. 1882, 519).

The acrimonious give and take over spending for the Mississippi lasted two full days. In the end, H. F. Page, from the Commerce Committee, rose to assure friends of the Mississippi that it would be treated well in the next rivers and harbors bill and that the bill would be open to amendment from the floor. King, prodded by two other members of the Commerce Committee sympathetic with his views, withdrew his motion. But, he also declared that he took Page's assurances as a public promise and that he would "watch carefully how far it [the Commerce Committee] will carry out its pledges to furnish the means necessary to effect the great work of Mississippi River improvements" (CR, 47-1, 19 Jan. 1882, 519–520; NYT, 20 Jan. 1882, 1).

The 48th House (1883–85) returned to Democratic hands, again providing malcontents with a greater hope that spending structure might be loosened up even further. Two developments helped to supply the initial optimism: The financially conservative Randall was replaced as the leader of the House Democrats by someone who was less conservative, though still in the Democratic mainstream; and the Commerce Committee's hold over rivers and harbors spending was broken. New leadership partly meant that southern and western Democrats might have a friendlier ear when it came to assaulting the conservative spending status quo. A new master over internal improvements could have meant even more generous oversight but mainly ended up providing a new target for high-demand legislators to snipe at.

Samuel Randall's tenure as the Democratic floor leader came to an unceremonious end at the beginning of the 48th House when he was deposed in party caucus by John Carlisle. Carlisle's main virtue, by all accounts, was that he was a known, undoctrinaire low-tariff man. Carlisle's ascent to the party leadership post did not put an end to Randall's dominance over budgetary matters, however, as the new Speaker turned around and appointed Randall to chair the House Appropriations Committee. This appointment was opposed by Carlisle's supporters, who tried to convince him that Randall would use the power and special privileges of the HAC to thwart tariff reform and other legislation. While sympathetic to these protests, Carlisle was ultimately unmoved. He expressed the faith that Randall's party loyalty would prevail; anyway, it was important not to alienate Randall's wing of the party by snubbing him altogether (Barnes 1931).

Less sensational was how the House changed the oversight structure for the omnibus rivers and harbors bill, but the impact on spending was arguably as significant. The rules change was simple enough: Two weeks after the 48th Congress convened, the Rules Committee returned with a report recommending that a Committee on Rivers and Harbors be created, with sole jurisdiction over the bill by the same name.

This proposal to split the jurisdiction of the Commerce Committee in half and create the Rivers and Harbors Committee attracted amazingly little attention or dissent. The lack of controversy was underlined when John Reagan, who again chaired the Commerce Committee, rose to support the reform. Reagan noted that his committee had become so overworked by this and other emerging commercial issues that they had been unable to report a rivers and harbors bill the previous session. Reagan argued that the rivers and harbors bill had become so large that his committee could handle either it or the rest of its pressing business, but not both (CR, 48-1, 19 Dec. 1883, 192).

There is nothing in the *Congressional Record* or the contemporary news accounts to suggest that there was any compelling reason for the creation of the Rivers and Harbors Committee other than the Commerce Committee's work load. The unanimity in the face of great underlying division over the structure of internal improvements decisionmaking suggests that this decision was indeed based on a concern that the Commerce Committee had become so overworked that the continued provision of internal improvements was hindered; the change did not occur because the preferences of Commerce Committee members had grown too dissimilar from those of the whole House. Widespread support for this reform was finally demonstrated when it was passed by a voice vote (CR, 48-1, 20 Dec. 1883, 215–216).

Nevertheless, it is important to note that remedying this overwork by division of the Commerce Committee was not forced on the House from above. The major structural alternative, expanding the committee, was apparently not considered. Instead, the easier route to reform was taken, with leadership agreeing to disperse the Commerce Committee's work more broadly around the House.

Although the Rivers and Harbors Committee was created with relative ease, the members of the Mississippi River Committee still coveted a portion of the omnibus water project bill; and a brief, unsuccessful effort was made to divert bills improving the Mississippi to that committee (CR, 48-1, 20 Dec. 1883, 215–216). Barely a month passed before the Mississippi River Committee had the opportunity to try again. On 9 January 1884, President Arthur sent a report to Congress requesting an additional $1 million for the improvement of the Mississippi (CR, 48-1, 9 Jan. 1884, 320). Albert Willis, who had been named to chair the new Rivers and Harbors Committee, routinely moved to refer the report to his committee. Floyd King immediately countered with a motion to refer the president's report to his Mississippi River Committee. After some debate, King's attempt lost by a narrow roll call vote of 123–144.

We can analyze this vote, as we have the others, first as a function of party, committee membership, and geography (Table 3.10). Not surprisingly, Democrats generally supported their leaders in this vote (voting no), members of Rivers and Harbors voted to protect their jurisdiction, and members of the Mississippi River Committee voted to send the report their way. The more interesting result of the vote analysis is the variable entered to capture geographic interest. This variable, District, is a dummy variable that takes on a value of 1 if the member represented a district that bordered on the Mississippi, 0 otherwise. The substantive size of the District coefficient in Table 3.10 indicates that members representing Mississippi River districts were slightly more likely to favor the Mississippi River Committee (the estimated probability of voting yes for these members is 0.56, compared to 0.44 for all others), but the standard error of the estimate is so large that the coefficient is nowhere near statistical significance.

Yet, if we disaggregate the District variable, another pattern emerges. Instead of assuming that all members from along the Mississippi had the same interest in improving that river, we can refine this premise by assuming that members differed in the degree and type of improvements they preferred, according to where on the river they lived. Specifically, we know (Frank 1930) that areas in the center of the Mississippi were primarily interested in routine maintenance and occasional dredging, while people in downstream areas were primarily interested in rebuilding the improvements that had been destroyed during the Civil War, along with further enhancements to flood control. Finally, because the areas furthest upstream had not benefited as extensively from improvements earlier in the century as had areas in the middle region, one could imagine that members from these geographic extremes had a greater interest in rapidly expanding spending on the Mississippi; they therefore may have voted differently than those in the geographic center.

The plausibility of characterizing this as an intraregional squabble is further bolstered when the regional memberships of the two committees

Table 3.10. *Effect of committee membership, district location, and party on vote to refer internal improvements report to the Committee on Levees and Improvements of the Mississippi River, 48th Congress, 1884 (logistic regression)*

Effect	Estimates[a]	
Intercept	1.574***	1.576***
Party (Democrats)	−2.895***	−2.909***
District	0.474	—
Mississippi River regions		
North and South	—	1.384**
Middle	—	−0.434
Committees		
Rivers and Harbors	−2.356***	−2.033***
Mississippi River	2.939***	2.868***
N	264	264
Proportion voting yes	45.8	45.8
Percent correctly predicted	80.3	80.7

Estimates that types of representatives would vote yes:[b]

1. By party
   Democrats: 0.209
   Republicans: 0.829

2. By committee membership
   Rivers and Harbors Committee: 0.098
   Mississippi River Committee: 0.936
   Neither committee: 0.435

3. By region
   Mississippi River, North and South: 0.760
   Mississippi River, Central: 0.339
   Non-Mississippi River: 0.442

Note: Estimates were produced using only members who were either Republicans or Democrats. The District variable denotes members whose districts bordered on the Mississippi River. The middle Mississippi River region includes congressional districts bordering the Mississippi in Iowa, Illinois, Missouri, and Kentucky. The northern and southern regions include districts bordering the Mississippi in Minnesota, Wisconsin, Arkansas, Tennessee, Mississippi, and Louisiana.
[a]Statistical significance: **, $p < .05$; ***, $p < .01$.
[b]Estimates based on second column of the table.

are compared. Although the Rivers and Harbors Committee had an over-abundance of members who represented districts bordering on the Mississippi, 20 percent of the committee compared to 5 percent of the House, each of these members came from one of the four middle-region states (Iowa, Missouri, Illinois, and Kentucky). None came from the southern

(Arkansas, Louisiana, Mississippi, and Tennessee) or northern regions (Minnesota and Wisconsin). On the other hand, only one of the four members of the Mississippi River Committee who represented river districts came from the middle region: Two were from the south and one was from the north. Thus, members representing districts near the head and mouth of the Mississippi River had clear geographic reasons to be mistrustful of Rivers and Harbors.

This view is bolstered by the results reported in the second column of Table 3.10, which replaces the District variable with two variables depicting members who represented districts along the head, mouth, and middle of the river. Members from the extreme north and south were much more likely to vote to support the Mississippi River Committee in this effort.

The pattern of this vote suggests that the intermittent skirmishing that was led by the Mississippi River Committee was an indicator of disunity among members who represented the Mississippi on the question of how the river should be improved. Members were particularly concerned that *their* stretch of the river get improved and that the type of improvement they most preferred receive high priority. Except for Republicans, who were simply interested in causing trouble for the Democratic leadership, the Mississippi River Committee had a difficult time convincing others to support them in this vote since it was clearly a parochial struggle. To have allowed members from the extreme north and south to oversee spending in their areas would have begun a splintering of the extraordinary coalition that had recently been marshaled to protect internal improvements in general. The potential for the disintegration of this coalition was clearly not worth it to other members, who viewed the continued provision of internal improvements to their districts as reliant upon the viability of the grand water project coalition.

THE DEVOLUTION OF 1885

In retrospect, one of the most important changes in the history of House budgetary politics occurred during the 49th Congress (1885–87). In the 49th House, party leadership finally acquiesced to increasing member demands for fragmentation. In doing so, leadership formulated its own reform plan that provided for a radical redistribution of appropriations power in the chamber, and this plan was finally approved by a comfortable margin. The end result was the creation of the budgetary regime of 1885, which shifted the locus of appropriations politics from the Appropriations Committee to the legislative committees for the next three decades.

Until 1885 formal leaders of both parties had generally taken the side of structural centralization and control. All of the successful efforts at fragmentation up until then, as we have seen, had been championed by various elements of the rank-and-file; if leadership entered the fray, it was on the side of the status quo, and their efforts were frequently in vain. The 1885 devolution was different because leadership changed sides and for the first time led the charge toward fragmentation. Leadership's change of heart may seem perplexing at first; but upon careful reflection, its conversion is readily understandable.

Ever since the middle 1870s, elements of the rank-and-file had expressed dissatisfaction with the HAC's handling of appropriations bills. The dissatisfaction had ranged from disapproval of the amounts recommended in the supply bills to grumbling about the committee's use of its privileged status in the House rules to influence substantive legislation. The continued efforts to extract certain bills from the Appropriations Committee (e.g., Rivers and Harbors and Agriculture), to limit the Appropriations Committee's use of suspension of the rules, and to grant other committees the right to privileged consideration of their business on the House floor were all indicators that certain quarters of the House rank-and-file were unhappy with Appropriations' behavior. The success of some of these efforts was an indicator that this dissatisfaction occasionally ran to a majority of the full House. The failure of other efforts was an indicator that dissatisfaction was either not always so widespread, or that party leaders could induce followers to oppose challenges to the status quo.

With the appointment of Randall to chair the Appropriations Committee, however, dissatisfaction became more universal. After Randall took the chair, a number of charges began to be leveled at the HAC more regularly. These charges can be divided into three general categories. First, it was charged that Randall had strategically used the privileged reporting position of the HAC to block the reporting of legislation from other committees. The most well-known issue that was delayed by Randall's actions was tariff reform, but Randall also managed to rile members for his obstruction of more minor, yet cherished, local programs. Second, it was charged that the HAC was becoming severely overworked, as indicated by the tardiness by which appropriations bills were reported in the 48th Congress (See CR, 49-1, 14 Dec. 1885, 168–171). Third, it was charged that the substantive recommendations of the committee were either too low or biased geographically.

The accumulation of these charges made it likely that a rank-and-file movement to severely sanction the HAC would emerge in the 49th Congress, with or without leadership action. Leadership could try to beat back this dissatisfaction, as it did in 1880; but dissatisfaction had only grown in five years, and it was not clear that leadership could prevail this time to preserve most of Appropriations' prerogatives. Thus, leadership moved to be in front of its followers, rather than be run over by them.

Leadership (i.e., Carlisle) acted through the Rules Committee, a body not noted for a fragmentary bias. Carlisle's appointees to the Rules Committee during the first session of the 49th Congress were drawn from the House finance committees, and thus they could not be charged with being imprudent big spenders. Those members were Carlisle, Randall, William Morrison (D-IL, Ways and Means Committee), Thomas Reed (R-ME, Ways and Means Committee), and Frank Hiscock (R-NY, Ways and Means Committee).

The Rules Committee began its work on the House rules shortly after it was appointed. In deciding how to handle pressures to alter the appropriations process, the committee had three options: (1) Expand the HAC, curing the committee's overwork yet enhancing Randall's power even further and inciting even greater rank-and-file policy discontent. (2) Depose Randall, placating low-tariff Democrats while alienating the high-tariff wing of the party, as well as doing nothing directly to ease the committee's burden or satisfy the rank-and-file over spending policy. (3) Disperse appropriations bills, relieving the work load by vastly expanding the division of labor, placating high-demand Democrats, and angering – but not alienating for long – the Randallites.

The word that the Rules Committee was crafting a change in appropriations jurisdictions was circulated throughout Washington before the House reconvened for its second session in December 1885. The *New York Times* reported:

The conduct of Mr. Randall during the last session of Congress in blocking the way of important legislation with the appropriation bills is likely to lead to a very important and very desirable amendment of the rules of the House. The distribution of the appropriation bills among the committees having charge of the various interests for which they provide would at once relieve the Appropriations Committee from a burden of labor which has been made an excuse for dilatory action and deprive its Chairman of a power of legislation which experience has shown may be grossly abused. (NYT 7 Nov. 1885, 4)

However, the *Times* did not give continued wholehearted endorsement to the proposal, and one week later proposed instead dumping Randall and keeping the House Appropriations Committee intact:

It is not necessary to distribute the bills. The desired object can be accomplished by distributing Mr. Randall and his associates, who showed so conclusively by their course that they were unfit to hold the places to which they had been assigned. (NYT, 13 Nov. 1885, 4; also NYT 22 Nov. 1885, 8)

The Rules Committee ignored the arguments of this latter editorial, and when it finally reported to the House on 14 December 1885, it recommended radical redistribution of committee jurisdictions, not radical redistribution of Randall and his associates. The plan reflected the difficult balancing act that Carlisle had to perform. First, Randall would continue as the chair of the Appropriations Committee. Second, the definitions of the annual supply bills would remain unchanged. Third, those annual bills would be distributed around the chamber to the logical legislative committees. The HAC would continue to oversee those bills that overlapped committee jurisdictions, and that would have created confusion and conflict had they been redistributed. These bills were the legislative, executive, and judicial; sundry civil; fortifications; pensions; District of Columbia; and deficiencies appropriations bills. The following committees were authorized to report the supply bills that corresponded with their jurisdiction: Military Affairs (army and military academy bills); Naval Affairs (navy bill); Post Office (postal service bill); Rivers and Harbors; Indian Affairs; Foreign Affairs (consular and diplomatic bill); and Agriculture.

The Rules Committee's report supporting this reform emphasized work load and minimized the strategic aspects of the situation, but the political significance of the plan was anything but subtle (CR, 49-1, 14 Dec. 1885, 168–171). Overnight, it more than doubled the number of House members directly overseeing appropriations.[26] And, most important for leadership, it put Democratic party leaders for the first time at the head of efforts to distribute appropriations decisionmaking about the chamber, demonstrating a determination on the part of Carlisle not to fall into the trap that had led to Randall's earlier ouster as Speaker.

The maneuvering between the time of the Rules Committee's report and final passage of its recommendations illustrates how hot this issue was, and how the final recommendation was the correct strategic solution as far as leadership was concerned. Randall filed a minority report, striking a theme that the few opponents of the proposed change would emphasize: The Appropriations Committee was the guardian of the treasury and reducing the Appropriations Committee's power would be a blow to government economy:

General appropriation bills are to be still further divided and scattered, and the result inevitably will be that it will be impossible to keep up any just relation between receipts and expenditures.

Experience and observation demonstrate such distribution leads to continually

26 Before the devolution forty-five members were on committees that directly oversaw some spending – Appropriations (fifteen members), Rivers and Harbors (fifteen), and Agriculture (fifteen). The committees that gained new spending jurisdiction in 1885 had a total of sixty-six members – Military Affairs (thirteen), Naval Affairs (twelve), Post Office (fifteen), Foreign Affairs (thirteen), and Indian Affairs (thirteen).

increasing appropriations, and renders it more difficult to keep expenditures within the limits of receipts. (CR, 49-1, 14 Dec. 1885, 171)

Randall's supporters moved immediately to quash the Rules Committee's recommendation, but their alternative was by far too little and too late. Joseph Cannon, who dismissed the Rules Committee recommendation altogether, simply moved that the recommendation be undone (CR, 49-1, 18 Dec. 1885, 313). James Blount also preferred leaving the appropriations system unchanged, but he objected to the ability of the HAC to monopolize floor time so easily. Thus, he amended the Cannon motion to allow the Foreign Affairs, Military Affairs, Naval Affairs, Post Office, and Indian Affairs committees special floor access (CR, 49-1, 18 Dec. 1885, 315). Blount's rather meager alternative, given chamber sentiment, was defended as follows:

I have reoffered the amendment of [Cannon] . . . because I was not willing that the House should be brought now to a direct vote on the proposition whether or not these bills should remain with the Committee on Appropriations. For one, I am not willing for them to remain where they are unless something shall be done giving to other committees of this House the right to report important legislation instead of allowing all such legislation to remain practically under the control of the Committee on Appropriations as heretofore. (CR, 49-1, 18 Dec. 1885, 316)

This compromise put forward by Blount was rejected by voice vote – the majority was so large that nobody even requested that tellers be taken – and the House proceeded to directly address the question of devolution.[27]

In the final debate that preceded voting on the Rules Committee plan, proponents of the devolution skirted away from complaining about the Appropriations Committee's historic economizing role – few wanted to admit publicly to being a spender. This is not to say that spending was entirely ignored by proponents of devolution. For instance, James Laird (R-NE) was one who was concerned about the distribution of past appropriations. He defended devolution as follows:

While the center of population of the United States has passed a thousand miles westward from the Atlantic coast, the center of appropriations and expenditures of public money will be found on a line drawn from this Capitol through the city of Philadelphia to Boston by way of New York.

To my mind the despotism of the Committee on Appropriations, as constituted in the last Congress, is in keeping with the domination which the East has

---

27 Both the Cannon and Blount amendments were rejected on a single vote because Cannon technically withdrew his motion so that Blount could offer his own amendment under a less complicated parliamentary environment. Blount responded by placing the entire text of the Cannon motion within his.

exercised over the West, since there has been a West. (CR, 49-1, 18 Dec. 1885, 323)

Laird continued by accusing the Appropriations Committee of ignoring the West, and stated that because of the Appropriations Committee's miserly attitude toward the Indian Bureau, New Mexico and Arizona were undergoing a "war of extermination" at the hands of "Geronimo and his band of Chiricahua Apaches."

The Committee on Appropriations last year scaled the estimates of the Indian Bureau $1,500,000 and upward. The bureau asked for nearly eight millions and got six millions. . . . Any economy, falsely so called, which turns loose the western savage upon the western settler is a disgrace. (CR, 49-1, 18 Dec. 1885, 324)

Before the devolution was finally adopted by a voice vote, two motions were voted on which help us to gauge the breadth of support in the House for this decentralization (CR, 49-1, 18 Dec. 1885, 338). The first was offered by Nathaniel Hammond (D-GA), and attempted to allow only the Appropriations Committee to report appropriations. This lost on a vote of 71 to 227. The second was a motion by Holman to restore a narrower version of the Holman Rule; this likewise failed by a roll call of 69 to 205.[28]

Leadership won this rules fight with a lopsided majority, and support for the Rules Committee report was strong throughout the chamber, with slight variation (Table 3.11). While the party coefficient in Table 3.11 indicates that Republicans and Democrats did not vote in a substantially different way this time, what the table hides is that this was the first time that a majority of all rank-and-file Democrats voted for fragmentation. (Previous fragmenting efforts had been led by Democrats, of course, with a minority of the rank-and-file going along.) While one could interpret this as testimony to the pulling power of Carlisle and other party leaders, it is more properly understood as an indicator of the need for Carlisle himself to follow the lead of his followers.

Regionally, the voting was also quite different from that witnessed on the previous structural votes. All regional coefficients are negative in Table 3.11, indicating that eastern representatives were the most inclined toward maintaining the status quo. The former Confederacy, which had previously showed the greatest tendency to favor loose controls over pork barrel spending, showed a slightly greater tendency to support the status quo. Because, however, the estimated probability is still low (0.256 for southern Democrats), this probably represents Hammond's ability to

---

28 The Rules Committee report recommended dropping the Holman Rule altogether. Holman's motion restored his rule, except that it would allow riders only to effect the "direct reduction of the number, salary, and compensation of officers and employes of the United States."

Table 3.11. *Effect of party, region, and committee on vote to retain HAC jurisdiction over spending, 49th Congress, 1885 (logistic regression)*

Effect	Estimate[a]
Intercept	−0.502*
Party (Democrats)	0.021
Regions (excluded = East)	
New England	−2.199***
Confederacy	−0.584
Midwest	−1.165***
West	−1.713***
Committees	
Appropriations	3.796***
Winners	−0.084

$N = 297$
Proportion voting yes = 23.9
Percent correctly predicted = 78.1

Estimated probabilities that types of members would vote yes:

1. By region and party[b]

Region	Republicans	Democrats
New England	0.063	0.064
East	0.377	0.382
Confederacy	0.252	0.256
Midwest	0.159	0.162
West	0.098	0.100

2. By committee membership[c]

Appropriations Committee: 0.937
"Winning" committee: 0.235
Neither committee: 0.251

Note: Estimates were produced using only members who were either Republicans or Democrats. "Winners" denotes membership in the 48th Congress on one of the committees that stood to gain spending jurisdiction: Military Affairs, Foreign Affairs, Indian Affairs, Naval Affairs, and Post Office and Post Roads. For regional definitions, see Table 3.1.
[a]Statistical significance: *, $p < .10$; ***, $p < .01$.
[b]Assuming the members served on neither the Appropriations Committee nor on any of the committees that stood to gain spending jurisdiction.
[c]Setting regional and party variables to their means.

bring a few of his fellow southerners along with him, not a general aversion of southerners to wholesale devolution.[29]

The variables measuring the voting behavior of members of affected committees show an interesting asymmetry of support and opposition.[30] The Appropriations Committee demonstrated that it was more concerned about losing power than the winning committees were interested in gaining power. Given the high level of support for fragmentation already existing in the chamber, being on a committee that stood to gain power did not boost one's tendency to favor decentralization any more. But, the general consensus to fragment did not stop members of Appropriations from making a last ditch effort to stave off diminution of its powers.

The high level of support in the chamber for devolution suggests finally that victory for decentralization did not come because the winners ganged up on the losers — or on the rest of the House — in an approximation of a minimum winning coalition. Rather, this was a classic case of universalism. Victory occurred because leadership showed a willingness to acquiesce to widespread desires to limit the Appropriations Committee's authority, allowing all who naturally wanted to vote for fragmentation to do so without fear of leadership retribution.[31]

29 This point is borne out by disaggregating the vote of the southern Democrats on Hammond's motion. (All eleven southern Republicans voted against Hammond and the status quo.) The Georgia delegation, which included Hammond, voted 6–4 on the motion. Of the states that adjoined Georgia, only Florida did not have a significant number of Hammond supporters: South Carolina supported Hammond 3–2; North Carolina, 5–1; Alabama, 3–5; and Tennessee, 4–3. Thus, Georgia, Tennessee, South Carolina, North Carolina, and Tennessee voted 21–15, while the rest of the former Confederacy voted 0–36 to maintain the status quo.

The East's support for Hammond, and by implication Randall, can similarly be interpreted by focusing on the voting of the Pennsylvania delegation, in which Randall was very influential: Pennsylvania Democrats voted with Hammond 6–1, with Pennsylvania Republicans voting 6–12. The strongest delegation vote in the East came from neighboring New Jersey, whose three voting Democrats and four voting Republicans stood unanimously with the status quo. The rest of the East's Democrats voted 7–15, and the Republicans voted 1–13.

30 Because most committees had not been appointed when the rules were considered, committee membership is measured as of the 48th Congress for members returning in the 49th.

31 One final word needs to be said about the degree to which this vote was a repudiation of Randall individually. Not only did most of his former followers refuse to go along with Randall's appeals to retain the HAC's power, there is evidence that members of the House wanted to rub Randall's nose in the dirt, as it were, in this Congress. Consider what happened later in the 49th Congress when Randall introduced a tariff reform bill: "Mr. Randall himself offered a bill embodying his own ideas of the proper extent and method of tariff reduction. The Committee on Ways and Means, having on its docket two or three score of tariff bills which it allowed to slumber and die in the committee-room [sic], singled out that of Mr. Randall for the honor of an adverse report. Neither the bill nor the report was considered by the House" (Stanwood 1903, II:326).

Thus, the support for sweeping devolution in 1885 was broad, though not entirely uniform. Democrats and Republicans supported it at approximately equal rates; support was widespread regionally, with the least supportive regions still supporting change by wide margins; and the Appropriations Committee showed greater aversion to losing power than the winners showed eagerness to gain power.

Although structural centralizers had lost in a major way in this rules fight, the fight for centralization had one last pathetic gasp in the 49th Congress, as several members who had sided with Randall made an effort to advance the presidential item veto. The item veto had first been proposed in 1876, but starting in 1885 centralizers began submitting the plan regularly as a symbolic beacon for centralizing reform.[32] Their persistence was in vain in the short run since the item veto proposals never got very far. The way the item veto proposals were first received in the House speaks to the level to which a decentralization ethos had pervaded congressional thinking in the 1880s.

In the 49th Congress, four members dropped different versions of the item veto constitutional amendment into the hopper. These resolutions were referred to the Judiciary Committee, and were adversely reported on 22 April 1886. What is interesting about the committee's report is that it attacked the item veto as being an impediment to logrolling. That is, to members of the Judiciary Committee, the most significant aspect of the item veto was not so much the claim that it could effect spending control, but that the item veto would make the president a more influential player in the deal-making process. Adding more people to deal making would only serve to heighten uncertainty. The committee argued:

All administration of popular government, where the people's interests are to be promoted, must depend on mutual concessions and compromises. One interest not only has no right to have exclusive benefit bestowed upon it, but can not in just administration obtain it. Equality of benefit is due by the Government to those who bear equality of burden. To separate bills in which these benefits are secured, instead of combining the just demands of all in one bill, may endanger the success of some of them, and by intrigue secure the monopoly to others. Combination may be necessary to insure justice to all, and prevent injustice to any, and while it may produce the evil consequence of what is known as logrolling, yet it will prevent the no less evil of partial and unjust appropriations.

The mandate of these [line item] amendments is that Congress shall not make *dependent* appropriations, or that if it does, the President may by his veto sever the *nexus* of dependence, and defeat either that he pleases and make the others *independent* of those defeated, and which Congress had made *dependent*. . . .

Whatever may be said of such a provision in a State constitution, the duties of Congress to the thirty-eight States of the Union make it necessary that the expenditure for all the States shall be made proportionate to their several needs.

32 For a history of the item veto issue see U.S. Congress (1984).

127

This involves the practice of dependent appropriations, because, if made for each in separate bills, the passage of one may be secured and of others defeated; a result which would be marked by injustice and be a violation of constitutional duty. (H. Rpt. 1872, 49-1, pp. 1–2)

Opposition from the Judiciary Committee was sufficient to kill consideration of the item veto before it got to the House floor.

Aside from occasional lone rumblings about undoing devolution and item veto proposals, after almost a decade of steady warfare over who would consider appropriations in the House, fighting ceased almost as if by magic. Those who had been interested in loosening budgetary control, having worked their will to what must have seemed to be its logical conclusion, no longer had reason to attack the rules; for the next decade centralizing proposals were regarded as quaint and were buried quickly and quietly. One emerging factor that served to control the excess of the newly fragmented system – and to regulate proposals to reverse it – was strong party rule enforced by the Speaker. Attempts to address substantive spending issues through House structure did not totally die out in the short term, however, but shifted form to become an informal activity, only to reemerge a quarter of a century later.

SUMMARY

In the middle and later nineteenth century, budget reform, seen as individual episodes and as a whole, emerged as the result of the interaction between certain key outcomes of the electoral connection on the one hand and the nature of the entrenched institution on the other. Knowing something about member spending preferences tells us a good deal about the types of structural arrangements they pursued. But, knowing something about electorally induced spending preferences is not enough. To understand fully the final outcomes of all the structural struggles, we also need to understand some important things about the institution in which those struggles took place.

Let us begin with the electoral connection. Between 1865 and 1885, electorally induced spending preferences helped, first, to regulate the order in which reform proposals were considered and passed and, second, to partially determine precisely who would be reform supporters and opponents at specific times. Let us first consider the order in which proposals were considered and passed. The order in which elements of annual appropriations were removed from the oversight of the Appropriations Committee and given to the legislative committees is consistent with the idea that electorally induced spending preferences guided reform activity. First, pensions spending was removed (before the opening of the study period).[33] Then came rivers and harbors (1878), followed by agriculture (1880). Only at the end of the sequence were most other programs removed. Thus, the general trend was one of liberating the most particularistic spending from the Appropriations Committee first, and then the least particularistic. Second, electorally induced spending preferences determined structural politics on a more micro level when, for instance, southerners consistently voted to decentralize internal improvements while easterners were steady supporters of centralization.

The fact that MCs did not always effect centralization when given the opportunity, and that all who had an objective interest in fragmentation did not always vote to do so, suggests that we need to look beyond simple spending preferences in order to round out our understanding of the dynamics of budget reform. In Chapter 1 I suggested that constraints on structural behavior came from five places: (1) the preferences of other members, (2) the nature of the budgetary problem, (3) the committee system, (4) the leadership system, and (5) the presidency. Not all of these constraints came fully into play between 1865 and 1885, but most did. Let us briefly rehearse how each of them constrained and molded the direction of budget reform during this period, making it more than just a story of brute grabs for pieces of the national treasury.

The preferences of other members

The unwillingness of the House to extend its fragmentation of water project oversight beyond the Commerce Committee and Rivers and Harbors Committee came, in part, because House members wanted to keep the flow of benefits to high-demand districts in check. The attempts by members of the Mississippi River and the Railways and Canals Committees to dislodge parts of the rivers and harbors bill was seen as an attack on universalism, and perhaps as the beginning of the slippery slope toward serial minimum winning coalitions. The rank-and-file refused to agree to these requests to fragment further because fragmentation would probably have jeopardized continued support for projects of interest to them.

---

33 One minor example of House administrative detail is illustrative on this point. In examining original bills in the National Archives, I discovered that almost all original bills in the nineteenth century, as thrown into the House hopper, were written in longhand by the members. The exceptions were appropriations bills, which were introduced in printed form by the Appropriations Committee, and private pensions bills. Pensioner casework had become so routinized after the Civil War that the House Clerk had printed private pension bill forms. All a member had to do to introduce private pension legislation for a constituent was to fill in the blanks giving the constituent's name, address, and the amount desired.

The nature of the budgetary problem

Concerns over the budgetary problem were expressed in words and in deeds all during this period. Through words, decentralizers often complained about the distributive consequences of the status quo, and centralizers always complained about the aggregate consequences of fragmentation. In deeds, all members realized that the Civil War had created severe strains on the federal financial system, and the creation of the Appropriations Committee was in large part a straightforward outcome of that consensus. Finally, the devolution of 1885 signaled how the priority afforded aggregation and distribution had shifted over the years. In 1865, when Appropriations was created, the problem was that of aggregation. By 1885, aggregational problems seemed to be taken care of – the government could not spend revenues fast enough – and the problem was clearly one of how to distribute a rapidly expanding pie.

The committee system

At almost every turn, the committee system found itself in the middle of budgetary structural politics. The first reason for this is the fact that every single reform episode before 1885 directly addressed some aspect of the committee system, from the conditions under which they could report legislation to the floor to their jurisdictions. The fact that these episodes centered on changes to the committee system was certain to elicit responses from members of those committees – and they did respond. Most reform proposals arose from one of the affected committees, members of affected committees were the most active when the proposals were discussed on the floor, and voting patterns revealed an eagerness on the part of committee members to expand, or at least protect, the prerogatives of their committees.

Committee members were not only active and vocal, typically voting in a self-interested way, but committee members were also willing to use the resources at their disposal as committee members to influence the outcome of structural battles. The Commerce Committee, for instance, openly bought-off members who challenged their authority, promising more favorable consideration of certain projects in the future. And, the willingness of John Reagan to challenge party leaders directly over the issue of his committee's jurisdiction and prerogatives most certainly must have had something to do with his committee's *preexisting* power. That is, he would not have confronted leadership had he been just any old member of any old committee. By being the chair or ranking minority member of the Commerce Committee for over a decade, he had accumulated enough goodwill among the rank-and-file to make party leaders hesitant about sanctioning him when he successfully challenged leadership's structural preferences.

The leadership system

Although party leaders did not always win when they entered into the structural debate – witness John Reagan's continued success – they were key features of the reform landscape nevertheless. First, they were the second-most frequent contributors of reform ideas to the agenda, next only to the committee system. Thus, even while frequently unsuccessful, leadership could still steer the direction of structural debate. Second, although leaders could not always sanction powerful committee chairs like John Reagan, they could impose sanctions against the rank-and-file more easily, and the threat of sanctions showed up in votes on structural issues. Reagan could propose change, for instance, but he had a hard time bringing other Democrats along with him. Therefore, Reagan's success came because he led a coalition of Republicans, who were always eager to vote against Democratic leaders on organizational matters, and those Democrats who experienced extraordinary constituency pressure. The influence of leadership was finally also seen in the outcome of 1885. With leadership proposing decentralization, the reform process ceased being a struggle and became a cake walk.

The presidency

Unlike subsequent periods, the presidency did not figure directly into most of what the House did to the budgetary process during this period. Concerns about the presidency, and the executive branch more generally, did surface when the Holman Rule was considered; but the issue there was not only about the presidency but also about the whole checks-and-balances system, including the typically Republican Senate. The movement for an item veto was not taken seriously at all, which is another sign of the unimportance of the presidency to many of these debates. The fact that the Judiciary Committee viewed the participation of the president in the budgetary process through the item veto as an expansion of fragmentation – not of centralization, as it began to be considered in later decades – suggests that the president was a nuisance, perhaps, but not an overwhelmingly powerful player who needed to be considered at every juncture.

In short, we see that the early development of the House appropriations process was partially driven by impulses easily traceable to the electoral connection. But, those impulses were consistently channeled in a variety of different directions, depending on the array of institutional characteristics and strategic situations facing members at any one given time. In the chapters to follow, we shall see how the constraints and politics of budgetary structure changed as the institution itself evolved.

4

Adaptation and adjustment to decentralization: post-1885 spending decisions

It is one thing to know that support for, and opposition to, decentralization in 1885 was largely based on predictions about what structural change would do to subsequent spending decisions. It is quite another thing to show that the predictions were borne out. Because members on both sides of the issue fought so hard for their positions in 1885, and because reform rhetoric early in the next century turned its fire on the regime of 1885, it is tempting to assume without second thought that the decentralizers ultimately triumphed in both their structural and substantive goals, gaining both spending independence and expansion.

Yet we should be slow in jumping to conclusions about the actual performance of the 1885 regime. The reasons for expressing caution are simple enough: Many factors influencing spending decisions were still beyond the direct control of members of Congress (MCs) after 1885. MCs could change structure, but structure was not the whole ballgame. The country and its demography, geography, economy, and politics had begun to change at an astounding pace by 1885. Certainly these changes would have some impact on subsequent House spending decisions, independent of the appropriations structure itself. Thus, if we are to develop a clear understanding of how changing the appropriations process changed spending decisions, we need to take these other factors into account.

The purpose of this chapter is to examine how appropriations decisions were affected by the change in the appropriations process in 1885, focusing primarily on incremental spending decisions made by agencies, committees, and the full House. The results confirm century-old suspicions that the decentralization of the appropriations regime indeed induced spending expansion after 1885. However, the findings also suggest that structural change was not the only factor inducing this spending expansion, and that the legislative committees were not alone in sanctioning higher spending levels after 1885. Thus a fuller explanation of post-1885 spending requires us to expand our range of explanations.

PROBLEMS WITH MEASURING CHANGES IN APPROPRIATIONS DECISIONS

In order to test the effects of the regime of 1885 on spending decisions, we need a good idea about what we are actually testing. Not only do we need a good theory that explains why decisionmakers choose particular budgets, in order to specify our statistical models correctly, but we also need a sense of how various ways of measuring spending decisions can guide our understanding of appropriations politics. In short, we need to answer the question: What is the most valid measure of spending choices that will allow us to judge whether spending decisions made by the legislative committees after 1885 were more generous than those made by the Appropriations Committee before 1885?

The few assessments that have been made about the spending consequences of the regime of 1885 have used aggregate spending levels to measure the degree to which post-1885 spending decisions were "profligate." While using total spending levels has a certain intuitive appeal and analytical simplicity – one simply looks at total spending before and after 1885 – aggregate levels can be misleading, both descriptively and theoretically.

Aggregate spending levels can be descriptively misleading if one does not control for other influences on spending levels. Of course, there is nothing inherent about using aggregate spending data that makes the analysis more prone to the problem of "specification error," but spending accelerated at such a pace after 1885 that one may be tempted to take this acceleration in total spending at face value without controlling for other factors that may have led to spending expansion.

Consider the specific case of congressional spending decisions from fiscal year (FY) 1871 to 1922. If one simply looks at a graph of total spending of the seven annual appropriations bills that were removed from the Appropriations Committee by 1885, it is clear that spending grew at a faster rate after 1885 (Figure 4.1).[1] The regression lines fit to the trends, before and after 1885, show that before calendar year 1885

---

1 This example excludes data from the rivers and harbors bill because it frequently did not pass every year during the 1870s and 1880s. The rivers and harbors bill has been excluded from this and subsequent analyses because I desired to have spending series that were uninterrupted for each bill. The rivers and harbors bill was not exceptionally large – containing 6.1% of the spending in the devolved bills during 1900, for instance – so that excluding it can probably be done with little

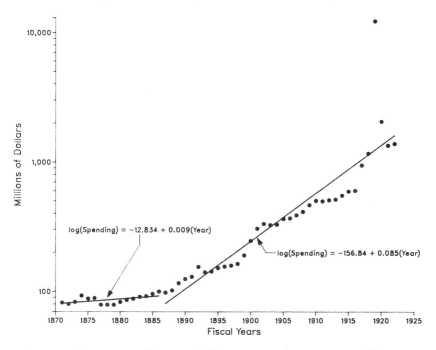

Figure 4.1. Aggregate spending contained in seven annual appropriations bills overseen by legislative committees after 1885, FY 1871–1922 (in millions of dollars). Data from House and Senate Appropriations Committees, *Appropriations, New Offices, Etc.*, various years; U.S. Statutes at Large, various years.

(FY 1887), the average annual spending growth of these seven bills was 0.9 percent, while they grew at an average annual rate of 8.5 percent afterward.

What simply looking at the graph in Figure 4.1 does not tell us, however, is how factors other than the structural change in 1885 may have also contributed to subsequent spending growth. Price changes; economic, population, and territorial growth; and wars have also been known to induce government spending growth. Each of these factors took on higher average values after calendar year 1885 and thus may

danger to the general points being made. For interesting, detailed analyses of rivers and harbors spending decisions during this period, see Wilson (1986a,b).

The period is confined to FY 1871–1922 for two reasons. First, FY 1871 marks the earliest period in which spending summaries for each bill are readily available. And in any case, immediately prior bills were so contaminated by the effects of the Civil War that the utility of their inclusion would be very low. Second, FY 1922 was the last year of the old regime. Following 1922, the annual appropriations bills were redefined, with a new set of annual bills established.

Table 4.1. *Average growth of annual spending bills, FY 1871–1922, controlling for military activity and prices (bills overseen by legislative committees after 1885)*

Time period[a]	Constant	Trend	Troops	Prices	Rho	R^2
Total	10.753	0.062			0.479	0.844
	(0.209)[b]	(0.007)				
Before	11.251	0.013			0.520	0.496
	(0.055)	(0.006)				
After	9.957	0.084			0.240	0.804
	(0.323)	(0.009)				
Total	9.153	0.048	0.433		0.077	0.881
	(0.355)	(0.005)	(0.093)			
Before	8.350	0.035	0.664		0.439	0.702
	(1.081)	(0.010)	(0.247)			
After	9.234	0.066	0.286		0.061	0.823
	(0.422)	(0.012)	(0.134)			
Total	3.551	0.044	0.151	1.516	−0.169	0.921
	(1.064)	(0.003)	(0.091)	(0.290)		
Before	6.737	0.038	0.633	0.380	0.421	0.708
	(2.351)	(0.010)	(0.257)	(0.492)		
After	3.297	0.041	0.138	1.604	−0.202	0.877
	(1.495)	(0.010)	(0.111)	(0.405)		

Note: Dependent variable: Logarithm of the sum of annual spending bills as they passed the House. The variable Trend is defined such that Trend = FY − 1871.
[a]Time period indicates whether the regression was run on the entire time series (total), the time series between FY 1871 and 1886 (before), or the time series between FY 1887 and 1922 (after).
[b]Standard errors are in parentheses.

also have contributed to spending expansion, independent of structural change.[2]

Table 4.1 demonstrates a simple attempt to disentangle the effects of these exogenous events on aggregate spending growth after 1885. First, I regressed the logarithm of the sum of the seven bills on a trend variable (Trend).[3] The Trend coefficient in this case measures the average percentage growth rate of all the bills before taking other factors into account. I conducted this regression on the entire spending series (time period Total), as well as splitting the sample and running the regression before the devolution (time period Before) and after the devolution (time period After). The first trio of regression results in Table 4.1 indicates

2 Between FY 1887 and 1922, GDP grew at an average rate of 3.6 percent, prices increased at an average annual rate of 2.2 percent, and there were two wars.
3 Trend = Fiscal year − 1871.

that the growth rate of the devolved bills averaged 1.3 percent before devolution and 8.4 percent afterward, a significant difference.[4]

The second trio of regression results in Table 4.1 indicates that some of the difference in growth rates can be explained in terms of the size of the army (Troops), a surrogate for military demobilization in the 1870s and military mobilization during the Spanish-American War and World War I. When we take demobilization into account, the annual pre-1885 growth rate jumps from 1.3 to 3.5 percent; taking the two wars into account reduces the post-1885 annual growth rate from 8.4 to 6.6 percent. There is still a substantively different annual growth rate between the two eras, but it is now less startling than the first comparison.[5]

The final trio of regression results in Table 4.1 adds inflation (Prices) into the model. Because the Prices variable is highly correlated with Troops, one result is to reduce the effect of the latter variable on spending. But more important, the introduction of a variable to measure price fluctuations eliminates the difference in annual percentage growth before and after devolution: The pre-1885 growth rate eases upward from 3.5 to 3.8 percent, while the post-1885 growth rate falls from 6.6 to 4.1 percent. Thus, there is plausible evidence to suggest that much of the difference in *aggregate* spending before and after 1885 rested in exogenous political and economic developments,[6] and that spending in large part accelerated because of inflation and the "ratchet effects" associated with the two wars that occurred after 1885.[7]

Spending aggregates can also be descriptively misleading because they do a very poor job of controlling for spending increases that occur because of decisions that are chiefly *legislative*. Most important, aggregate spending levels can change when Congress passes a new law through the regular

---

4 An F test to determine whether the lines were statistically different yields an F statistic with $p < .01$. The lines described in the first trio of results in Table 4.1 differ from those described in Figure 4.1 because the results reported in Table 4.1 take into account the presence of autoregressive errors.

5 The difference in coefficients in the second trio of regressions is significant only at $p < .25$.

6 In a strict sense, inflation, economic growth, and war are not exogenous to government spending. Keynesians, monetarists, and supply-side economists all agree that government spending affects inflation and economic growth, although they disagree about what those effects are. And, high military spending certainly makes subsequent war-fighting far from the nation's borders, as happened in the Spanish-American War and World War I, more likely. Dealing with the endogeneity of inflation, economic growth, and war is beyond the analysis of this chapter; further, allowing for this endogeneity would not alter the conclusion that events outside the structural politics of the House may have had an independent effect on spending expansion after 1885.

7 No control for GDP was included in the equations because the size of GDP was correlated with Trend at a level of .984.

legislative process that adds programs, missions, or agencies to a department. If, for instance, Congress passed a law after 1885 dramatically expanding the range of free postal delivery throughout rural areas, resulting in an expansion of post office appropriations to pay for such expanded services, it would be misleading to attribute that spending expansion to the devolution of 1885. (It may be possible to show that the spending expansion due to the introduction of rural free delivery occurred at a faster pace than it would have if the appropriation had been overseen by the Appropriations Committee, but this line of inquiry would lead us to examination of *marginal* spending decisions, not aggregate ones. I return to this point below.)

To understand how the additions to agency missions can present problems in aggregate spending analysis, consider agricultural spending between FY 1871 and 1900. (I stop in FY 1900 in order to avoid compounding the analysis with estimation problems associated with the two wars.) The Agriculture Department has been a primary focus in the study of the spending consequences of devolution because it was the first full department that was removed from the purview of the HAC and because post-1880 spending outstripped pre-1880 spending by so much (see Brady and Morgan 1987).[8] It also makes a good example because it was a relatively small department, and thus legislatively induced expansions to its structure and mission are readily visible.

Why did agricultural appropriations grow so fast after 1880? Was it because the Agriculture Committee was so generous? That is certainly part of the explanation. But, before concluding specifically how generous the Agriculture Committee was, we need to get a sense of how much of this spending growth can be attributed to *legislative* changes that, while perhaps related to changes in the appropriations process, are still conceptually different.

The first thing to know about agricultural appropriations after 1880 is that by FY 1900 over three-fourths of the budget of the Agriculture Department went to three bureaus and major programs that were not part of the department's activities in 1880, when the annual bill was transferred to the legislative committee. In 1884 Congress passed an act that created the Bureau of Animal Industry within the Agriculture Department; this bureau received one-third of the department's budget within two years of its creation. In 1887 Congress created a system of agriculture experiment stations; in the first year of funding (FY 1890), these stations received 36 percent of the department's budget. And, finally, Congress transferred the Weather Bureau from the army signal

8 The average annual growth rate in agricultural appropriations before FY 1881 was 5.2 percent; afterward, 13.6 percent.

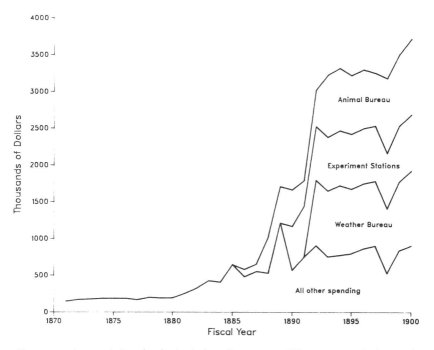

Figure 4.2. Appropriations for the Agriculture Department, FY 1871–1900 (in thousands of dollars). Data from U.S Statutes at Large, various years.

corps to the Agriculture Department in 1891, and along with it, the bureau's $890,000 budget (in a year that the entire agriculture budget was just over $3 million). Between FY 1880 and 1900, the appropriation for the Agriculture Department grew at an average annual rate of 12.3 percent; if we exclude the effects of the addition of the Weather Bureau, the Animal Industry Bureau, and the experiment stations, the average annual growth rate was only 7.0 percent. Thus, the "old" functions of the Agriculture Department grew after 1880, and at a faster rate than they did before;[9] but, about half of the growth in the department's appropriation after 1880 was due to functions and programs that were added through the legislative process (see Figure 4.2). When the major programs and bureaus were added, their budgets caused the entire appropriation for the Agriculture Department to expand in step fashion: These one-time budgetary shocks had long-term consequences.

In general, in examining aggregate spending, it is very difficult to separate out appropriations increases that are due to these sort of legislative

9 The agricultural items that were in the legislative, executive, and judicial bill before FY 1881 grew at an annual rate of 2.1 percent in the 1870s.

activities from increases that are due to changes in the appropriations process itself. It would certainly be a Herculean task to comb through the histories of hundreds of government departments and bureaus for half a century to discover just the *major* new functions, missions, and bureaus that were added after 1885. And, even if we could discover all those cases where spending grew because of legislative activity, we still would not want to discard information about these new spending programs, we would only want to place the new programs within their proper context. After all, once the Weather Bureau was in the Agriculture Department, how the Agriculture Committee handled the bureau's appropriation in *subsequent* years is an important piece of information to have. Therefore, absent knowing the detailed histories of all government programs during this period, the next best strategy is to abandon spending aggregates all together and look at *changes* in spending.

If we examine changes in spending levels from year to year, the effects of a one-time-only expansion of spending are felt only in the year in which it occurs. Thus, the effects of legislative changes are not totally removed from the analysis, but there is a greater chance that the idiosyncratic effects associated with sudden surges in appropriations in any given year will enter the random error component of the model.

Moving away from spending aggregates toward *changes* in spending has a final advantage that is even more important than the methodological one: theory. The budgetary studies undertaken by Wildavsky, Fenno, and their followers have fairly conclusively shown that, ceteris paribus, budgetary decisionmakers usually do not make decisions by looking at aggregates; rather, they concentrate on *changes* to the aggregates.[10] Given the persistence of incrementalist spending strategies over time, what is important is not so much how much was contained in various appropriations bills at the end of each appropriations cycle, but what the relevant actors did to the bills at each stage of the process.[11]

Of course, if we are interested in applying the incrementalist model,

10 The ceteris paribus argument is a strong one – all things are not equal all of the time. There have clearly been cases in the history of budgeting when decisionmakers were concerned with the aggregates and when they have made substantial, "nonincremental" changes in spending levels. For the moment, though, I want to concentrate on "normal budgeting," bringing in the political world and the causes for nonincremental decisionmaking later in the chapter.

11 For this analysis, I am assuming that the practice of incrementalism that has been so widely observed in modern budgeting was the norm in budgeting a century ago. Several years of work in the area of budgetary politics in Congress after the Civil War lead me to believe that this assumption is a safe one to make. In fact, the behavioral antecedents to incrementalism, namely limited information and processing capacity, made incrementalist strategies even *more* compelling during the nineteenth century than they have been during the twentieth century.

we will not be looking at the changes in appropriations year to year; rather, at changes step by step. That is, we are interested in how much the bureau requests above the appropriation received last year, how much the committee cuts from the agency's request, and how much the House adds back to the committee recommendation. By further disaggregating the appropriations process, we not only get closer to the decisionmakers themselves, whose behavior was supposedly changed by structural reform, but we further lessen the probability that findings concerning the growth of appropriations are created by principally legislative events.[12]

THE APPROPRIATIONS SYSTEM, 1871–1922

In many respects, appropriations politics a century ago conformed to the patterns ascribed to modern budgeting by Wildavsky (1964) and Fenno (1966). In short, spending decisions were made incrementally, meaning that changes in spending levels were made in small amounts, and that decisions made at step s were a function of decisions made at step $s - 1$. Not only were decisions made at step s a function of those made at step $s - 1$, they were also a function of what was anticipated to happen at step $s + 1$. Agencies asked for more, not only to make up for the previous year's cut, but also to compensate for the cut sure to come in the House committee that year. And, the committee cut the agency's increment not only to excise the fat added by the agency, but to counteract the certain increase to come on the House floor.

That budgetary decisionmakers made their decisions to compensate for what had happened previously and to anticipate what was to come next suggests that within budgetary cycles, spending levels oscillated in predictable ways consistent with the Wildavsky-Fenno model. Specifically, agencies almost always asked for increases over the previous year's appropriation, committees typically cut this "increment" (leaving the "base" intact), and the full House added back a small amount of what the committee cut. The end result was that the annual bills typically grew each year, but at a slower rate than was preferred by the agencies.

12 The dichotomy I am creating between purely legislative and appropriations politics is clearly too neat for the real world of congressional politics. Still, the distinction is an important one to make for conceptual reasons. Legislative and appropriations politics are distinct to the extent to which the latter is typically routine and the former is typically not. As well, appropriations committees typically are strategically advantaged when they bring measures to the floor since (1) the annual appropriations bills "must pass," (2) the committees can easily hide provisions deep within the recesses of voluminous appropriations bills, and (3) the reversion level if a bill fails is often zero. The floor is at less of a disadvantage in legislative matters since (1) fewer pieces of legislation "must pass" and (2) the reversion level is less likely to be zero (i.e., a complete lack of policy).

Of course, there was a great deal of latitude afforded to budgetary decisionmakers during this time, and decisions were by no means automatic: Committees occasionally augmented agency spending, agencies sometimes asked for less, and some agencies underwent sustained periods of retrenchment. Still, even within this behavioral variation, decisions gravitated around a set of expected outcomes. Even though the 1885 reform may have upset decision patterns at the margin, broad decisional patterns associated with the major budgetary actors were clear both before and after FY 1887, the first year decisions were made under the new regime.[13]

Upon casual inspection of the data (Table 4.2), it is easy to see these incremental decision rules applied during the period of interest; changes across the 1885 intervention are also evident. (For instance, the size of the cut made in committee went down on average after 1885.) Less easy to see are (1) how *variations* in the behaviors of some actors (e.g., agencies and the full House) systematically affected *variations* in the behaviors of others (e.g., the committees) and (2) how exogenous political and economic factors affected incremental budgetary decisionmaking.

To see how budgetary actors changed in their relations to each other after 1885, and also to see how budgetary actors took exogenous political and economic events into account, it is necessary to specify and test statistical models of the appropriations process. The models to be specified here are very similar to those that have been tested to explain budgetary decisions in modern times (e.g., Kiewiet and McCubbins 1985a,b). Although the models are similar, largely because basic aspects of budgetary politics have been similar over the past century, they are not identical because there are some obvious differences of detail that must be taken into account.

As a general matter, the spending decisions in which we are interested can be modeled as follows:

$$\text{Decision}_s = (\text{Decision}_{s-1}, \text{Decision}_{s+1}, \text{Elections, Partisan politics,}$$
$$\text{Institutional developments, Economic conditions,}$$
$$\text{War, Error)} \qquad (4.1)$$

Let me now move through the elements listed in equation (4.1) and discuss how they were specified and measured.[14]

---

13 Throughout this chapter there will be possibility of confusion about the dividing line after which the "regime of 1885" began to exist. The devolution itself started in *calendar year* 1885, although the decisions that were first made under the new regime were first effective in *fiscal year* 1887.
14 An even more detailed discussion of the variables and statistical analysis can be found in Stewart (1987a,b).

Table 4.2. *Changes in spending levels at various stages of the appropriations process, FY 1871–1922*

	Cut >10%	Cut 5–10%	Cut 0–5%	No change	Add 0–5%	Add 5–10%	Add >10%	Total
Difference between appropriations at time t − 1 and agency estimate at time t								
Before	8	3	12	2	24	34	76	159
FY 1887	(5.0)	(1.9)	(7.5)	(1.3)	(15.1)	(21.4)	(47.8)	(100.0)
After	40	19	36	6	73	64	163	401
FY 1887	(10.0)	(4.7)	(9.0)	(1.5)	(18.2)	(16.0)	(40.6)	(100.0)
Total	48	22	48	8	97	98	239	560
	(8.6)	(3.9)	(8.6)	(1.4)	(17.3)	(17.5)	(42.7)	(100.0)
Difference between agency estimate and House committee recommendation								
Before	88	27	26	15	8	4	2	170
FY 1887	(51.8)	(15.9)	(15.3)	(8.8)	(4.7)	(2.4)	(1.2)	(100.0)
After	130	67	106	11	52	12	23	401
FY 1887	(32.4)	(16.7)	(26.4)	(2.7)	(13.0)	(3.0)	(5.7)	(100.0)
Total	218	94	132	26	60	16	25	571
	(38.2)	(16.5)	(23.1)	(4.6)	(10.5)	(2.8)	(4.4)	(100.0)
Difference between House passage and committee recommendation								
Before	4	3	25	58	58	7	15	170
FY 1887	(2.4)	(1.8)	(14.7)	(34.1)	(34.1)	(4.1)	(8.8)	(100.0)
After	15	8	104	140	115	6	13	401
FY 1887	(3.7)	(2.0)	(25.9)	(34.9)	(28.7)	(1.5)	(3.2)	(100.0)
Total	19	11	129	198	173	13	28	571
	(3.3)	(1.9)	(22.6)	(34.7)	(30.3)	(2.3)	(4.9)	(100.0)
Difference between final appropriation and initial agency estimate								
Before	70	28	39	8	12	7	6	170
FY 1887	(41.2)	(16.5)	(22.9)	(4.7)	(7.1)	(4.1)	(3.5)	(100.0)
After	110	53	102	14	54	24	44	401
FY 1887	(27.4)	(13.2)	(25.4)	(3.5)	(13.5)	(6.0)	(11.0)	(100.0)
Total	180	81	141	22	66	31	50	571
	(31.5)	(14.2)	(24.7)	(3.9)	(11.6)	(5.4)	(8.8)	(100.0)

Note: Row percentages are in parentheses. Cell entries indicate the number of times specific types of decisions fell within particular ranges. For instance, the first cell of the table indicates that before FY 1887, agencies requested budgetary cuts exceeding 10 percent only 8 times (or 5 percent of all agency requests during that period). The data set consists of all regular annual appropriations bills except the rivers and harbors and the District of Columbia bills.

Decisions. The endogenous variables of interest in this analysis are the spending decisions made by federal agencies, House committees, and the full House. As I have already discussed, the theoretical starting point in describing the spending decisions made by any of these budgetary actors is the set of spending decisions made by others, thus the inclusion of lagged and leading decisions on the right-hand side of the equation.

Decisions are measured as the logged ratio of the amount contained in the bill at step s to the amount contained at step $s - 1$. Thus, agency decisions are defined as

$$\Delta \text{Agency}_t = \log\left(\frac{\text{Agency request}_t}{\text{Appropriation}_{t-1}}\right)$$

Committee decisions are defined as

$$\Delta \text{Committee}_t = \log\left(\frac{\text{Committee recommendation}_t}{\text{Agency request}_t}\right)$$

House decisions are defined as

$$\Delta \text{House}_t = \log\left(\frac{\text{House passage}_t}{\text{Committee recommendation}_t}\right)$$

And congressional decisions for an entire appropriations cycle are defined as

$$\Delta \text{Congress}_t = \log\left(\frac{\text{Final appropriation}_t}{\text{Agency request}_t}\right)$$

Agency decisions (ΔAgency_t) are a partial function of last year's congressional decision and the expectation about the committee decision ($\Delta \text{Congress}_{t-1}$ and $\Delta \text{Committee}_t$); committee decisions are a partial function of agency decisions and anticipated House decisions; and House decisions are a partial function of committee decisions.[15]

Because spending decisions were made in response to and anticipation of other spending decisions, it is clear that the decision variables must be considered to be endogenous. Therefore, in order to deal with the

---

15 I assume that House decisions were made without anticipating what would happen in the Senate. This assumption is justified in three ways. First, in numerous appropriations debates in the *Congressional Globe* and *Congressional Record* during this period, the anticipated reaction of the Senate rarely emerged as a justification for amending committee recommendations. Second, even if the anticipated behavior of the Senate *were* a factor in amending committee recommendations on the House floor, albeit an unspoken one, it is unclear which step in the Senate members of the House were anticipating – committee or Senate floor. Third, and more practically, the data-gathering job necessary to include the Senate in the House floor equation would have doubled the (substantial) work already necessary to conduct the analysis here, with rapidly diminishing marginal returns.

endogeneity of the decision variables, I used three-stage least squares to estimate the following models.[16] Instruments to take the place of right-hand side endogenous variables are designated with superscripted stars (i.e., $\Delta\text{Committee}_i^*$ is the instrument for $\Delta\text{Committee}_i$).[17] Finally, because the leading indicators measure decisions that were reached *after* the values of the dependent variables were determined, I am assuming that the relevant actors were responding to unbiased estimates of what would come next.

Elections. Recent research (Kiewiet and McCubbins 1985a,b) has shown that in addition to the traditional incrementalist process, aspects of the "electoral connection" have had strong effects on post-World War II congressional spending decisions. Although turn-of-the-century legislators were less likely to seek reelection than current MCs, the consequences of electoral politics were still likely to be felt, either as some members actually sought reelection (as most did) or as others attempted to impress local party officials with their skill at bringing home benefits to the community. Therefore, as with more recent MCs, those under study here may have had an interest in expanding appropriations right before congressional elections. The presence of congressional elections is indicated in the models by a dummy variable (Election), which takes on a value of 1 if the appropriation was *passed* in an even-numbered year, 0 otherwise. This dummy variable should pick up the hypothesized biennial surge and decline pattern.

Partisan politics. In addition to the electoral calendar, spending decisions were obviously influenced by partisan fluctuations since the parties differed in their general and specific spending preferences. But, the nature of many of those preferences stood current relationships on their head. Generally speaking, *Republicans* preferred higher spending aggregates

16 *Two*-stage least squares (2SLS) is the more common way of dealing with the problems associated with having endogenous variables on the right-hand side of the equation. *Three*-stage least squares (3SLS) extends 2SLS by taking into account the correlation of the errors between the different equations in the models. The advantage of 3SLS is that it is more efficient than 2SLS. Structural parameters estimated using 3SLS are interpreted the same way as the better-known ordinary least squares (OLS) parameters.

17 The instrumental variable estimates were created by imposing the exclusionary restrictions implied in the tables reported below, regressing the right-hand endogenous variables on the exogenous variables in the model, and then using the fitted values of the endogenous variables thus obtained as predictor variables. In addition to the exogenous variables already available in the model for the creation of instruments, I included several other additional variables, as well: a dummy variable for each bill (in pooled regressions) and variables for the president's party and the occurrence of presidential elections. Even before the addition of these other exogenous variables, all of the equations described are strictly overidentified.

during this period. *Democrats* desired to reduce spending generally because during most of this period the federal government was essentially a Republican preserve. High aggregate spending meant the expansion of Republican policy interests, and Democrats saw retrenchment as one way of reining-in the Republican state. Like modern-day Republicans, however, late-nineteenth-century Democrats were willing to pursue higher spending for *specific* programs if this would benefit their own constituents and interests. Thus, Democrats, as well as Republicans, were willing to utilize the benefits that could accrue from the skillful provision of federal services, especially those enacted in election years. But, all-in-all, Republican-passed spending should have been higher than Democrat-passed spending.[18]

Although lower spending should be associated with the presence of more Democrats in the House, and established patterns should have been upset when Democratic Houses faced Republican presidents, the effects of partisanship are hypothesized to have entered into decisions in different ways in the two congressional steps. First, consider the committee step. The partisan effect in the committee is measured with a dummy variable, equal to 1 when Democrats controlled the House, 0 otherwise (Control). The effect of *split partisan control* of the House and the presidency is also measured with a dummy variable (Split), equal to 1 when majority House Democrats faced a Republican president, 0 otherwise.

Second, consider the full House step. Unlike the binary nature of partisanship specified for committees, partisanship on the House floor is specified to have operated in a continuous fashion. Three justifications can be offered for this assumption:[19]

1. The (small) size of the committees was such that shifts in partisan balance in the full House could not be simply transferred into shifts in the partisan balance on individual committees. Changes in party control would significantly upset a committee's partisan balance; but once party control was stable, shifts in the size of the party's majority in the House had a less important influence on subsequent shifts in the committee's partisan balance (Stewart 1987b, 19, fn. 14).

2. Although levels of party-unity voting were much higher during this period than in the present, reaching historic levels in the 1890s, party coalitions did not cohere perfectly. Therefore, as margins were closer, it was more likely that the preferences of minority party members would be felt in decisions

18 The assertion in this paragraph about relative Republican and Democratic spending preferences may seem to contradict the pattern discovered in Chapter 3, whereby the appropriations process was decentralized during Democratically controlled Houses. There is in fact no contradiction since the Democratic assaults on the conservative appropriations process were concentrated on *particular* spending items.

19 See Stewart (1987b, 18–20) for a more detailed examination of these justifications.

made on the floor. In practical terms, this means that as more Democrats were in the House, House spending decisions would be lower, even if Democrats were not in the majority.

3. Specifying partisanship to affect committee and full House decisions differently helps to identify the committee equation. Given the substantive arguments I have just given for making two types of specifications, it is clear that practicality is not the only, or most important, argument. However, in estimating models where specification can determine whether estimation is even possible, this practical argument cannot be overlooked.

This continuous partisanship variable is defined as

$$\text{Margin}_t = \log\left(\frac{\text{Democratic House members}_t}{\text{Republican House members}_t}\right)$$

If changing partisanship influenced committee and floor decisionmaking differently, then split partisan control of the House and presidency would also influence floor decisions as a continuous function. Therefore, in the case of floor decisions, I measure split partisan control with an interaction term, $\text{Split}_t \times \text{Margin}_t$.

Institutional developments. The devolution of 1885 was not the only institutional development after the Civil War that could have affected spending outcomes. Two other major, and related, developments come quickly to mind: the "institutionalization" of the House in the late nineteenth century and the appearance of "czar rule" around the turn of the century (Busbey 1927; Galloway 1962, 52–53, 134–136).

Congressional institutionalization has come to refer to a series of secular changes in the House following the Civil War that were related to the rise of House membership as a career, the solidification of committee jurisdictions and House rules, the rise of a series of property rights and the operation of seniority in settling questions about committee membership, and the routinization of the procedures by which the agenda for the consideration of legislation on the House floor was established (Polsby 1968; Polsby, Gallagher, and Rundquist 1969; Price 1971, 1975, 1977).

The period of strong speakerships, or czar rule, coincided with much of the rapid rise of institutionalization. Czar rule was symbolized by the establishment of the Reed Rules in 1890 and was characterized by a rapid increase in the degree to which the Speaker could (1) control proceedings on the floor and (2) affect congressional careers through appointments to committees. Although the Reed Rules provided a potent symbol for the coming of a new age, later-to-be-Speaker Joseph Cannon reports that the full weight of czar rule did not become fully entrenched in the House until Reed's second term as Speaker (Busbey 1927, 184). Therefore, I consider czar rule to have lasted from the 54th Congress until the revolt against Speaker Cannon in the 61st.

Although these two related developments are somewhat distinct analytically, their hypothesized effects on spending decisions are the same. Both served to bolster the authority of decisions made by committees and to limit the range of flexibility in changing committee recommendations on the floor. If there is by nature a slight "positivity bias" in appropriations proceedings on the floor, then the period of greatest institutionalization and czar rule should have produced a counter "negativity bias" in floor decisions.

Although both institutionalization and czar rule were important developments that affected spending decisions after the Civil War, in the models tested below I include only a measure for the existence of czar rule. I offer three justifications for this. First, the two developments coincide so much (and are therefore collinear), that disentangling their unique effects is nearly impossible; therefore it is important only to account for the effects of the development that was the *more significant* of the two. Second, therefore, I would argue that czar rule was a more significant influence than secular institutionalization. Coming as it did on the heels of high drama on the House floor, the imposition of czar rule was certainly more noticeable to members of the House *at that time* than institutionalization, which was making slow (albeit steady) progress. Third, the concept of institutionalization is a vague one, so that any attempt to measure it here would certainly yield a variable that was full of measurement error, resulting in attenuated measures of relationships. Although czar rule is not a concept measured perfectly without error, there is less error in measuring it than in measuring institutionalization.

Thus the variable Czar is a dummy variable that takes on a value of 1 if the bill was considered between the 54th and 61st Congresses (inclusive), 0 otherwise. I further assume that the effects of czar rule were only felt on the floor. Although there is evidence to suggest that Speakers brought committee leaders into party leadership councils during the period of strong Speaker dominance (Busbey 1927, 219), the most obvious effects of czar rule were those observable on the House floor itself. These include a drop-off in the number of roll call votes during this period (Stewart 1987b, 22) and a decline in the degree to which challenges to leadership-initiated rules changes were pursued on the floor (Stewart 1985, 269), in addition to the well-known imposition of the Reed Rules, which of course applied primarily to floor behavior.[20]

---

20 One could argue that yet another institutional development, the experiment with caucus government carried out by the Democrats immediately upon the end of czar rule, should be accounted for in the model. I have refrained from doing so in the interest of both parsimony and substance. First, the experiment started off with a bang, but quickly lost steam. Second, it is not clear that any binding votes taken by the Democratic caucus related to appropriations items anyway (see Haines 1915; Busbey 1927; Roady 1951).

Economic conditions. Fluctuations in prices and in economic prosperity are hypothesized to have affected spending decisions during this period. In general, given full information about the state of the economy, spending decisionmakers would tend to prefer higher spending when the economy is more prosperous and less spending when it is suffering under inflation.[21] These are the relationships found in modern decisionmaking (Kiewiet and McCubbins 1985a,b), and these are the two relationships I expected in the case of post-Civil War spending.[22]

The speeches of nineteenth century politicians made it clear that most desired to expand spending during deflationary periods and to retrench during depressions. However, the quality of national macroeconomic data was very poor indeed, and responses to exogenous economic changes were filled with error.[23] Therefore, we should expect a positive relationship between economic growth and federal spending and a negative relationship between prices and spending, but we should also expect many mistakes to have been made as a consequence of these adjustments, and therefore for statistical description of the relationships to be attenuated and noisy.[24]

21 Arguing that spending decisionmakers prefer retrenchment during panics or recessions is certainly counter to Keynesian notions of countercyclical fiscal policy, yet it is clear that these notions never fully established themselves in the agencies and spending committees. And certainly before the New Deal, few thought in countercyclical terms (Kimmel 1959). Seen through the eyes of bureaucrats, committee members, and the House rank-and-file, an expanding economy increased tax revenues and thus eased the balanced budget constraint, making it more likely that the search for increased spending could be satisfied.

While on the topic of inflation, I want to make it clear that the spending models discussed and tested here are developed in *nominal* terms. It is clearly the case that any model of modern spending decisionmaking must take into account the discounting that decisionmakers do to account for inflation. However, in the years I have spent reviewing budget debates following the Civil War, I have never seen one of these latter-day budgeters making a comparison between nominal and real spending; in the pre-World War I world, the two were not differentiated. Therefore, in this discussion I adopt the conventions of those whose behavior I am attempting to explain, and operate in nominal terms.

22 The assumption about the negative relationship between inflation and spending levels would seem to contradict the finding reported earlier in this chapter that prices were strongly related to total spending. Two things could be said about this apparent contradiction. First, the earlier finding concerned price and spending *levels*; the analysis in this part of the chapter is interested in *changes* in levels. Second, the finding reported earlier in the chapter is largely picking up the effects of inflation during wartime; if we exclude the war years from the analysis, the earlier findings approach null findings.

23 Also, lacking the existence of a fully integrated national economy, crises in particular sectors did not necessarily mean crisis, or even concern, elsewhere.

24 Attenuation is due to the "errors in variables" problem. Noisiness is due to sporadic adaptation to economic fluctuations, an inconsistency that would have remained even if the economic variables were measured better.

The annual measures of prices and gross domestic product (GDP) were based on data reported by the *Economist* (1982). The price and GDP variables were measured in terms of changes, as follows:

$$\Delta\text{Prices}_t = \log\left(\frac{\text{Price index}_t}{\text{Price index}_{t-1}}\right)$$

$$\Delta\text{GDP}_t = \log\left(\frac{\text{GDP index}_t}{\text{GDP index}_{t-1}}\right)$$

Finally, I assumed that the economic variables, inflation and economic growth, entered the picture only at the agency and committee steps of the process. Agencies, of course, have an interest in using economic changes to their advantage and are therefore likely to have responded accordingly. Of the two decisionmaking steps in the House (the committee and the floor) the more likely place for economic conditions to have had an impact is in committee. Taking economic conditions into account is routine in making a spending decision and therefore is the type of matter most likely entrusted to the committee in the division-of-labor deal defining the committee system.

War. The effects of war on federal spending are well-known; because two wars (the Spanish-American War and World War I) occurred in the period we are studying, we need to make allowances for war's effects in our statistical models. The effects that war had on spending decisions during this period are unmistakable, but also highly variable.[25] The domestic bills were not obviously affected by war at all. The foreign and military bills, which were all affected by war, were all affected differently. And, in the case of the army bill, wartime spending results produced such severe outliers that statistical analysis involving this bill was driven by just a few data points, even controlling for hostilities in a number of ways. All the military and foreign affairs bills seemed to be affected the same way by *demobilization*, however. Therefore, I concluded that the most straightforward way to deal with the analytical problems caused by war was (1) to remove the observations for all variables during war years, in this case FY 1900–1902 and FY 1917–19 and (2) to create a variable that captured the three-year, postwar demobilization effect present in all foreign and military bills.[26]

This variable, Demobilization, was measured as follows:

25 See Busbey (1927, 186–198) for Joseph Cannon's first-hand recollection of how exceptional the spending process was for the beginning of the Spanish-American War.
26 Among the devolved bills, these were the army, consular and diplomatic, military academy, and naval affairs bills; each of the bills that remained with the HAC after 1885 contained substantial military and foreign affairs spending.

$$\text{Demobilization}_t = \begin{cases} -3 \text{ if } t = 1902, 1920 \\ -2 \text{ if } t = 1903, 1921 \\ -1 \text{ if } t = 1904, 1922 \\ 0 \text{ otherwise} \end{cases}$$

DATA ANALYSIS

As I have already suggested, it would be inappropriate to estimate the statistical models summarized by equation (4.1) using ordinary least squares (OLS) regression. To take into account the endogeneity of the spending decision variables, I had to use two- or three-stage least squares (2SLS, 3SLS) to estimate statistical models. Because I had to use a technique such as 3SLS, the small number of observations for each spending bill presented further problems. There were only fifty-two observations for ten of the spending bills, fifty-one for the military academy. By pooling each set of bills, those that were devolved after 1885 and those that remained with the HAC, I gained statistical leverage by increasing the N in each set of regressions, as well as allowing for the testing of the major hypotheses by examining a limited number of coefficients. Finally, by expressing the spending variables in terms of logged ratios, I avoided heteroscedasticity, which is often a problem with pooled analyses.

Of course, pooling the data comes with some costs and adds complexities to the analysis that must be addressed. First, pooled time-series analysis assumes that the coefficients associated with the explanatory variables are the same for all spending bills and do not vary across time. To test whether this constraint resulted in an unacceptable increase in residual sum of squares, I calculated a series of F tests that compared the errors produced in the restricted and unrestricted models.[27] Second, pooled time-series analysis assumes the lack of cross-sectional correlation of errors. That is, it is assumed that the factors producing error in a decision for bill i at time t are uncorrelated with the factors producing error in a decision for bill j at time t. If the errors are correlated, then the estimated standard errors will be biased. To test whether this assumption held, I calculated the correlation between the residuals of the

---

27 I conducted two types of tests. First, I tested the gain produced when all restrictions about equal coefficients were relaxed, and all coefficient parameters were allowed to vary across all bills. This is essentially asking whether the bills as a whole should be estimated separately or pooled together. When this test proved negative, I then tested whether the constraint that *specific* coefficients be equal across bills produced an unacceptably large increase in error sum of squares. For instance, I tested whether the coefficient associated with the ΔPrices variable was equal across bills, then whether the ΔGDP coefficient was equal across bills, and so on. Third, I then interacted all of the explanatory variables with a trend variable and entered them together and in blocks, also with negative results.

various appropriations bills. Third, the analysis assumes the lack of serial correlation. The commonly used Durbin-Watson statistic to test for autoregression is inappropriate in pooled analysis, and therefore I examined the serial correlation of errors separately for each bill. In only one case, which I report later, did any of the diagnostics yield a positive result.

The data analysis that follows was performed on two pooled time series. In each pooled series, the cross-sectional items were annual appropriations bills and the time series ranged from FY 1871 to 1922.[28] The first data set was constructed using seven of the annual appropriations bills that had been transferred away from the HAC by 1885: agriculture, army, consular and diplomatic, Indian affairs, military academy, naval affairs, and post office. The only relevant annual bill that was left out of this set was the rivers and harbors bill, which did not pass every year in the 1880s.

The second set was constructed using four of the annual appropriations bills that remained with the HAC after 1885: fortifications; legislative, executive, and judicial; pensions; and sundry civil. This second set omitted the District of Columbia bill, because a full time series was unavailable, and the various supplemental and deficiency bills, because their contents varied considerably.

The empirical core of this chapter is the question of whether the character of spending decisions changed after 1885 among those bills that were removed from the HAC, and whether similar changes occurred among bills that remained with the HAC. The criteria that were most likely to change and to be of major consequence in determining final appropriations were those related to the incrementalist portion of the spending model. In other words, we are interested in discovering whether reactions to past and anticipated spending decisions remained unchanged after 1885, controlling for exogenous political and economic variables. In the specific case of committee decisions, did the legislative committees cut as much out of agency requests as the HAC did, and did the legislative committees also try to counter additions on the House floor with the same vigor as did the HAC?

To assess this series of empirical questions, I proceeded as follows. First, I estimated models explaining agency, committee, and House floor behavior based on equation (4.1). Second, I estimated models that added two or three more variables to each equation, to test whether the key coefficients remained unchanged after 1885. These added variables were (a) a dummy variable (After) that took on a value of 0 before and including FY 1886 and 1 afterward, (b) the interaction of After with the

---

28 The only exception is the time series for the military academy appropriations bill, which ended in FY 1921.

variable describing the previous decision, and (c) (where appropriate) the interaction of After with the variable describing the following decision. I then conducted an F test to see whether the values associated with these three (or two) new variables equaled zero. A positive F test would indicate that the interaction terms measure the degree to which the relevant parameters changed after 1885.

For instance, consider the simple incrementalist case where

$$\Delta \text{Committee}_t = (b_0 + b_1 \text{After}_t) + (b_2 + b_3 \text{After}_t)\, \Delta \text{Agency}_t$$
$$+ (b_4 + b_5 \text{After}_t)\, \Delta \text{House}_t \qquad (4.2)$$

Before devolution, After = 0; thus equation (4.2) reduces to

$$\Delta \text{Committee}_t = b_0 + b_2\, \Delta \text{Agency}_t + b_4\, \Delta \text{House}_t \qquad (4.3)$$

After devolution, After = 1; thus equation (4.2) can be rewritten as

$$\Delta \text{Committee}_t = (b_0 + b_1) + (b_2 + b_3)\, \Delta \text{Agency}_t$$
$$+ (b_4 + b_5)\, \Delta \text{House}_t \qquad (4.4)$$

b_1 measures the extent to which the intercept changed, while b_3 and b_5 measure the extent to which the two relevant slopes changed. If the F test that evaluates whether $b_1 = b_3 = b_5 = 0$ allows us to reject the null hypotheses, then we can conclude that the slopes and intercept did indeed change following devolution.

Third, I conducted the same type of procedure involving interactions with the variable After to see whether the coefficients associated with the exogenous variables changed after 1885. Fourth, I conducted the necessary diagnostics described previously.

Because the findings associated with the devolved bills differ from those associated with the bills that remained with the HAC, I will discuss the findings separately.

THE FATE OF THE DEVOLVED BILLS

The equations used to test the decision patterns for bills that were removed from the HAC, estimated using 3SLS, were as follows (for bill b and fiscal year t):

$$\Delta \text{Agency}_{b,t} = (a_0 + a_1 \text{After}_t) + (a_2 + a_3 \text{After}_t)\, \Delta \text{Congress}^*_{b,t-1}$$
$$+ (a_4 + a_5 \text{After}_t)\, \Delta \text{Committee}^*_{b,t}$$
$$+ a_6\, \Delta \text{Prices}_{t-1} + a_7\, \Delta \text{GDP}_{t-1}$$
$$+ a_8 \text{Demobilization}_t + a_9 \text{Army}$$
$$+ a_{10} \text{Indian} + \text{Error}_{1,b,t} \qquad (4.5)$$

$$\Delta\text{Committee}_{b,t} = (b_0 + b_1\text{After}_t) + (b_2 + b_3\text{After}_t)\,\Delta\text{Agency}^*_{b,t}$$
$$+ (b_4 + b_5\text{After}_t)\,\Delta\text{House}^*_{b,t}$$
$$+ b_6\,\Delta\text{Prices}_{t-1} + b_7\,\Delta\text{GDP}_{t-1}$$
$$+ b_8\text{Election}_t + b_9\text{Control}_t + b_{10}\text{Split}_t$$
$$+ b_{11}\text{Demobilization}_t + b_{12}\text{Post}$$
$$+ b_{13}\text{Agriculture} + \text{Error}_{2,b,t} \tag{4.6}$$

$$\Delta\text{House}_{b,t} = (c_0 + c_1\text{After}_t) + (c_2 + c_3\text{After}_t)\,\Delta\text{Committee}^*_{b,t}$$
$$+ c_4\text{Election}_t + c_5\text{Margin}_t + c_6\text{Split}_t \times \text{Margin}_t$$
$$+ c_7\text{Demobilization}_t + c_8\text{Czar}_t + c_9\text{Indian}$$
$$+ c_{10}\text{Agriculture} + \text{Error}_{3,b,t} \tag{4.7}$$

In each equation, I added dummy variables to account for different mean levels of the dependent variables for particular bills [for instance, the inclusion of variables Army and Indian in equation (4.5)]. The results from this estimation are reported in Table 4.3.

I first tested to see, in terms of equations (4.5), (4.6), and (4.7), whether $a_1 = a_3 = a_5 = 0$, $b_1 = b_3 = b_5 = 0$, and $c_1 = c_3 = 0$. The p levels associated with these tests were, respectively, .766, .074, and .083. Based on these results, I concluded that the decisionmaking criteria had changed in committee and on the House floor but not among the agencies.[29] Because I concluded that agency decisionmaking criteria had remained unchanged, I reestimated the agency equation, omitting the intervention terms, and report those results as well. Let us now turn to the specifics in the findings.

As a general proposition, the coefficients in Table 4.3 are in the right directions, although some of the exogenous variables do not reach standard levels of statistical significance. Only one variable is of the wrong sign, and it is not statistically significant.[30]

---

29 I should report that I was willing to reject the null hypothesis at $p < .20$.

30 Three-stage least squares does not produce an R^2 statistic for each individual equation, but it does produce an estimated R^2 for the entire system of equations. In the case of Table 4.3, the system R^2 is 0.188. This may strike some as low, but recall that we are analyzing *changes* in appropriations, not *levels*. Also, R^2 is low because I have not included all of the variables that went into deciding appropriations levels. For instance, I leave out measures of substantive issues that affected decisions on particular bills. If I were interested in building comprehensive spending models, this would be a cause for concern. However, I am only interested in testing the degree to which the incrementalist system was upset because of the devolution of 1885. What is important to examine in the findings here is the estimated coefficients, which should be unbiased if the omitted variables are uncorrelated with the variables in the models.

For those who are still interested in R^2s for the individual equations, the 2SLS R^2s were .160, .260, and .117 for the last three equations in Table 4.3; the OLS R^2s for the same equations were .345, .387, and .183.

Table 4.3. *Structure of spending decisions concerning seven annual appropriations bills overseen by legislative committees after 1885, FY 1871–1922 (three-stage least squares, N = 314)*

Variable	Dependent variables		ΔCommittee$_t$	ΔHouse$_t$
	ΔAgency$_t$			
Intercept	0.025	0.054[b]	−0.043	−0.013
	(0.042)	(0.020)	(0.040)	(0.015)
Intercept × After	0.032	—	0.001	0.031[e]
	(0.043)		(0.041)	(0.020)
ΔCongress$^*_{t-1}$	−0.518[e]	−0.289[c]	—	—
	(0.387)	(0.118)		
ΔCongress$^*_{t-1}$ × After$_t$	0.240	—	—	—
	(0.403)			
ΔAgency$^*_t$	—	—	−0.841[b]	—
			(0.268)	
ΔAgency$^*_t$ × After$_t$	—	—	0.389[e]	—
			(0.287)	
ΔCommittee$^*_t$	−0.368[e]	−0.454[a]	—	−0.195[c]
	(0.271)	(0.117)		(0.081)
ΔCommittee$^*_t$ × After$_t$	−0.151	—	—	0.247[c]
	(0.300)			(0.100)
ΔHouse$^*_t$	—	—	−1.049[c]	—
			(0.439)	
ΔHouse$^*_t$ × After$_t$	—	—	0.904[e]	—
			(0.622)	
ΔPrices$_{t-1}$	−0.413[e]	−0.310	−0.882[b]	—
	(0.318)	(0.290)	(0.274)	
ΔGDP$_{t-1}$	0.152	0.097	0.285[d]	—
	(0.201)	(0.193)	(0.172)	
Election$_t$	—	—	0.003	0.002
			(0.020)	(0.009)
Democratic House$_t$	—	—	−0.048[d]	—
			(0.027)	
Democratic margin$_t$	—	—	—	−0.029[c]
				(0.013)
Split control$_t$	—	—	−0.020	—
			(0.034)	
Democratic margin$_t$ × Split control$_t$	—	—	—	0.025
				(0.021)
Czar rule$_t$	—	—	—	−0.025[d]
				(0.014)
Demobilization$_t$	0.062[c]	0.057[c]	0.061[b]	0.023[c]
	(0.025)	(0.024)	(0.023)	(0.009)
Agriculture	—	—	0.075[c]	0.023[d]
			(0.031)	(0.014)

Table 4.3 *(cont.)*

	Dependent variables		
Variable	ΔAgency$_t$	ΔCommittee$_t$	ΔHouse$_t$
Army	-0.099^b -0.098^b	—	—
	(0.033) (0.033)		
Indian affairs	-0.109^b -0.113^b	—	0.024^d
	(0.036) (0.035)		(0.014)
Post office	— —	0.075^c	—
		(0.031)	

R^2 with intervention terms: 0.188.
R^2 without intervention terms: 0.187.

$^a p < .001.$ $^b p < .01.$ $^c p < .05.$ $^d p < .10.$ $^e p < .20.$

Agencies

The agencies represented in these seven bills made their annual requests by, first, asking for an automatic 5.5 percent[31] increase over the previous year's appropriation (indicated by the Intercept term).[32] In addition, each agency also took into account the amount that Congress had cut from its request the previous year and the amount that it predicted the committee would cut in the current year. On average, agencies tried to recover about a quarter of what had been removed from their budgets previously and attempted to preempt committee decisions by adding to their requests about half of what they estimated would be cut in committee.

While the coefficients do not reach statistical significance, the signs associated with ΔPrices and ΔGDP are in the right direction, indicating perhaps some cutting during inflationary times and some expansion when the economy was growing. Still, the standard errors of both coefficients and the substantively small size of the ΔGDP coefficient should make us hesitant about drawing this conclusion too strongly. The Demobilization variable indicates that the four military and consular bills were retrenched immediately following wars, being reduced 15.7 percent in the first year

31 Change variables in the analysis are all expressed as logged ratios. Because logged ratios have less intuitive meaning than percentages, I have converted the estimated logged ratios determined by the 3SLS parameters into percentages, for ease of exposition. Logged ratios can be converted into percentage change by the following formula: $(x - y)/y = \exp[\log(x/y)] - 1$.
32 Strictly speaking, this "automatic" 5.5% increase would only occur if the values of all of the other variables in the model were zero, which, while improbable, is not impossible.

after the end of hostilities, and being further cut 11.8 and 5.5 percent the next two years.

Finally, the army and the Indian bureau followed relatively more frugal paths than the other agencies throughout this period, each year asking for approximately 10 percent less than other agencies, given identical circumstances. The finding that the army was typically in a retrenching mode during peace time is not surprising, given the general societal distrust of a standing army during this period of the nation's history. The Indian affairs finding is a little more surprising, but an explanation is partially hinted at in the final column of Table 4.3. The Indian affairs bill was volatile on the House floor as well as in the Senate. Led by western members, the House and Senate both frequently added considerable amounts to the Indian affairs bill that had not been requested. The following year, the bureau would leave off these added items, resulting in the pattern shown in the tables.

Although the agency coefficients remained stable across time, this does not mean that agency requests remained unchanged after 1885. This is because the coefficients in the analysis only describe the process the agencies went through in deciding how much to ask for; the change in coefficients does not take into account whether the variables on which the coefficients operated also remained unchanged.

To illustrate this point, we consider the structural coefficients and mean values associated with the most important variables in this analysis, $\Delta Congress^*_{i-1}$ and $\Delta Committee^*_i$. While the coefficients remained unchanged, the mean value of $\Delta Congress^*_{i-1}$ went from -0.090 to -0.045 after 1885 and the mean of $\Delta Committee^*_i$ moved from -0.163 to -0.087. The change in the values of these variables means that before 1885, an average cut in Congress the previous year would induce an additional request of 2.6 percent, while an average congressional reduction would only produce an additional 1.3 percent increase after 1885.[33] Likewise, if an agency anticipated an average cut in committee before 1885, that agency would add another 7.7 percent to its request; after 1885 an average anticipated committee cut would only produce an addition of 4.0 percent.

Thus, if we examine the variables that describe the effects of the incremental spending process on agency decisions, we conclude that they produced smaller agency requests after 1885. Of course, with committees

---

33 This calculation was performed as follows. First, we held every other variable in the equation constant. Second, we multiplied the coefficient by the pre-1885 mean and convert the result into a percentage change: $-0.289 \times -0.090 = 0.02601$; $\exp(0.02601) - 1 \approx 0.026$. Third, we multiplied the same coefficient by the post-1885 mean and converted the result into a percentage change: $-0.289 \times -0.045 = 0.013005$; $\exp(0.013005) - 1 \approx 0.013$.

specifically and Congress generally cutting less after 1885, the end result may have been higher spending once the entire congressional process had been completed. If that was indeed the case, then the devolution produced a boon for the agencies: After 1885 they could reduce their estimates and still receive higher appropriations in the end. But, in order to tell whether this was indeed the case, we need to turn to the analysis of committee decisions.

Committees

Some of the criteria by which House committees made decisions about these seven appropriations bills remained unchanged by devolution. Both the HAC and the legislative committees reduced appropriations in response to agency requests and in response to anticipated changes on the House floor, although the *levels* of those responses were different. Both types of committees reduced appropriations during inflationary periods and were more likely to honor agency requests for increases when the economy was growing. Democratic committees reduced appropriations by almost 5 percent more than Republican committees. During the first three years following wars, the legislative committees reduced related appropriations requests a further 16.7, 11.5, and 5.9 percent. Finally, both the post office and agriculture departments fared especially well in committee, generating an average of 7.8 percent more than other agencies.

Although there were similarities between the HAC and the legislative committees, there were significant differences in the *degree to which* these committees responded to agency requests and anticipated full House reactions. First, consider the response to agency requests. Before 1885, the HAC granted very little in the way of agency requests for budget increases. The size of the relevant coefficient in Table 4.3 (-0.841) indicates that if an agency were to ask the HAC for a 10 percent increase over the previous year, the HAC would only grant a 1.5 percent increase. This changed after 1885. The size of the coefficient after 1885 ($-0.841 + 0.389 = -0.452$) indicates that if an agency were to ask a legislative committee for a 10 percent increase over the previous year, that committee would grant a 5.6 percent increase.

Another way of demonstrating the effects of changes in these coefficients is to compare the predicted fates of average agency requests before and after 1885. If an agency asked the Appropriations Committee for an average increase over the previous year before 1885 (12.1 percent), it could expect to receive an increase of only 1.9 percent. If an agency asked a legislative committee for an average increase over the previous year after 1885 (7.3 percent), the agency could expect an actual increase of 4.1 percent. Thus, the changes in how legislative committees took into account agency requests show a strong tendency toward greater generosity after 1885.

The point raised in the previous paragraph is the complement of the point raised at the end of the discussion about agency decisions. The fact that agencies requested smaller increases on average after 1885 did not result in their receiving smaller committee recommendations. In fact, by reducing their requests by almost half, agencies could still coax recommendations out of the legislative committees that were more than double the recommendations of the Appropriations Committee.

Likewise, changes in how committees anticipated House reactions to their decisions also produced a movement toward greater generosity after 1885. If the HAC anticipated that the House would add 10 percent to the appropriations bill on the floor, it would reduce its recommendation by another 9.5 percent, while a legislative committee in the same position would cut the bill by only another 1.4 percent. Comparing responses to actual average changes on the House floor, the pre-1885 coefficient would predict an average cut of 3.4 percent by the Appropriations Committee in anticipation of floor action, while the post-1885 coefficient would predict an average cut of only 0.05 percent.[34]

The House floor

Finally, we can turn our attention to the decisions made on the floor of the House before and after 1885. First, as the House became more Democratic, the floor was more inclined to cut committee recommendations even further; Republican Houses were more inclined to expand agency budgets on the floor. The extent to which fluctuations in party strength influenced spending politics on the floor can be easily demonstrated. The average value of Margin during this period was −0.036, indicating that Republicans held a slight advantage in House membership overall. Moving one standard deviation (0.484) in a Republican direction would add another 1.6 percent to any given bill; moving one standard deviation in a Democratic direction would produce a cut of 1.3 percent.[35] In the Congress during the period with the greatest Republican membership (54th, 1895–97), the model predicts that 2.5 percent more was added to each bill; it further predicts that in the Congress with the greatest Democratic membership share (52nd, 1891–93), an additional 2.8

34 The relevant means of the ΔHouse,* variable before and after 1885 were 0.033 and 0.003.
35 The average value of −0.036 translates into a party ratio favoring the Republicans of 51–49. The one standard deviation move in a Republican direction produces a Republican advantage of 61–39; the move in a Democratic direction produces a Democratic advantage of 37–63.

percent was deducted from each bill. The effects of changing party ratios in making spending decisions on the House floor combines with the party-related findings in the committee equation to demonstrate the appropriations-cutting tendencies of Democrats during this period: Democratic committees would cut an extra 5 percent, followed by an additional cut on the floor of about 1 percent.

The coefficient in Table 4.3 identifying czar rule suggests that this was a period of greater economy on the House floor: Bills leaving the floor during this period were on average 2.5 percent smaller than bills that moved through the House in other times. Demobilization also sparked economy moods on the floor, but not of the magnitude witnessed in committees and among the agencies: the coefficient shows that the House approved cuts to bills of the order of 6.7, 4.5, and 2.3 percent in the three years immediately following wars. Finally, both the agriculture and Indian affairs bills fared especially well on the House floor, in each case receiving a little over 2 percent beyond what was allocated to other bills in identical situations.

But the most important set of coefficients are those that describe the floor's reaction to committee decisions, in addition to the change in the intercept term. First, consider the variables that test the House's response to committee decisions. Before 1885, these coefficients show a set of feeble attempts to overcome the HAC's retrenchment strategy: A 10 percent committee cut yielded an average 2.1 percent increase on the floor. After 1885, any attempt to overcome committee decisions disappeared, as the same 10 percent cut would yield a substantively insignificant *cut* on the floor of 0.5 percent. The comparisons of the responses to committee decisions are even stronger when the basis of comparison is the response to *average* committee cuts. Before 1885, the average committee cut (15.0 percent) would have yielded an increase on the floor of 3.2 percent; after 1885, the average legislative committee cut (8.4 percent) would have yielded a further cut on the floor of 0.5 percent. The intercept term did change after 1885, although the change is only marginally significant. Still, this shift in the size of the intercept suggests that instead of responding to unsatisfactory committee decisions after 1885, the floor took a different tack, augmenting bills by small amounts for idiosyncratic reasons.

Summary

The findings discussed so far confirm the conventional wisdom that has associated the expansion of federal spending with the change in appropriations regime in 1885. Most of the changes in spending criteria point in one direction: toward greater spending generosity. However, these findings also suggest some more subtle points that must be made if we are to understand fully the behavioral changes that infected the appropriations process late in the past century.

First, the greater committee generosity came even as the size of average agency requests went down. Before 1885, the average agency request was for 12.1 percent more than the previous year; after 1885, for 7.3 percent more. Yet, the reception the HAC gave to agency requests was such as to reduce that 12.1 percent increase to a miserly 1.9 percent recommendation; the legislative committees would take the more modest 7.3 percent agency request and turn it into a more substantial increase of 4.0 percent. What an ideal world for federal agencies! They could reduce their recommendations, appear to embody greater fiscal responsibility, and still come out more than twice as well off as before.

Second, although the change in committee regimes produced more generous appropriations decisions, perhaps the more significant change from the viewpoint of institutional development is how the change in committee regimes ended the war between the committees and the House floor. The pre-1885 coefficients in Table 4.3 show an Appropriations Committee interested not only in scaling back agency plans, but also in protecting the Treasury from the designs of House members. While the legislative committees were more subdued guardians of the purse along the committee-agency axis, they ended their guardian roles altogether along the committee-floor axis.

THE FATE OF NONDEVOLVED BILLS

This analysis would not be complete without a discussion of spending patterns among the bills that remained with the HAC after 1885. Such an analysis can confirm whether the patterns discovered among the legislative committees were a product of the new committee structure per se or were simply a product of a changing political landscape that pervaded all of the House, reaching the legislative committees and Appropriations alike.

I proceeded to carry out the same analysis I conducted in the previous section, this time using data about the appropriations bills that remained with the HAC after 1885. From the outset, this analysis was more tentative because there were fewer such bills, reducing the N by almost half (four bills instead of seven), and thus making statistical inference less certain.

What I discovered during this latter analysis made the findings even more tentative. First, the House floor amended these four bills much less than it amended the seven bills that were removed from the HAC. Thus, there was practically no variation of interest in the $\Delta House_t$ variable, reducing the utility of the equation in which it was the dependent variable, and producing implausible coefficients with ballooned standard errors when its instrument was included in the committee equation. Therefore, I reduced the number of equations estimated in this section to two, the agency and committee equations, and deleted $\Delta House_t^*$ from the committee equation.[36]

Also, it was readily apparent, upon examination of a graph of the spending time series of these four bills, that the spending series for fortifications was "different" from the other three in two senses. The first was its range of variability: For about half of the study period the armed services produced wish lists to be considered by the HAC, resulting in both tremendous cuts in committee and in gargantuan recommended increases the following year.[37] The simple case of variability would not be a problem, however, if it simply meant that fortifications spending decisions were made at one extreme of an otherwise constant process. Yet, this was not the case. Diagnostics, described previously, to test whether the regression parameters were equal across all four bills yielded the conclusion that this was not the case for fortifications spending, and in fact the fortifications bill drove the results of the pooled analysis. Therefore, I had to remove the fortifications bill from the pooled data set, reducing the N even further, and thus making statistical tests even more tentative.

I still proceeded with the analysis because the overall findings do correspond with the conventional wisdom, while providing some new and interesting perspectives. Therefore, I present the following analysis of spending decisions made by the HAC as a tentative exploration that provides interesting comparisons between decisions made by the legislative committees and the HAC after 1885.

Before discussing the particular results, let me discuss the general pattern of estimation. As with the devolved spending bills, I began by testing the following models for the three remaining nondevolved bills (legislative, executive, and judicial; pensions; and sundry civil):

36 This is not to say that the HAC did not take House preferences into account in making its decisions. One could argue that the dearth of floor amendments reflected general satisfaction with committee decisions and a tendency of the committee to adapt to floor preferences. Unfortunately, we simply do not have enough information on which to make any sort of inference along these lines.

37 For instance, from FY 1871 to 1885, the average fortifications recommendation was 270.3% above the previous year and the average committee cut was 64.5%. The average recommendation for every other bill was 14.9% and the average committee cut was 5.6%.

$$\Delta\text{Agency}_{b,t} = (a_0 + a_1\text{After}_t) + (a_2 + a_3\text{After}_t)\,\Delta\text{Congress}^*_{b,t-1}$$
$$+ (a_4 + a_5\text{After}_t)\,\Delta\text{Committee}^*_{b,t} + a_6\,\Delta\text{Prices}_{t-1}$$
$$+ a_7\,\Delta\text{GDP}_{t-1} + a_8\text{Election}_t + a_9\text{Control}_t$$
$$+ a_{10}\text{Demobilization}_t + \text{Error}_{1,b,t} \qquad (4.8)$$

$$\Delta\text{Committee}_{b,t} = (b_0 + b_1\text{After}_t) + (b_2 + b_3\text{After}_t)\,\Delta\text{Agency}^*_{b,t}$$
$$+ b_4\,\Delta\text{Prices}_{t-1} + b_5\,\Delta\text{GDP}_{t-1} + b_6\text{Election}_t$$
$$+ b_7\text{Control}_t$$
$$+ b_8\text{Split}_t + b_9\text{Demobilization}_t + b_{10}\text{Pensions}$$
$$+ b_{11}\text{Sundry} + \text{Error}_{2,b,t} \qquad (4.9)$$

The inclusion of the variables Pensions and Sundry are to account for the different mean levels of the ΔCommittee variables for both of these bills. I also estimated analogous equations for the fortifications bill alone.

I first tested whether $a_1 = a_3 = a_5 = 0$ and $b_1 = b_3 = 0$. These tests produced F statistics that were significant at levels of 0.932 and 0.524 in the 3SLS analysis. Based on these findings, I concluded that the values of the intercepts, $\Delta\text{Congress}^*_{t-1}$, $\Delta\text{Committee}^*_t$, and ΔAgency^*_t did not change in a step fashion among these three bills after 1885. Finally, I ran the series of diagnostics necessary to test whether the assumptions of pooled time-series regression held. All of the tests proved negative except one, which is relevant to the analysis.

I tested to see whether, controlling for the other variables, there was a time trend in both dependent variables in equations (4.8) and (4.9). There was no statistically significant trend in the agency equation, but the trend was significant in the committee equation.[38] Thus, while the HAC did not become more generous toward these three bills in a step shift after 1885, the positive direction of the trend indicates that the HAC became *gradually* more generous toward these three bills as time went on.

Let us now turn to the specifics of the analysis, reported in Table 4.4.

Agencies

On the whole, the agency findings in Table 4.4 are similar to those reported in Table 4.3 for the seven devolved bills. The responses to previous congressional action and anticipated committee action are slightly different – HAC-overseen agencies asked for slightly less in response to previous congressional cuts but asked for slightly more in anticipation of committee cuts – but the differences are probably not significant. What is most different is the agency responses to price and

38 A test for separate trend variables for each bill proved negative.

Spending reform and its consequences, 1865–1921

Table 4.4. *Structure of spending decisions concerning three annual appropriations bills overseen by the Appropriations Committee after 1885, FY 1871–1922 (three-stage least squares, N = 135)*

Variable	ΔAgency$_t$		ΔCommittee$_t$	
	\multicolumn{2}{}			
Intercept	−0.035	−0.007	−0.122^c	−0.134^b
	(0.039)	(0.023)	(0.043)	(0.043)
Intercept × After$_t$	0.036	—	0.035	—
	(0.043)		(0.040)	
ΔCongress$^*_{t-1}$	−0.002	−0.123	—	—
	(0.376)	(0.170)		
ΔCongress$^*_{t-1}$ × After$_t$	−0.149	—	—	—
	(0.416)			
ΔAgency$^*_t$	—	—	−0.881^a	−0.772^a
			(0.160)	(0.136)
ΔAgency$^*_t$ × After$_t$	—	—	0.145	—
			(0.260)	
ΔCommittee$^*_t$	−0.841^c	−0.627^a	—	—
	(0.328)	(0.161)		
ΔCommittee$^*_t$ × After$_t$	0.279	—	—	—
	(0.422)			
ΔPrices$_{t-1}$	−0.617^c	−0.617^c	−0.621^d	−0.754^d
	(0.455)	(0.427)	(0.368)	(0.394)
ΔGDP$_{t-1}$	0.770^b	0.743^b	0.695^b	0.678^b
	(0.261)	(0.254)	(0.226)	(0.225)
Election$_t$	—	—	0.035^d	0.034^c
			(0.021)	(0.022)
Democratic House$_t$	—	—	−0.048^d	−0.043^c
			(0.029)	(0.029)
Split control$_t$	—	—	0.018	0.009
			(0.036)	(0.033)
Demobilization$_t$	0.013	0.012	0.026	0.027
	(0.029)	(0.029)	(0.023)	(0.022)
Trend$_t$	—	—	—	0.002^c
				(0.001)
Pensions	—	—	0.058^c	0.066^c
			(0.026)	(0.028)
Sundry civil	—	—	0.089^b	0.098^b
			(0.030)	(0.031)

System R^2 with intervention terms: 0.329
System R^2 without intervention terms: 0.316

$^a p < 0.001.$　　$^b p < 0.01.$　　$^c p < 0.05.$　　$^d p < 0.10.$　　$^e p < 0.20.$

other economic fluctuations. In the case of the HAC-overseen bills, the coefficients associated with ΔGDP and ΔPrices are substantively larger and are always statistically different than zero. Thus, unlike the agencies that answered to legislative committees, those that answered to the HAC were more likely to take the economic climate into account in making their requests, a pattern that was reinforced by the HAC itself.

Committee

The committee decisions described in Table 4.4 are likewise similar in many respects to those reported in Table 4.3. The response to agency requests was approximately the same, as was the response to prices and split partisan control. The HAC responded to a greater degree to changes in GDP and was more sensitive to elections, but it was less sensitive to demobilization. Finally, the pension and sundry civil bills typically did better than the legislative, executive, and judicial bill in committee.[39]

What is of most interest in the committee model is the operation of the trend variable. The trend variable is defined such that it compares the committee action in any given year to that of the base year, 1871, when Trend = 0. Thus, the trend variable predicts that the HAC granted these three bills 0.8 percent more in 1875 compared to 1871, incrementing as follows over the decades:

Year	Percent difference
1871	0.0
1875	0.8
1885	2.8
1895	4.9
1905	7.0
1915	9.2
1922	10.7

Fortifications

The values of most of the coefficients in Table 4.5, which report the results of the analysis of the fortifications bill, are of an order of magnitude larger than the coefficients reported in previous tables, reflecting

39 This latter finding is just as one would expect, given the composition of these three bills. Pensions was the largest direct benefit program in government at the time. The sundry civil bill contained sizable amounts of pork in the nature of public building and water project appropriations. The legislative, executive, and judicial bill provided the salaries and support of bureaucrats who were headquartered in Washington, D.C., an eminently incidental expense.

Table 4.5. *Structure of spending decisions concerning the fortifications bill, FY 1871–1922 (three-stage least squares, N = 45)*

Variable	Dependent variables			
	ΔAgency$_t$		ΔCommittee$_t$	
Intercept	−0.382	0.154	−0.640	−1.084[b]
	(0.665)	(0.216)	(0.593)	(0.429)
Intercept × After	0.546	—	0.304	—
	(0.731)		(0.715)	
ΔCongress$^*_{t-1}$	0.183	−0.564[a]	—	—
	(0.596)	(0.152)		
ΔCongress$^*_{t-1}$ × After$_t$	−0.677	—	—	—
	(0.650)			
ΔAgency$^*_t$	—	—	−0.388	−0.079
			(0.535)	(0.255)
ΔAgency$^*_t$ × After$_t$	—	—	0.124	—
			(0.640)	
ΔCommittee$^*_t$	−1.295[c]	−0.157	—	—
	(0.609)	(0.128)		
ΔCommittee$^*_t$ × After$_t$	1.081[d]	—	—	—
	(0.640)			
ΔPrices$_{t-1}$	−6.517[b]	−6.172[b]	−1.066	−2.429
	(2.667)	(2.190)	(3.545)	(3.453)
ΔGDP$_{t-1}$	2.449[e]	2.247[d]	1.840	2.016
	(1.626)	(1.295)	(1.880)	(1.713)
Election$_t$	—	—	−0.085	−0.124
			(0.228)	(0.210)
Democratic House$_t$	—	—	−0.591[c]	−0.565[c]
			(0.281)	(0.266)
Split control$_t$	—	—	0.263	—
			(0.377)	
Demobilization$_t$	0.223	0.244[e]	0.363[d]	0.351[d]
	(0.171)	(0.142)	(0.185)	(0.176)
Trend$_t$	—	—	—	0.021[c]
				(0.010)

System R^2 with intervention terms: 0.486
System R^2 without intervention terms: 0.469

[a] $p < .001$.   [b] $p < .01$.   [c] $p < .05$.   [d] $p < .10$.   [e] $p < .20$.

the much greater range through which the dependent variables moved. *F*-tests revealed that there was no discontinuous break in the character of the spending decisions the HAC made about fortifications after 1885, but the HAC did become more generous toward fortifications secularly, matching the pattern of spending growth in the other three Appropriations-overseen bills.

Table 4.6. *Average effects of changes in prices, gross domestic product, and partisan control of the House on committee spending decisions, before and after 1885*

Variable	Average		Devolved bills		Nondevolved bills	
	Pre-1885	Post-1885	Pre-1885	Post-1885	Pre-1885	Post-1885
$\Delta Prices_{t-1}$	0.050	0.019	−0.044	−0.017	−0.038	−0.014
ΔGDP_{t-1}	−0.131	0.040	−0.037	0.014	−0.089	0.027
Democratic House$_t$	0.486	0.442	−0.023	−0.021	−0.021	−0.019

The army and navy tried to restore previous congressional cuts in fortifications when they made their requests, and they reacted much less to anticipated committee cuts. In addition, the services were particularly sensitive to changes in prices and fluctuations of the economy. The coefficients in Table 4.5 indicate that the services would ask for a cut of 6.0 percent following a 1 percent increase in prices and would ask for an increase of 2.3 percent following a 1 percent increase in GDP. The HAC was almost equally reactive, cutting service requests 2.4 percent following a 1 percent price increase and granting 2.0 percent more following a 1 percent GDP increase.

The fortifications bill's relationship to real problems of war fighting is also revealed in the size of the demobilization coefficient: Fortifications appropriations plummeted following the end of hostilities. Agency requests declined by 48.8, 36.1, and 20.1 percent the first three years after wars, and committee recommendations were reduced an additional 65.1, 50.4, and 29.6 percent in those years.

The findings also reveal the partisanship associated with fortifications spending: Republicans liked it much more than Democrats. Ceteris paribus, during periods of Democratic control of the House, the fortifications bill was reduced 43.2 percent more than it was during periods of Republican control.

Finally, the findings in Table 4.6 show how the HAC warmed to fortifications spending over time, just as it warmed to other spending. The trend variable suggests that compared to 1871, the HAC cut 8.8 percent less in 1875, and proceeded to cut the fortifications bill even less as time went on. By 1885, the HAC was granting 34.2 percent more to fortifications than it was in 1871, and by 1922 the HAC was almost 200 percent more generous toward fortifications than it had been in the middle of Reconstruction, controlling for everything else.

These numbers suggest a rather radical change of affairs for fortifications over time. However, the estimates following the turn of the century should not be taken too literally since this is the period of greatest inflation and also includes an eight-year string of Democratic Houses, both of which served to bring final recommendations down substantially. Still, the general point here is that controlling for everything else, as time went on, the HAC radically relaxed its immediate impulse to reduce fortification appropriations.

Summary

Overall, the Appropriations Committee was not immune to changes in national politics that were producing pressures to expand federal spending during this period. Natural membership turnover eventually brought new members onto the committee who were more sympathetic to greater spending. And, having been burned once before on the House floor because of perceived unresponsiveness to floor preferences, the HAC was likely to change its criteria to head off even more challenges to its authority in the future. Still, because the changes infused the Appropriations Committee gradually, spending expansion within the HAC also occurred more gradually. There may have been greater generosity "all around" in the House during the late nineteenth century, but the way that greater generosity was allowed to express itself institutionally influenced the actual pattern of spending expansion.

CONCLUSION

The members of the House who argued about the appropriations process on 14 December 1885 had a theory about the ability of structures to induce outcomes independent of preferences. The findings in this chapter show that the theory was essentially correct. But to go beyond the theory as it was expressed on the floor of the House, a change in committee jurisdictions certainly induced more than behavioral changes in committees. As far as the bills that were overseen by the legislative committees after 1885 are concerned, the shift in the appropriations process also gave political room to the agencies to expand their budgets by lowering their average requests. And it served as a signal to the House floor that the war between committees and the whole House had ended, inducing members of the rank-and-file to be less prone to monitor committee recommendations closely or to amend them at all.

The politicians and reformers who would argue about the appropriations process three decades later also had a theory about the ability of structure to induce outcomes independent of preferences. But they now also had data that, to those in favor of added centralization, confirmed the theory: Spending was higher in 1910 than it had been in 1885, therefore devolution was the culprit. However, as the findings in this chapter also show, while devolution was *a* culprit, it was not the only culprit.

To begin with, if devolution were the only culprit, then the exogenous political and economic variables added to the models tested in this chapter would have been of no consequence. Yet these variables were of consequence. Consider the two exogenous economic variables, changes in prices and GDP. While both the legislative committees and the Appropriations Committee were about equally responsive to changes in prices and GDP (Tables 4.3 and 4.4), both prices and GDP changed in different ways before and after 1885 (Table 4.6). Prices grew on average faster before 1885 than they did afterward. And probably more important, the average growth rate of the economy between FY 1871 and 1887 was *negative*, while the economy grew at an annual pace of about 4 percent after the devolution. Thus, as prices rose before 1885, the HAC cut an increment to the agency's budget (about 4.4 percent on average); and then because the economy was on average contracting, the HAC cut another increment (about 3.7 percent on average). Thus, given a year with average price changes and economic decline, the Appropriations Committee would reduce an agency's request by about 8 percent, simply on account of these two economic conditions, even before taking into account the agency's request. After 1885, the net effects of inflation and economic growth about canceled each other out in an average year.

One of the consequences of this is that the basis of comparison – spending levels in 1885 – is a bad point of departure. Following a decade and a half of rough economic times, aggregate spending in that year was significantly lower than it would have been had the previous decade been a period of robust economic growth and lower inflation. And, the post-1885 period is a difficult one to compare with pre-1885 since the latter period was characterized by more sustained economic expansion along with lower inflation (and in some years, actual deflation).

This is all to say that had the legislative committees been overseeing spending in the same economic climate as the 1870s and early 1880s, aggregate spending reported from those committees also would have been lower than it turned out to be. I am not claiming that the entire expansion of federal spending after 1885 was produced by changes in the macroeconomy – the findings in this chapter certainly would not support that claim – but I am arguing that in addition to the effects of the regime of 1885, the changing nature of the macroeconomy in the late nineteenth century should also be given its due.

The third "unindicted co-conspirator" in the post-1885 spending expansion, in addition to the legislative committees and the economy, was the Appropriations Committee. It is simply the case that as time went on after 1885, the Appropriations Committee did not cut agency budgets with the same zeal with which it had before. The difference between the legislative committees and the Appropriations Committee, of course, was the *pattern* by which the two types of committees became more generous. In fact, it is the suddenness with which the legislative committee produced more generous results and the gradualness in the Appropriations Committee that suggests that the structural change did have an impact on spending decisions.

There are two explanations for this gradual shift toward generosity, neither of which excludes the other. The first concerns membership replacement: As members retired and left the Appropriations Committee, they were replaced by new members who, given generational replacement in the House as a whole, were probably more prone to grant spending requests than those members who had been elected on the heels of the Civil War and Reconstruction. The second explanation concerns committee strategy: Members on the HAC could take a hint. They understood that the devolution of 1885 might be only the beginning, and that if the HAC continued to slash agency requests, further bills might be withdrawn from its oversight. This type of strategic thinking on the part of members of the Appropriations Committee – that some sort of change in spending decisions was necessary in order to preserve the committee's prerogatives – would have set members of the committee off on a search to find that level of spending expansion that was sufficient to ensure continued maintenance of the committee's jurisdiction but at the same time did not give away the store.

The final partial contributor to the aggregate spending rise around the turn of the century was the general expansion of governmental activity, much of which was initially sanctioned through legislative channels before being turned into new appropriations. In other words, what occurred in the Agriculture Department, with the addition of significant new programs and bureaus, occurred throughout the government at this time. Much of this expansion was associated with reform movements of many types – social, governmental, military – and the implications were quite expensive. It is important to remember that the congressional political agenda had been largely monopolized by the South during the three decades preceding 1885. Once the nation's attention had turned away from reconstructing the South, there remained a whole host of issues that had gone unattended for a quarter of a century, among them army and navy reform, reform in relations with Native American tribes, and rebuilding the destroyed productive centers of the South (Sprout and Sprout 1939; Priest 1942; Wiebe 1967; Skowronek 1982; Coletta 1987).

To take only the most obvious example, one of the most hotly contested institutional reform efforts was that of moving the navy from a sailing to a steam fleet (Sprout and Sprout 1939). In both substantive and spending issues, the Naval Affairs Committee was in the middle of the controversy. But the general decision that resulted in an acceleration in naval construction, to refurbish and expand the fleet, was one that had to be resolved as part of a broad-ranging policy debate. Regardless of how spending was considered in the House after 1885, once Congress had decided to convert the navy to steam, that switch was a very expensive proposition. Expenses may have been held down marginally under the pre-1885 regime, but the major decisions to increase spending dramatically were largely independent of the appropriations process.

Thus, on aggregate, a number of independent influences resulted in the expansion of government spending after 1885. But, although we cannot partial out the separate effects each of these influences had on aggregate spending after 1885, we can conclude that the spending induced by structural change was significant. The devolution provided an immediate opening for spending. But, probably more important, once new issues came on the legislative agenda, or once economic conditions changed to allow expanded spending, then the members of the legislative committees were in a good position to influence the *final form* of the expanded spending, including its distribution. Structural change was an important contributor to spending changes, even if it was not the only contributor.

5

The reappearance of formal reform,
1885–1921

The devolution of 1885 significantly altered the orientation of structural politics in the House. Most obviously, the new regime represented a shift in the status quo, altering the basic orientation of leaders, committee members, and backbenchers toward structure. Legislative committee members, who had previously been the old regime's strongest opponents, became the new regime's staunchest supporters; members of the traditional money committees became its biggest critics. Leaders could not openly assault the regime of 1885 since their followers obviously supported the new arrangement, but they could work quietly to effect their own wills through the appointment process and their efforts to coordinate committee decisions informally.

As I suggested in Chapter 1, however, the devolution was likely to have *indirect* institutional consequences as well. Most importantly, now that seven legislative committees could oversee appropriations bills, resources available to protect the new status quo were dispersed throughout the chamber. As members of these legislative committees went about their jobs, they were bound to generate support for their own institutional positions by doing favors for other members. As these favors proliferated, so too did the institutional currency necessary to withstand structural challenges. In short, membership on these legislative committees was valuable not only because members could more easily aid their own constituents, but also because members could assist the constituents of others, extracting a price in the process.

Because of largely exogenous leadership changes, most of these institutional chits never had to be called in, however. Almost immediately following the devolution of 1885, the parties (Republicans especially) began developing mechanisms of party power centered in the Speaker. These strong Speakers moved to assert their power, in part, by firmly controlling the flow of business on the House floor. This control cut off challenges to the appropriations regime of the style that characterized the House during the decade before 1885: The House floor became a much less chaotic place.[1]

The other important exogenous change that occurred after 1885 was growing revenue scarcity. In the short term, this revenue scarcity reduced pressures to decentralize even further. In the long term this scarcity, compounded by the effects of World War I and the expansion of direct taxation through the income tax, increased the usefulness of centralization to the rank-and-file; it resulted in the creation of the executive budget, with the Budget and Accounting Act of 1921, and in the overthrow of the regime of 1885, with reconsolidation of spending authority in the HAC in 1919.

While the continuing fiscal difficulties that began around 1890 made the consideration of recentralization more likely, fiscal difficulties alone go only a little way toward explaining the ultimate move back to centralization. The particularizing impulses associated with the electoral connection and committee behavior interacted with the centralizing impulses associated with "fiscal responsibility" to produce a transformed budgetary process that was more susceptible to central direction than before, but that also continued to be amenable to the distributive impulse of legislative life.

THE REED RULES

It was a long time after 1885 until formal budget reform reemerged as a salient issue. Reform activity went immediately underground after 1885, in part because of the nature of structural reform itself. Structural issues are not the kind to elicit much excitement from most MCs, structure rarely rivals substance as a vehicle for credit claiming and position taking, and therefore becomes highly salient only when the gains to be had by changing it are tremendous and exceed the animosity that will be generated by attacking somebody's valuable institutional turf. Most MCs most of the time can get more from working within the appropriations system than from working to change it.

The resilience of the regime of 1885 was demonstrated two Congresses after its creation when the Republicans moved to consolidate their reestablished hegemonic control of the House. In the history of the House's institutional development, the 51st Congress (1889–91) is noted for the most far-reaching of all rules changes – the Reed Rules. As far-reaching as these rules were, however, they left appropriations alone. The only

---

1 The ability of the leadership to control the floor was probably a function of a unique configuration of the two parties' constituencies. See Cooper and Brady (1981).

attempt to address budgeting during the formalization of the Reed Rules came from the Democratic side of the chamber. This attempt to highlight the budgetary costs of military pensions met a resounding, and partisan, demise.

The Reed Rules dismantled a number of devices that minority party members had used over the years to obstruct action by the majority. The two most commonly used obstructionist tactics were (1) the *disappearing quorum*, which was the practice whereby minority party members refused to respond to the roll call although physically present and (2) *dilatory motions*, the practice of offering a series of motions simply to delay business (Galloway 1955, 55–56; Bolling 1968, 55; *Congressional Quarterly* 1982b, 120–122). The Reed Rules were reported from the Rules Committee on 6 February 1890 and were adopted by a 161–144 vote on 14 February (CR 51-1, 6 Feb. 1890, 1105–1109; 14 Feb. 1890, 1347). They allowed the Speaker to count toward a quorum those members who were physically present but who refused to respond to the roll call; they prohibited the Speaker from recognizing anyone for the purpose of dilatory tactics; and they reduced the size of a quorum of the Committee of the Whole from 175 (half of the whole House) to 100. The proposed changes in the rules were branded "tyranny" by the Democratic minority, and the debate and final vote were by strict party line.

Given the willingness of the Republicans to aggressively seize control of the House by revising the rules, one would have imagined that if there had been dissatisfaction with the 49th House's devolution of appropriating power, the Republicans would have attacked this as well. But no mention of the regime of 1885 was made at all in the Rules Committee report or in the four days of debate that preceded the adoption of the rules.

However, this is not to say that budgeting more broadly defined was totally ignored in the rules debate. John Bynum (D-IN) broached a new budgetary issue bound to raise partisan hackles: military pensions. Toward the end of the debate on the Reed Rules, Bynum proposed that legislation to raise revenues be in order whenever any bill was brought to the floor granting a pension increase (CR 51-1, 14 Feb. 1890, 1327). This proposal "raised a storm on the Republican side" of the House (NYT 15 Feb. 1890, 4). It stimulated nine pages of partisan debate in the *Congressional Record*, as Democrats verbally battled Republicans. The storm broke open the raw nerve between the two parties over the Civil War, and the "bloody shirt" was waved freely about the House floor. Joseph Cannon (R-IL) stated:

We have revenues enough now to fully meet liberal . . . pension legislation for the soldiers of the late war, and I know of no reason why a proposition to properly pension them should be harnessed up and embarrassed with revenue legislation.

[Bynum] does not seek an amendment to make revenue legislation in order upon a public building bill, or upon a river and harbor bill, . . . but he singles out pension legislation and proposes to tack this provision onto that. (CR 51-1, 14 Feb. 1890, 1327)

Ormsby Thomas (R-WI) declared:

I have never before during my political life seen manifested so plainly as I have to-day the opposition of the Democratic party to the granting of pensions to the men who defended the life of this nation. (CR 51-1, 14 Feb. 1890, 1328)

In an interesting constituency-based twist, Edward Allen (R-MI) noted that a Bynum Rule would backfire on the Democrats and hurt them just as much as the Republicans since most Democrats represented northern districts with pensioned constituents:

The Gentleman from Missouri [Bland] the other day, when a provision went through this House for clearing out the snags of the Missouri River, did not ask that the money should be raised by taxing any particular class or any particular interest. . . . And of all the interests in this country, the rivers and harbors, the coast defenses, everything, the only thing that is sorted out by gentlemen on the other side [i.e., Democrats] for a particular stigma, for the purpose of defeating it, is pension legislation. . . . [B]ut let me tell you, further, that the speeches you make belittling pensions, the efforts you make to tie them up . . . will react against you in your constituencies in the North, for there are Democrats in that region who were soldiers. (CR 51-1, 14 Feb. 1890, 1329)

The Bynum Rule fell in a partisan 96–164 vote, with the Republicans opposing the measure 0–146 and the Democrats favoring it 91–18 (the remainder being from other parties). The most potent pockets of Democratic opposition to the measure came from midwesterners and easterners who nevertheless *favored* the Bynum Rule by majorities of 17–10 and 15–5, respectively; no southern Democrats opposed Bynum.

Because this was clearly a partisan measure, there was obviously no chance for the Bynum Rule to have passed. Had the rule passed, it would have provided a continuing source of Republican embarrassment each time a special or general pension bill was considered. Republicans would have been embarrassed because they consistently championed expanded pensions spending, pockets of Democratic support not withstanding (Stewart 1985, 273–274).

The attempt to enact a Bynum Rule in the 51st Congress can only be termed partisan harassment. It was a convenient way for Democrats to take positions against pension profligacy at a time when legislative control was out of their hands. The fate of the Bynum Rule, however, is indicative of the state of the general structural environment that House members faced in the 1890s and first decade of the 1900s. Democrats found that their reform efforts could simply be outvoted by Republican majorities.

And, Democrats ultimately were denied the ability even to bring harassing motions to the floor as a series of Republican Speakers took the full reigns of agenda control characteristic of "czar rule." Because of the growing power of the Speaker, rank-and-file Republicans also found it increasingly difficult to publicly float reform proposals.

FISCAL DISTRESS AND REFORM BY PROVISO

Neither lopsided partisan majorities nor powerful party leaders could keep the lid on efforts to alter the appropriations process in the House forever. The firm control exercised by party leaders was predicated on an exogenous partisan and policy system that was changing even as it emerged (see Brady 1978; Cooper and Brady 1981; Bullock and Brady 1983). Although most members of the House restrained their attacks on the regime of 1885 for twenty years, the aggregational budgetary problem loomed larger and larger on the horizon. Continued problems with balancing the federal budget ultimately undermined the regime's legitimacy, much as the distributional problem had undermined the legitimacy of the 1865 regime. But, unlike the 1870s, when the centralized regime began to be undermined, the 1890s posed new institutional constraints on reform actors. So, while challengers to the regimes of 1865 and 1885 were ultimately driven by policy dissatisfaction, the dissatisfaction was channeled through different institutions, one under loose partisan control and the other under strict party discipline, thus leading to different reform dynamics in each era.

Budgeting met new regular fiscal constraints in the 1890s on a magnitude not experienced in the 1880s nor even in the 1870s. During the decade before 1885, the fiscal picture of the federal government was relatively positive, even given occasional stresses. When there were stresses on the federal budget caused by a contraction of economic activity, as in 1874, the centralized regime reacted quickly to reduce expenditures, thus keeping the budget in balance. The final result was that during the decades immediately following the Civil War, the federal government experienced almost thirty years of unbroken budget surpluses. These surpluses helped to absorb the expansion of programmatic spending after 1885, as well as allowing payments into the sinking fund, enlarged reserve deposits into national banks, an expanded pork barrel, and an expanded state apparatus. In short, the regime of 1885 began its life within a benign fiscal environment.

As the regime lived out its life, its macroeconomic environment became significantly less benign. Beginning with 1894, surpluses could no longer be assumed. Between 1894 and the beginning of World War I, the federal government had to contend with a deficit for fourteen out of twenty-two years. Congress therefore had to continually contend with the political and financial problems of deficit spending.

The onset of these chronic deficits was caused by a shortage of revenues brought on by the unfortunate coincidence of lower tariff rates and the panic of 1893. Because of the large surpluses that had been run up after the Civil War, deficits could be financed in the short term without new borrowing, through reducing payments into the sinking fund and re-calling surplus deposits that had been placed in the national banks. Yet by 1903 the future of this strategy became limited, as bank reserves dwindled to almost nothing. With revenues and expenditures running very close to each other and the previous fiscal cushions depleted, the House began to awaken from its structural slumber and to address spend-ing reform in some tentative ways.

The first movements toward reform skirted the issue of congressional fragmentation all together and were handled as second thoughts to the annual appropriations process. At first, riders were placed on appropri-ations bills essentially exhorting executive departments to follow the law and not to spend more than was appropriated. For instance, the following condition was placed on the general deficiency bill (H.R. 19150) during the 58th Congress (28 February 1905):

No Department of the Government shall expend, in any one fiscal year, any sum in excess of appropriations made by Congress for that fiscal year, or involve the Government in any contract or obligation for the future payment of money in excess of such appropriations unless such contract or obligation is authorized by law. (U.S. Statutes at Large, 58–3, vol. 33, pt. 1, chap. 1484, sec. 3679, p. 1257)

The functional purpose of this proviso was to prohibit a common practice in which agencies obligated funds beyond their appropriations, and then presented Congress with a fait accompli (see remarks of James Hemen-way, CR 58-3, 3687). Members of the Appropriations Committee illus-trated the extent to which this was a real problem in 1905 by noting that the general deficiency appropriations bill to which this proviso was attached carried $31 million while the same bill the previous year had been reported out at a sum of $10.4 million – deficiencies would surely grow without this type of limitation on executive discretion.

This proviso did allow agency heads to waive its implementation under loosely defined conditions, and agency heads quickly proved willing to do so without a second thought. So, a further condition was placed on the next urgent deficiency bill (H.R. 12320, 59th Cong.), again prohib-iting departments from expending funds in excess of appropriations, but also directing that funds be allocated to agencies on a monthly basis "as to prevent expenditures in one portion of the year which may necessitate deficiency . . . appropriations to complete the service of the fiscal year" (U.S. Statutes at Large, 59–1, vol. 34, pt. 1, chap. 510, sec. 3679, p. 49).

In addition to having a functional utility, these two provisos were also politically useful. These amendments were a way for members of Congress to buy time and to deflect budgetary dissatisfaction away from themselves. It was hoped that using these amendments to buy time would allow deficits to run their own course, thus quieting calls for fundamental reforms. But if deficits did not end, as proved to be the case, then members of the House were bound to be forced into a more earnest search for a noncosmetic solution.

By orienting dissatisfaction away from Congress, legislators were further demonstrating the age-old love/hate relationship with the bureaucracy and symbolic preoccupation with waste, fraud, and abuse (see Fiorina 1977). The provisos were predicated on the assumption that the deficits were of agency, not congressional, origin. The provisos allowed MCs to continue to profess support for programs while blaming improper implementation for deficit problems. And by targeting these provisos toward purely administrative behavior, the Appropriations Committee, which originated them, avoided direct conflict with the legislative committees about programmatic questions.

THE RISE OF PRESIDENTIAL INTEREST IN CONGRESSIONAL REFORM

Continued deficits after 1905 undercut the ability of the House to adjust to deficits by making small, incremental changes and by amending appropriations bills. With the activist presidency concurrently being defined by Theodore Roosevelt, the willingness of the president to play an observer role in the budget game also diminished. Any glimmering hope that the aggregational problem could be solved by administrative riders to appropriations bills ended in 1908 when a dramatic drop in tariff revenues dried up the very last of the surplus national bank deposits. The revenue crunch experienced in 1908 also prompted the first recorded direct intervention by a president into the budget process when Roosevelt moved to actively shape agency requests. Roosevelt was reported to be "genuinely aroused over the growing deficits" and ordered both the army and navy to pare back their fiscal year 1910 requests substantially (NYT 9 Mar. 1909, 1). The 1908 revenue crunch also incited the first public call for congressional budget reform by a Treasury secretary. Secretary George Cortelyou, in his final annual report to Congress, argued that the problem with chronic deficits could be partially cured through a consolidation of all spending oversight into one joint congressional budget committee:

It would perhaps be competent for the Congress to vest in a joint committee the power of revising the appropriation bills, with a view to distributing reductions and increases in an equitable manner and with a view also to the relative importance of the objects for which appropriations are sought. It would seem that such a committee on budget revision should be charged with the responsibility of keeping the expenditures of each year approximately within the revenues of the year, ... By such a committee needless and wasteful expenditure might be checked and the amounts saved diverted to more necessary or more beneficial purposes. (U.S. Secretary of the Treasury 1909, 87)

Advocacy for budget reform moved closer to being an ongoing executive branch concern when William Howard Taft came to office in 1909. The most persistent voice within the Taft administration for consolidation of congressional appropriations oversight came in the annual messages of Treasury Secretary Franklin MacVeagh. In his first annual report, sent to Congress in December 1909, MacVeagh called for coordination among appropriations and revenue bills both within and between the executive and legislative branches. But in his message of the following year MacVeagh could only regret "that the movement has not as yet gone far" (U.S. Secretary of the Treasury 1909, 4–5; 1910, 22). In the latter report he went on to express the hope that the consideration of appropriations could be as "practically one bill" and that a budget board, representative of Congress and the executive branch, could be created. This cajoling of Congress about reform continued throughout Mac-Veagh's four-year tenure, but he never saw his desires translated into action at the east end of Pennsylvania Avenue.

While MacVeagh's (and later, Taft's) calls for budgetary consolidation resulted in little *formal* action, the level of *informal* coordination between the two branches reached a new high during the first two years of Taft's term. The informal coordination showed up in occasional meetings between congressional leaders and administrative officials about ways to address the deficit problem. For instance, within the first week of Taft's term, Sen. Nelson Aldrich, the chair of the Finance Committee and de facto Senate majority leader, and Speaker Joseph Cannon met in a "finance conference" to discuss the coming difficulty in reducing the deficits while at the same time tariff schedules were being revised (NYT 9 Mar. 1909, 1). This type of informal consultation was formalized somewhat in a rider to the FY 1910 sundry civil bill (H.R. 28245, 60th Cong.), which served to vest further power in the president and Treasury secretary over the control of agency estimates. In part, the rider read:

Immediately upon the receipt of the regular annual estimates of appropriations needed for the various branches of the Government it shall be the duty of the Secretary of the Treasury to estimate as nearly as may be the revenues of the Government for the ensuing fiscal year, and if the estimates for appropriations, including the estimated amount necessary to meet all continuing and permanent appropriations, shall exceed the estimated revenues the Secretary of the Treasury shall transmit the estimates to Congress as heretofore required by law and at once transmit a detailed statement of all of said estimates to the President, to the end that he [the president] may ... advise the Congress how in his judgment the estimated appropriations could with the least injury to the public service be reduced so as to bring the appropriations within the estimated revenues, or, if such reductions be not in his judgment practicable without undue injury to the public service, that he may recommend to Congress such loans or new taxes as may be necessary to cover the deficiency. (35 U.S.C. chap. 299, sec. 7, 1909)

The willingness of Congress to entrust much of the leg work in balancing the budget to the president and to work with the executive branch continued throughout 1909 as estimates continued to be pared down.

That Taft and MacVeagh were serious about reducing estimates to balance the budget was clear as news leaked out all spring and summer about planned reductions to estimates. For example, Taft is reported to have sent one unnamed department, probably Agriculture, back to square one with the order to trim its estimates 15 percent (NYT 26 May 1909, 1). In all, it was reported that Taft had wrung $100 million in estimates from original department requests for FY 1911 (NYT 7 Dec. 1909, 3).

Evidence of Taft's active interest in shaping budget requests to reduce the deficit was also provided directly from the president himself. In Taft's first annual message to Congress, he noted that "perhaps the most important question presented to this Administration is that of economy in expenditures and sufficiency of revenues" (Richardson 1913, 15:7422). He suggested that part of the problem could be solved by selling bonds for one of the federal government's largest cash drains, building the Panama Canal, and went on to note:

In order to avoid a deficit for the ensuing fiscal year, I directed the heads of Departments in the preparation of their estimates to make them as low as possible, consistent with imperative governmental necessity. The result has been . . . that the estimates for the expenses of the Government for the next fiscal year ending June 30, 1911, are less than the appropriations for this current fiscal year by $42,818,000. (Richardson 1913, 15:7423)

All of the activity and concern for the chronic deficits was not confined entirely to the executive or the House. Some concern and movement was also evident in the Senate. A month after the "finance conference" between Taft, Aldrich, and Cannon, Sen. Aldrich announced that a Senate Committee on Public Expenditures would be created. He expressed the hope that it would consider together all of the appropriations bills as they came from the House (NYT 3 Apr. 1909, 8; 15 May 1909, 8). Aldrich went so far as to name nineteen senators to this committee, six of whom were taken from money committees and thirteen from legislative committees. But it turned out that Aldrich was ahead of general congressional sentiment for appropriations consolidation, and the Senate withheld from the committee authority to actually consider appropriations.

Instead of being empowered to deliberate on the appropriations bills themselves, the Senate simply allowed the Committee on Public Expenditures to study the issue of budget reform (S. Res. 50, 61st Cong.; CR 61-1, 29 May 1909, 2525). The committee did report out a bill (S. 6168, 61st Cong.) creating "the government business methods commission" to be composed of senators and representatives who would be charged with studying methods of government management and recommending reform that would effect significant retrenchment. The bill passed the Senate but failed to get out of committee in the House (CR 61-2, 28 Feb. 1910, 2494). In the 62nd Congress the Senate Committee on Committees concluded that the Committee on Public Expenditures "had not done anything to justify its continuance" and dropped it (CR 62-1, 1 May 1911, 788–789).

While the Senate was unable to initiate reform on its own, it did ensure the provision of money to support the President's Commission on Economy and Efficiency, better known as the Taft Commission.[2] The commission came into existence through a floor amendment to the sundry civil bill "in compliance with the wishes of the President" (CR 61-2, 9 June 1910, 7656–7658; NYT 10 June 1910, 1; Taft 1916, 64). An amount of $100,000 was added to the bill through an amendment by Eugene Hale (R-ME), who noted that the commission was a good idea even if the matter had never been considered by the Senate or House Appropriations Committees:

I think it is worth while to endow the President with this appropriation, to see if he can report to us something that will tend to limit and bring into reasonable space the enormous, the increasing, and alarming and appalling expenditures of the Government. (CR 61-2, 9 June 1910, 7656)

Sen. Newlands agreed with his Maine colleague and hoped that the economy commission could extend the retrenchment that the Taft administration had begun:

The President has inaugurated a new system of preparing a budget and of bringing his Cabinet into cooperation in the ... revenues. They did good work in their last recommendations to Congress. They cut down the estimates to the expected revenue, and if Congress has not exceeded the appropriations which they asked for, in all probability the expenditures will approximate our revenue. (CR 61-2, 9 June 1910, 7656)

The amendment was approved by the House conferees, though there was no discussion of the item on the House floor when the bill was brought up for final passage. Thus, acquiescence by the House to the

---

2 Contemporary accounts frequently referred to it as the "Cleveland Commission" after the chair of the group, Frederick Cleveland.

Taft Commission's creation occurred out of a desire to suit the president on a "motherhood" issue, not out of deliberative reasoning (H. Rpt. 1631, 61st Cong.; CR 61-2, 21 June 1910, 8646–8649).

I hrough this little-noticed amendment the ground began to be laid for the ultimate overthrow of the regime of 1885. Yet almost as soon as the money had been appropriated for the Taft Commission the political climate on Capitol Hill had begun to change, spelling difficulties for the commission's efforts as well as a general shift in legislative style. The internal political climate changed because two conditions that had facilitated the coordination between Congress and the president over the previous decade were coming to an end: (1) unified party control of the federal government and (2) czar rule by party leaders.

First, during the first decade of the century, unified party control of both the presidency and Congress had facilitated informal contacts between the two. Unified party control meant that MCs were less suspicious of the attempts by Roosevelt and Taft to retrench agency requests. But with the election of 1910, Democrats were returned to majority control of the House after wandering in the minority desert for eighteen years, and they were ill-inclined toward cooperation with the opposition. This new element of partisan conflict was revealed in the ongoing efforts to address the fiscal crisis directly, and in the House's reception to the Taft Commission's work.

Second, the strong Speakership system that had dominated the House for two decades had served to facilitate informal coordination among legislative committees, as it also helped to impose a climate of predictability onto structural issues. The well-known 1909–1911 revolt against Speaker Cannon had specific implications for the ensuing debate about appropriations structure. The revolt indicated widespread dissatisfaction with twenty years of czar rule, while its success changed the institutional context of budget reform yet again. On the one hand, the end of czar rule introduced greater uncertainty about the House's institutional future. On the other hand, the loosening of institutional control that created this uncertainty also lent the rank-and-file a freer hand in shaping their collective institutional future.

The partisan shift in the House after the 1910 election gave the Democrats a free hand in adjusting the rules to their liking in the 62nd Congress (1911–13). One of the chief changes that the Democrats made was the reinstitution of the Holman Rule. In Chapter 3 I argued that the Holman Rule served as a partisan instrument during the 1870s and 1880s. Thirty years later, its reemergence excited partisan animosities yet again (NYT 6 Apr. 1911, 1). During the general debate on the rules, Republican after Republican rose to attack the resurrection of the Holman Rule (CR 62-1, 5 Apr. 1911, 60–68). John Dalzell (R-PA) carried the most extensive attack on the rule, as well as on the total package of rules changes proposed by the Democratic leadership. Dalzell remarked in his summary:

> Mr. Speaker, aside from the question of selecting committees,[3] the only material change, in my judgment – the only serious change in my judgment – made in the rules of the Sixty-first Congress is in Rule XXI, section 2, by the adoption of what is known as the Holman amendment. I can not, in view of the parliamentary history of this country, do otherwise than regard that as a most dangerous innovation in the rules of the House....
>
> ...[The Holman Rule] is a provision for legislation on appropriations bills. That is a provision which renders useless and unnecessary any other committee of the House.... It is wrong in theory, because, in the first place, the Committee on Appropriations ought not to legislate, for the reason that the other branch of Congress is entitled to have an appropriation bill not containing legislation which they have not considered; and, secondly, because the President of the United States is entitled to have an appropriation bill that does not require consideration at his hands of legislation. (CR 62-1, 5 Apr. 1911, 61)

Republicans continued to complain bitterly about the Holman Rule throughout the debate, recounting numerous examples culled from the 1870s and 1880s in which amendments were proposed cutting minimal amounts off of an appropriation while changing broad swatches of statute. But Democrats remained silent throughout the debate, relying on their majority to pass the rule by voice vote (CR 62-1, 5 Apr. 1911, 80).

While Democrats were adjusting to their new-found majority status in the 62nd House, the Taft administration continued to act as if nothing had changed between the two branches. Taft continued to supervise the preparation of agency estimates, frequently ordering budget cuts, a point MacVeagh reiterated in his report submitting the requests for FY 1913. MacVeagh continued to call on Congress to consolidate its appropriations oversight into one joint committee (NYT 2 June 1912, 14). And, the Taft Commission was finally organized on 9 March 1911 with the appointment of Frederick A. Cleveland (chair), Merritt Chance, and William F. Willoughby to be members.[4]

In the preliminary reports made to Taft that year, the commission identified the study of a national budget system as its top priority (Taft Commission 1913, nos. 29 and 30). The centerpiece of this national budget system was the "executive budget," in which the president would take formal responsibility for framing the annual budgetary debate by shaping agency requests to his liking. The executive budget plan also

---

3 The change to which Dalzell was referring formalized one of the outcomes of the revolt against Speaker Cannon in the previous Congress, by which the House, and not the Speaker, would formally elect committee members.
4 Two others, Walter Warwick and Frank J. Goodnow, would be appointed later.

called for a new institutional capacity for the president, by expanding the number of financial and budgetary experts at his call. Finally, the executive budget idea – yet to become a plan – envisioned an ambiguous role for Congress. A truly executive budget might require Congress to subordinate its flexibility altogether to presidential preferences. Or, it might simply represent an incremental increase of presidential power along with no diminution of formal congressional authority – only an increase in interbranch conflict. In either case, the implementation of any type of executive budget presupposed a demise of the regime of 1885 since the logic of the national budget system required Congress to match the president in institutional centralization.

The preliminary 1911 Taft Commission reports outlining key aspects of a national budget system served as the basis of Taft's 1912 message to Congress dealing with economy and efficiency. In that message, Taft cast the national budget issue in terms of bringing the United States into the company of other developed nations by arguing that

the United States is the only great Nation whose Government is operating without a budget. This fact seems to be more striking when it is considered that budgets and budget procedures are the outgrowth of democratic doctrines and have had an important part in the development of modern constitutional rights. . . . The constitutional purpose of a budget is to make government responsive to public opinion and responsible for its acts. (U.S. President n.d., 8094)

In this first report by Taft on economy and efficiency, he also was aware of rumblings of dissatisfaction with the Taft Commission's business brought on by the recent partisan realignment in the House. Taft justified the work of his embryonic efficiency commission by claiming that its recommendation had already saved the federal government $2 million in nine months of existence – a figure that was difficult to substantiate.

At this time Taft also recognized that the issue of budget reform was an esoteric one that would excite no natural political support without a thorough effort of political education. Thus, Taft's 1912 message also contained a request for an additional $50,000 so that the findings of the Commission could be "widely publicized" (U.S. President n.d., 8099). Taft was eager for this publicity to begin. Two days after his message was delivered, even before Congress had had time to appropriate the funds, commission member Chase reported that "the President has given us direct instructions to resolve ourselves into a publicity commission . . . to get the importance of this subject of efficiency and economy in the administration of the Government understood by the people" (NYT 19 Jan. 1912, 6).

Overt congressional support for executive branch propagandizing has never been very high, and there was no exception in this case – the money for publicity was never appropriated. In fact, even as the commission was helping Taft draft his economy and efficiency message, many Democratic representatives had already made known their displeasure with the commission's work, and its budget was considered to be imminently threatened (NYT 1 Jan. 1912, 5).

Widespread, spontaneous popular support for the commission's work was not immediately forthcoming, and the Taft Commission soon found its appropriation successively reduced, restricted, and finally eliminated by a Congress leery of the implications of its work. This difficulty arose most seriously when the Appropriations Committee considered its 1913 appropriation. In the appropriations hearing, and later in the Appropriations Committee's report, the committee expressed impatience at the commission's tardiness in reporting out its results (H. Rpt. 826, 62nd Cong.). More importantly, many Democratic members of the House Appropriations Committee expressed suspicion that the commission, while demanding economy of others, was trying to build up its own large administrative empire without direct congressional approval – a sticky political position for the commission to find itself in. Thus, Congress found a potent symbolic avenue for attacking the commission. Consider the following exchange between Cleveland and the committee when he was asked what, beyond the $75,000 requested for FY 1913, would be needed for the commission's total work:

John Fitzgerald (Chair): How long, appropriating at that rate [$75,000] will it take to complete the work now in contemplation?

Cleveland: ... I may say that the $250,000 [sic] requested is not to be considered to be the limit of amount of money that could be effectively used. It was thought that request for larger amount might provoke hostile criticism. . . . The probability is that half a million dollars could be used with very great effect during another year. . . .

R. N. Page: What amount of appropriation, Mr. Cleveland, would most effectively accomplish the work – a large one or a small one?

Cleveland: A large one, a large appropriation . . . .

Fitzgerald: The trouble in considering your suggestion is that while the President has sent some messages as to the amount desired, the official and legal estimate before this committee is $75,000, and even the White House must comply with the law, which controls the submission of estimates, and it does not do so. . . .

Cleveland: Of course, I do not know what has been the machinery at this end for handling such requests on the part of the President, but on two occasions he has officially asked Congress for $250,000, and I understand these were referred to your committee in the regular way.

Fitzgerald: I know; and that is the curse of the system, that the President in messages violates the law which we are trying to compel the administration

185

to live up to in order to get...a comparison between the estimates and the appropriations. But the President does not pay any attention to the law in that respect....

Cleveland: I understand that the law does not apply to the President....

Fitzgerald: If we could get the Executive to comply with these requirements we would have less trouble with his subordinates. (U.S. Congress, House Appropriations Committee 1912, 152–154)

The FY 1913 sundry civil bill ended up containing an appropriation of $75,000 for the commission, but it required the commission to cut its membership and the salaries paid to the remaining members.[5] By the time the sundry civil bill reached the House floor, it was clear that the Appropriations Committee, the one House committee that should have been sympathetic to the Taft Commission's work, had become lukewarm in its support. Page chastised the commission for calling on Congress to change its budgetary ways while the commission's recommendations to the president had gone unheeded by Taft:

[The commission members] have made partial reports to the President and to the Congress of the United States. The subcommittee had before it representatives of this commission and patiently for three days listened to their testimony touching not only what they had accomplished but the plans they had for the accomplishment of other things.... It is somewhat significant...that the commission of the President, of his creation and reporting to him, made reports to the President of reforms that might be effected, saving thousands of dollars to the Government, as long ago as last December – reforms that required absolutely nothing except the Executive order of the President of the United States to put them into operation – and while six months have elapsed no order has been issued to put into effect these reforms that have been recommended by his own board. (CR 62–1, 6 June 1912, 7763)

The strongest recommendation for the commission that Page could give was that the Appropriations Committee "did not feel that there had been sufficient time for them to demonstrate whether or not their work was of real value." Page went on to relate the commission's further existence to the upcoming presidential elections:

I think they may be of value, and we were willing to give them a chance. Personally I had this sort of mental reservation – that if they did not make good, after the 4th of next March a Democratic President could discontinue them [Applause on the Democratic side]. (CR 62–2, 6 June 1912, 7765)

---

5 The amendment allowed only three members to receive $4,000 a year in salary; up until then, there were five members who each received over $6,000 in salary, Cleveland receiving $10,000.

Try as they might, the commission and Taft could not get the unfavorable response of the House to their work overturned.[6]

Amid clear trouble in maintaining support for the Taft Commission on Capitol Hill, Taft proceeded to unilaterally implement the commission's key innovation: the executive budget. In July 1912, similarly to what he had done in the previous three budgets, Taft issued an executive order requiring department heads to submit their FY 1914 estimates to him for approval and reduction. This time, however, Taft ran into resistance from the Democratic House. As soon as Taft's executive order was made public, the following proviso was attached to the legislative, executive, and judicial appropriations bill:

Section 10. That until otherwise provided by law, the regular annual estimates of appropriations for expenses of the Government of the United States shall be prepared and submitted to Congress, by those charged with the duty of such preparation and submission, only in the form and at the time now required by law, and in no other form and at no other time. (H.R. 26321, 62nd Cong.; H.Rpt. 1201, 62nd Cong.)[7]

Taft remained insistent that the submission of an executive budget was necessary and that Congress's action was unconstitutional. In an open letter to MacVeagh, Taft made one of the classic arguments in favor of strong executive leadership in shaping the federal budget:

If the President is to assume responsibility for either the manner in which business of the Government is transacted or results obtained, it is evident that he cannot be limited by Congress to such information as that branch may think sufficient for his purposes. In my opinion, it is entirely competent for the President to submit to Congress and to the country a statement of resources, obligations, revenues, expenditures, and estimates in the form he deems advisable. And this power I propose to exercise.... Under the Constitution, the President is entrusted with the executive power, and is responsible for the acts of the heads of departments, and their subordinates as his agents.[8]

6 See Cleveland to Taft, 13 July 1912, and Sen. Francis Warren (chair of Senate Appropriations Committee) to Taft, 17 July 1912, in personal letters, William H. Taft Collection, Manuscript Division, Library of Congress, Washington, D.C.

7 Neither committee records nor other reports are helpful in determining the exact origin of this proviso. The committee's work had originally been done in the spring of 1912, before Taft's executive order requiring that estimates be cleared through him. The legislative bill was being considered in August of that year because it had earlier been vetoed by Taft because it abolished the Commerce Court (H.R. 24023, 62nd Cong.; H.Rpt. 633, 62nd Cong.). Thus, subsequent action on the legislative bill focused almost totally on the matter of the court. The only mention of the Section 10 restriction came in H.Rpt. 1201: "An additional section is recommended in the bill prohibiting the preparation of estimates of appropriations except as authorized and required by law" (p. 2). No mention of this section was made in floor debate.

8 Taft to MacVeagh, 19 Sept. 1912, 5, in personal letters, series 8, William H. Taft

The hyperbole surrounding the production of the first widely recognized executive budget flew all around Washington. Partisans on both sides of the controversy accused the others of irresponsibility and unconstitutionality. The height of rhetoric was reached when Frederick Cleveland, in supporting Taft's stance, argued that an executive budget would save the federal government $300 million, at a time when total federal spending reached between $600 and $700 million per year (NYT 29 Sept. 1912, 2).

To Taft's dismay, the budget that he finally submitted was never even considered or consulted by any committee in either chamber. Simply as a courtesy to the lame duck president, the Republican Senate, but not the Democratic House, printed the document (S.Doc. 1113, 62nd Cong.).

Taft's defeat in the 1912 election also paved the way for the abolition of the Taft Commission itself. Further money for the commission was denied in the 1914 sundry civil appropriations bill, forcing it out of business (H.R. 28775, 62nd Cong.; H.Rpt. 1526, 62nd Cong.). The fact that no mention of the commission was made on the floor when the 1914 sundry civil bill was reported speaks to the low levels of congressional interest and support that it commanded by then.

The genesis, mixed congressional reception, short life, and quick death of the Taft Commission reveals much about the ability of Congress to support reform efforts, especially when those efforts promise to infringe upon congressional policy flexibility. The creation of the commission itself was not very remarkable; ideas about what the commission would actually do, would find, and would recommend were ill-formed at the beginning. The concept of a government study commission on efficiency was one primarily of symbolic significance. Members of Congress could easily support its creation because it had acquired no really substantive content as of yet. In their search for ways out of the deficit problem, MCs had already expressed a willingness to delegate limited authority to the executive branch. Because the commission was created with simple reporting authority, its anticipated functions did not stray too far from what had already been delegated to the president and Treasury secretary over the past few years.

Creating the commission was also facilitated by the fact that Congress and the presidency were controlled by the same party. Those who had inklings that a government efficiency commission might recommend a fundamental reshuffling of the relationship between the two branches could momentarily swallow their objections, assuming that any such

Collection, Manuscript Division, Library of Congress, Washington, D.C. The letter was made public in NYT 20 Sept. 1912, 7.

recommendation would at least have partisan compatibility, if not institutional compatibility.

The response of the House to the commission's short life was shaped by the changing nature of the two factors – lack of clear substantive content to the commission's work and partisanship – that had facilitated its creation in the first place. First, as the commission did its work and its efforts acquired greater substantive content, the symbolic attractiveness of a government efficiency commission diminished. On the one hand, much of the commission's production was mundane in the extreme. Aside from the budget plan, the other reports of the commission ran to the pedestrian side, with titles such as "Use of Window Envelopes in the Government Service" and "Memoranda of Conclusions Concerning the Principles that Should Govern in the Matter of Handling and Filing Correspondence." Given that the movement for greater efficiency within the federal government was still nascent, this concentration upon the mundane did not help to broaden the commission's base of public support.

It could, however, have been sustained had the content of its most cherished and well-known proposal, the executive budget, not been so fundamentally objectionable to the sensibilities of most members of Congress. When the commission had been authorized in 1910, it was easy to lend general and vague support to the president in his quest to increase government efficiency. Once it became clear that the commission's "Public Efficiency Enemy Number One" was Congress, however, the general, vague support quickly became specific, focused opposition.

The loss of congressional support for the commission's enterprise can be traced back in part to the commission casting the executive budget debate in terms of the British model; MCs read the commission as favoring a system in which the president would present Congress a take-it-or-leave-it budget plan. Whether or not the congressional perception of the commission's actual attitudes was accurate, the damage to the commission's credibility had been done. The continued insistence by the commission and its supporters that the president was the only legitimate budget writer continued to grate on the sensibilities of many members of Congress, even those who favored consolidation and retrenchment. The prospect that Congress would lose its budgetary preeminence if the commission's reforms were enacted led to the open hostility of MCs toward the commission.

Even the leading fiscal conservatives in the House, such as J. Swagar Sherley (D-KY) and John Fitzgerald (D-NY), had a hard time accepting the commission's proexecutive arguments. For MCs like Sherley and Fitzgerald, increased budgetary control might require reestablishing a strong Appropriations Committee or creating an umbrella budget committee, along with an enhanced financial reporting capacity in the executive branch, but broad unilateral policy powers for the president were not required (CR 62–2, 7 Aug. 1912, 10399–10401; CR 62–3, 28 Feb. 1913, 4349–4355). The commission sealed its institutional fate when it was viewed as the prime mover behind Taft's assertion of the right to submit an executive budget regardless of explicit legislation to the contrary.

The fact that the Taft Commission was seen as championing a strong reorientation of budgetary power toward the executive was not aided by the subsequent partisan division between the House and the presidency. It bears repeating that Taft had crafted his own budgets before 1912; but he had not done so within the same charged partisan environment, had not done so as an act of executive will, and had never *called* the result an executive budget. Taft's 1912 budget-writing exercise provided a convenient focus for dissatisfaction within the House.

While the generally rocky reception of the Taft Commission in both the House and Senate can be attributed to its antilegislative tendencies, the vehemence with which the House attacked the commission and Taft's own independent efforts after the 1910 election can be attributed to the consequences of partisanship. Certainly the Republican Senate did very little to protect the Taft Commission from House attack after 1910, but no Senate Republican leader *actively* sought the commission's demise.

Finally, it must be said that the House would probably have rejected nonincremental structural change at this time anyway, regardless of its content or origin. The death of the message was assured, and killing the messenger was simply the most direct way of accomplishing it. At this time, the general orientation toward addressing deficits was incremental, and the executive figured into congressional designs only as a source of information and enforcement of spending limits. Nobody in either House had even speculated about allowing the president to act unilaterally. Members of Congress were trying to face rising budgetary problems through incremental changes that preserved maximal congressional prerogatives. While continued deficits were troublesome politically and financially, they had not reached true emergency proportions as they had during the Civil War.

A fiscal emergency would move Congress off the incremental course. Barring an emergency, however, time would provide incrementalism the opportunity to accumulate small changes, give proconsolidation MCs the opportunity to build reform coalitions, and allow everyone to cope with the other institutional changes being wrought by the demise of czar rule. Fundamental changes in the distribution of influence in the House could not occur until questions about the resulting power distribution could be easily explained and justified in terms of the unique goals and constraints facing members of Congress. The Taft Commission and the Taft administration had failed in putting the issue to members of Congress in language they could accept. With the commission's death, the focus on reform shifted away from the executive branch back to Congress.

CONGRESS TAKES ON THE REFORM MANTLE

The first tangible move away from the regime of 1885 toward the regime of 1921 occurred through a series of fits and starts, governed by the success of reformers in building coalitions, the partisan compositions of the White House and Capitol Hill, and the unfolding of new macropolitical and economic crises.

With the elections of 1912, the Democracy entirely controlled both ends of Pennsylvania Avenue for the first time in twenty years, and the movement toward budget reform that had been interrupted during the 62nd Congress regained some momentum. The shift of reform activity to Congress also altered the mix of reform proposals on the agenda: Executive budget plans were exchanged for legislative plans. As we shall see, legislative budget plans were varied, but all of them approached reform by striving to maximize budgetary power *within* Congress and by proposing the establishment of formal, centralized structures either to mitigate the effects of the regime of 1885 or to overthrow the regime altogether.

The first plan to reform *internal* budgetary practice that emerged within the House and gained wide support and discussion proposed the creation of a House Committee on Estimates and Expenditures. This reform was closely associated with Rep. J. Swagar Sherley (D-KY), who first submitted it during the 61st Congress in 1910 (NYT 18 Dec. 1910, 11; H. Res. 878, 61st Cong.; H. Res. 141, 62nd Cong.). Under the Sherley plan, the Committee on Estimates and Expenditures would

as soon after the convening of each regular session of Congress as may be, report to the House the amount of revenue probably available for appropriation for the next fiscal year, and apportion the amount to the several appropriation bills within the jurisdiction of the committees empowered by the rules and practice of the House to report appropriations from the Treasury.[9]

9 Thus, while the membership was conceived of as being different, the function of the proposed committee was quite similar to that as embodied in the 1974 Congressional Budget and Impoundment Control Act. The incubation period of the reforms that did occur between 1919 and 1921 was about ten years, but the creation of congressional budget committees incubated for over half a century.

The committee would be composed of five members each[10] from the Ways and Means and Appropriations committees and two members each[11] from the Rules Committee and the legislative committees endowed with the authority to report appropriations. The committee membership was designed explicitly to balance the aggregational and distributive budgetary problems; of the total membership of twenty-six, twelve would be drawn from control committees – the ten from Ways and Means and Appropriations and the two from Rules – while the other fourteen would come from the legislative committees.

Sherley's proposal was significant in at least two respects. First, it shows how even fiscally conservative Democrats were reluctant to cede budgetary authority to the executive branch. Sherley's proposal said nothing about strengthening the hand of the president through the submission of agency estimates. Sherley's aversion to the executive budget was also shared by others who made competing reform proposals in the House.[12]

Second, the Sherley plan was significant because it represented an estimate of the practical limit to which some fiscal conservatives believed they could bring House budgetary centralization. Sherley tempered his reform zeal with a grasp of the strategic reality involved in enacting reform: Any centralization proposal would certainly meet opposition from the 147 (out of 391) House members who were on legislative committees endowed with appropriations jurisdiction, in addition to opposition from other members who had gained under the dispersion of power. This strategic consideration was on Sherley's mind in the closing days of the 62nd Congress when he analyzed the relative merits of his plan and a proposal made by John Fitzgerald to simply return all appropriations bills to the HAC. In opposition to the Fitzgerald plan, Sherley stated that "bringing back to the Committee on Appropriations jurisdiction of all the supply bills" would be an "impossible task" politically (CR 62–3, 28 Feb. 1913, 4351). In response to the charge that his reform would give too much institutional power to too few, Sherley replied:

10 Four majority party members and one minority party member. The majority party members would be the chair and the three most senior members; the minority party member would be the ranking minority member from those committees.
11 The chair and ranking minority member.
12 The most important of Sherley's competitors was John Fitzgerald, who chaired the Appropriations Committee for six years. Fitzgerald spoke consistently for economy and retrenchment, yet he also opposed Taft Commission proposals in favor of restoring the HAC to its full past glory (see CR 62–2, 7 Aug. 1912, 10399–10401). Although both Sherley and Fitzgerald differed in their approaches to reform and argued over where authority would lodge in the House, they were united in opposition to strengthened presidential budgetary power.

[That criticism] really applies to the proposal urged in lieu of mine, of giving back to the Appropriations Committee exclusive jurisdiction of supply bills. That is what destroyed it [the HAC] before. That committee would determine what is the real function of the House alone to determine – the relative size of the various bills. Now, I believe in power and with it responsibility, but what I particularly want is the power of a party and not a committee of a party, and then, as a true sequence, party responsibility. (CR 62–3, 28 Feb. 1913)[13]

Both Sherley and Fitzgerald laid the groundwork for more active pursuit of House reform in the next Congress. Once the 63rd Congress (1913–15) convened in March 1913, leaders of the Democratic Caucus elevated the issue of budget reform to a party matter.[14] A report of business held during the first meeting of the House Democratic Caucus in the 63rd Congress stated that

the most important action taken by the caucus was the selection of the Democratic membership of the Ways and Means Committee and the adoption of a resolution offered by Mr. [Oscar] Underwood [D-AL] directing the new caucus Chairman, A. Mitchell Palmer [D-PA] . . . to appoint a special committee of seven to consider the wisdom of adopting a National budget in handling the regular annual appropriations "to the end that the total of appropriations may the better be controlled, reductions in expenditures may be attained, and confusion in and duplication of appropriations avoided." (NYT 6 Mar. 1913, 2)

Membership on that caucus study committee is not clear because specific official records of the caucus have disappeared over the years. The names of four members of the study committee were reported by the Washington Post: Oscar Underwood (AL, Ways and Means chair and majority leader), John Fitzgerald (NY, HAC chair), Swagar Sherley (KY,

13 Sherley's appeal to the ideology of responsible parties was consistent throughout his defense of a budget committee. His defense also revealed that the Ways and Means Committee operated through excluding the minority party members from its deliberations (CR 62–3, 28 Feb. 1913, 4351). It is not surprising that the decline of the popularity of the Sherley plan paralleled the decline of the strength of partisan rule during this decade.

14 The move to caucus government for part of this decade presents some methodological problems. While the Democratic Caucus had published rules (see CR 63–1, 13 Sept. 1913, 4903) and made the journal of its proceedings available to the press (see CR, 63–1, 17 Apr. 1913, 224; Haines 1915), no verbatim records of the caucus deliberations were kept and the caucus journals – along with the roll call votes taken in caucus – are available only in fragments. I have been able to reconstruct most of the *Journal* beginning in 1911 from various archival sources, including the papers of Lynn Haines (located in the Minnesota Historical Society), Claude Kitchin (University of North Carolina, Southern Manuscript Collection), and the Democratic Caucus of the House of Representatives (Library of Congress). Unfortunately, the largest gap in the reconstruction occurs between 1913 and 1915. Therefore, much of the caucus activity is reconstructed here through newspaper accounts and other secondary sources.

HAC), and Finnis Garrett (TN, Rules) (WP 23 June 1913, 2). The membership was drawn from committees closely identified with budget control, along with party leadership. The fact that both Sherley and Fitzgerald were put on the committee indicates that leadership either had not taken sides in the dispute or wanted to coopt their support for whichever plan emerged, or both. The presence of both Sherley and Fitzgerald on the committee also guaranteed a sufficient level of group energy to actively pursue the issue, even if it did not guarantee agreement.

The committee met intermittently for the next two months and reported its recommendation to the caucus in the summer of 1913. Its recommendation was essentially the Sherley plan already described (NYT 26 June 1913, 5). The study committee called for the creation of a budget committee that would meet early each year to allocate spending totals to all committees authorized to report appropriations. These committees would then work within their own totals. The proposed budget committee would be representative of all spending committees but be weighted heavily toward Appropriations, Ways and Means, and Rules.

If party leaders had meant to coopt Fitzgerald by including him on the study committee, they failed. Fitzgerald continued to endorse reconsolidation back into the Appropriations Committee and worked in caucus to defeat the Sherley plan. The caucus fight over budget reform was said to "shake the democratic party in the House to its very foundation" (Washington *Evening Star* 25 June 1913, 1). In the meeting, Oscar Underwood reported the recommendation and acted as the floor leader for reform supporters, among whom was Speaker Champ Clark. John Fitzgerald was among the leaders of the opposition (NYT 26 June 1913, 5).

While the caucus study committee produced a recommendation, it did not produce a majority. The caucus committee was unable to build a party majority because Fitzgerald's faction joined with representatives opposed to any reform whatsoever. Opposition to any reform was led by two Georgians, Samuel Tribble and Charles Hardwick. Tribble objected that the proposed budget committee would constitute the "most gigantic trust ever formed." Hardwick moved to table the reform, and the vote carried 95–80.

Because the caucus *Journal* from this meeting apparently no longer exists, we do not know the exact breakdown of the caucus vote. The *New York Times* (26 June 1913, 5) did report how New York Democrats voted, and we can use this account to gain some feel for where support for the measure rested at this time. Concluding anything about Democrats generally from the New York vote is risky because Fitzgerald was a senior and very influential member of that delegation. On the other hand, New Yorkers had proved to be among the most consistent supporters of budgetary consolidation over the previous forty years, so analyzing their votes may help us to understand the structural preferences of more control-oriented members.

New York Democrats opposed the Sherley plan more than other Democrats (63 percent opposed versus 51 percent).[15] Among New York Democrats, support for the Sherley reform plan came more strongly from members of committees that could currently report appropriations than from nonmembers. Of the six New York Democrats who served on legislative committees that could report appropriations, the vote was split evenly; the ten who did not serve on one of those committees voted three to seven in opposition.

The New York Democratic delegation vote and press accounts of the meeting suggest a couple of tentative conclusions about the basis of reform support at this stage of the process. First, there was probably majority support among House Democrats for some kind of consolidation or greater formal coordination. More accurately, it is probably true that a majority of Democrats would have assented to consolidation or coordination had the general proposition been put to a vote. Of course, a *specific* proposition was put for a vote, not a general one. The majority level of support for some sort of added institutional coordination is suggested by the close vote in caucus – the switch of eight votes among ninety-five would have brought the issue up for a vote on substance. Given historic voting patterns of procedural versus substantive issues, we can safely assume that (almost) all Democrats who voted against tabling would have supported the Sherley plan on a straight vote on the issue, and that there would have been switches toward Sherley's position if the vote were on the substance.

Second, actual passage of reform was thwarted in a classic "ends against the middle" voting pattern, which suggests that the radical centralizers saw it in their interests to oppose compromise in the short run in order to achieve even greater institutional benefits in the long run. As far as Fitzgerald and the Appropriations Committee were concerned, the creation of a budget committee under the Sherley plan would directly gain them no greater authority while it might diffuse agitation for further centralization. Thus, they had little to lose by opposing Sherley and potentially much to gain.

The reasonableness of this speculation about Fitzgerald's strategic calculation is bolstered when we consider the behavior of New York Democrats who served on the legislative committees bound to see their appropriations power diminished under either plan: they were more likely to support Sherley than other New York Democrats. If some type of

15 To aid in clarity of discussion, a vote to table is equated with opposition to the Sherley plan while a vote against tabling is equated with support.

reform was likely, which may have been the perception before the caucus vote, then Sherley's plan of coordination was preferable to members of the legislative committees compared to the Fitzgerald plan.

At this juncture reform stalemated because neither the radical nor moderate reform faction was willing to compromise. But, the closeness of the caucus margin suggested that reform supporters might still be able to craft an acceptable compromise if they continued to work at it.

The Democratic Caucus budget study committee was reconstituted in the 64th Congress (1915–17). Its membership once again was weighted heavily toward control committees.[16] Only two members of the study committee were not either party leaders or members of the finance committees.

The group decided not to seek a repeat of the previous year, and they looked to the White House for assistance, soliciting Wilson's help in drawing up a reform plan. Wilson had earlier voiced his support for a budget plan and had run on a presidential platform that endorsed reform; thus hope that Wilson would actively work for centralization in the House was not far-fetched. And given the closeness with which Wilson worked with party leaders (especially during his first term), presidential support in this matter could have aided in any reform's passage. Absent a push from their party's president, the study committee was pessimistic about reform's chances.

The delegation that solicited Wilson's assistance was disappointed in its quest to get the president to endorse a specific budget reform plan, although we do not know why. All we know is that within a month of meeting with Wilson to gain his support, it was reported that

after a preliminary investigation by a special committee named by the Democratic caucus of the House, plans for the establishment of a budget system of appropriations have been practically abandoned for the present legislative session. (NYT 26 Dec. 1915, 13)

Thus budget reform, after a brief glimpse of the limelight, was pushed far down the political agenda, even by those who favored it the most. Although the proximate cause of reform's loss of luster may have been the inability to convince Wilson to come along, reform's declining salience was also due to rising preoccupation with the emerging foreign crisis. While passing a consolidating reform in 1915 might have had a positive impact on the prosecution of the coming war effort, decisionmakers began

---

16 Members were Champ Clark (MO, Speaker), Claude Kitchin (NC, Ways and Means chair), John Fitzgerald (NY, HAC chair), Swagar Sherley (KY, HAC), James Hay (VA, Military Affairs chair), Tom Stout (MT, Expenditures in the Interior Department chair), and John Garner (TX, Ways and Means) (Sherley to Kitchin, 10 Mar. 1915, in the Claude Kitchin Papers of the Southern Historical Collection, University of North Carolina Library).

to focus more and more on crisis management of the problems themselves and less and less on the structures in which the problems were solved.

The entry of the United States into World War I served to reduce the premium put on frugality, and thus to reduce the level of congressional search for budget control. In the short term even the politicians who had most often argued for structural and substantive budgetary control conceded that frugality was the last thing needed in a war. In an interview upon taking the chair of the House Appropriations Committee in early 1918, Sherley summarized the thinking of many congressional budget reform supporters on this point when he said:

> Under normal conditions we should consider every expenditure with reference to whether it is worth the burden it puts upon the people. In times of war there is only one side to that vital question. In time of war, we, as the representatives of the people, must spend to the last of all that the people have, if necessary, to save the people themselves.
>
> I would not care to be chairman of the committee to which all the appropriating power was conferred at this time, even if the majority of Congress approved such concentration, because the resentment of the minority at such a change would so cripple the efficiency of the Appropriations Committee as to practically destroy it. (NYT Magazine, 17 Mar. 1918, 1)

Yet, in the process of spending "to the last of all that the people have," the stage was set for support for centralization to broaden. Two consequences of the war brought about this heightening of support: expansion of the income tax and the general state of the government's administrative apparatus during and immediately following the war.

Income taxation had resumed after the ratification of the Sixteenth Amendment in 1913, but the ramifications for budget reform politics were not fully clear before the war. The significance of the income tax was not broadly conceived because, first, it was a popular proposal and, second, it did not generate much revenue. The immediate function of the first income tax that passed in 1913 was to replace revenues lost through a concomitant reduction in tariff rates. As a replacement for lost tariff revenues, the first income tax rates were set at very low levels, raising only $68 million and $180 million in the first two years, and represented only 16 percent of all revenues collected by 1917 (U.S. Census Bureau 1975, series Y352–372).

In response to the war, however, rates were not only raised for those already paying, but the income base was dramatically broadened. Internal

197

revenue collections in FY 1918[17] were $3.7 billion, a 357 percent increase over collections from the previous year.

The effect that the rapid expansion of income tax incidence had on the salience of public spending and taxing issues did not escape national politicians. Even before the income tax's enactment, members of the House most closely acquainted with fiscal matters had noted that the prevailing taxation system, which relied on indirect revenues such as the tariff and excises, served to lower the salience of general government spending. These prescient House members anticipated that the enactment of the income tax would eventually heighten popular awareness of federal activity. Such a point was made by James Tawney in 1910, when he chaired the Appropriations Committee:

The fundamental cause of our greatly increased expenditures is found in the fact that these expenditures are met from revenues secured indirectly – from customs duties, internal revenue taxes, and miscellaneous receipts, the burden of which the people do not directly feel. The citizen who must go into his own pocket, and therefrom contribute directly his share toward a public improvement or a public service, is not indifferent as to the necessity for such improvement or service, nor is he tardy in complaining if the weight of the burden of taxation becomes excessive in proportion to the benefits he receives. (Tawney 1910, 343)

After the war, James Good, who had assumed the HAC chair, related the popular demand for greater control over spending to the changes in the methods of taxation:

It is thus seen that the number of corporations and persons who are affected by direct taxes is rapidly increasing and with that increase there will come an increased demand for the practice of economy and efficiency, both on the part of the executive departments and of Congress. (CR 66-1, 17 Oct. 1919, 7083)

The fiscal burdens imposed on citizens and corporations on account of the war was only one of the reasons why an interest in fiscal control emerged after 1917. More fundamental problems emerged during the war that called into question the efficacy of a large, fragmented government that was now required to survive in a more complex, dangerous world. The whole history of the growth of the federal government's administrative apparatus after the Civil War had been a story of conflict between the fragmented orientation of Congress and the centralizing desires of professional reformers and certain presidents. While the fragmentation of administration could continue relatively unchallenged during peacetime, the fragmented governing apparatus proved unable to prosecute the war with a reasonable degree of efficiency (Skowronek 1982, 163–284).

17 Internal revenue collections were predominantly from the income tax.

Several stop-gap measures were adopted by the federal government to solve the problems of coordinating the massive industrial war effort, the most significant being the infusion of "dollar-a-year men" and intellectuals into the government. The weakness of governmental administration in meeting the initial challenges of war mobilization demonstrated to many, private and public citizens alike, the dangers inherent in leaving the survival of the country in the hands of a fundamentally fragmented, uncoordinated governing system. The success that the private-turned-public officials had in coordinating the war effort convinced many that government should be run more on a "business basis."

Increased taxes, the initial failure of government to respond efficiently to mobilization, and the resultant turn to business leaders in order to meet the war challenge all interacted politically with the return of Republicans to the control of Congress after the election in 1918 (66th Congress) to produce budget reform. An important issue that helped to return Republicans to congressional control was the Democrats' handling of the war, and thus they returned with a unique sense of popular support for governmental reform.

Republicans gained control of the House intent upon passing both an executive and legislative budget plan. At the beginning of the first session of the 66th Congress, Speaker Frederick Gillett announced that he favored a change of the budgetary rules, and James Good (R-IA), who had succeeded into the chair of the Appropriations Committee, began to draft a bill to concentrate all appropriations into one committee (see NYT 3 Mar. 1919, 7; 7 May 1919, 8).

Good did not prepare the plan unaided. William F. Willoughby, formerly of the Taft Commission and now director of the Institute of Government Research, was called in to aid Good's effort at writing and defending the budget reform proposal in the House.[18] While Good was preparing his plan, a number of representatives and senators jumped on the reform bandwagon, submitting various budget reform plans of their own.[19]

By the summer of 1919, enough interest had been shown in budget reform, along with enough support, that a special committee was appointed to study a budget system and to reconcile the viewpoints of members with conflicting reform approaches (H. Res. 168, 66th Cong.; H. Rpt. 192, 66th Cong.). The resolution to create the committee passed

18 Robert Brookings to Trustees of the Institute of Government Research, letter, 22 October 1919, Archives of the Brookings Institution, Washington, D.C.; Saunders (1966); Skowronek (1982).
19 See H.R. 1201; H.Res. 168; H.J.Res. 59, 83; S.Res. 58; Sen.J.Res. 11, 12, 50 (all 66th Cong.).

by voice vote, but not without some members expressing tentative opposition to the prospect of stripping the legislative committees of their spending power (CR 66-1, 31 July 1919, 3431–3437).

Two months later, Gillett appointed the Special Budget Committee.[20] The membership of the committee reveals an interest on Gillett's part to proceed expeditiously with formulating a reform plan that would work, while simultaneously formulating a plan that could pass. Given the level of organizational expertise resident in and out of government at this time, developing a workable plan was a minor problem. Given the fact that a significant minority of the House benefited directly from the existing fragmentation, formulating a plan that could pass was more problematic. In an effort to diffuse the opposition from the legislative committees that would stand to lose from a strengthening of the Appropriations Committee, only half of the members of the Select Budget Committee came from one of the two control-oriented finance committees, Ways and Means and Appropriations. Of the six members from Ways and Means or Appropriations, three were Republicans and three were Democrats. The other six slots were filled by people who were members of neither of these two committees. Four members (all Republicans) were named from legislative committees that were allowed to report appropriations; the other two members (both Democrats) served on committees that did not have the right to report appropriations.

The membership balance between finance committees and nonfinance committees was an attempt to lessen the appearance that the succeeding reforms would be railroaded through without the consent of the committees that stood to lose power. But, the fact that all of the members of the Select Budget Committee who were chosen from the committees that would stand to lose something under reform were Republicans suggests that Gillett was concerned that the representatives from these committees be "controllable" in some way. Thus, he provided for representation on the Select Budget Committee for the "losers," but these representatives were inherently cross-pressured between committee and party.

While these formal steps building toward reform passage stretched over months, Good was active in the interim building his case for reform.

---

20 Republican members were James Good (IA, HAC chair), Philip Campbell (KS, Rules and Indian Affairs), Martin Madden (IL, Post Office), Willis Hawley (OR, Ways and Means), Henry Temple (PA, Expenditures in the State Department and Foreign Affairs), George Tinkham (MA, HAC), and Fred Purnell (IN, Agriculture). Democratic members were Joseph Byrns (TN, HAC ranking minority member), Claude Kitchin (Ways and Means ranking minority member), John Nance Garner (TX, Ways and Means), Edward Taylor (CO, Irrigation of Arid Lands and Public Lands), and Everette Howard (OK, Expenditures in the Interior Department).

On the same day the Select Budget Committee was appointed, for instance, it began its hearings (Select Budget Committee 1919).[21] While disagreement continued in the chamber over reform details, most notably around whether the Sherley or Fitzgerald option would be taken, the depth of that disagreement was not evident in the committee's deliberations. The witnesses that Willoughby arranged to appear before the committee presented a unified case in favor of both consolidation of appropriations decisionmaking in the House and enhanced presidential power in setting the budgetary agenda. The list of witnesses that appeared before the committee reads like a *Who's Who* of budget reform politics. Witnesses included former members of the Taft Commission,[22] officers of reform organizations,[23] business and professional organizations,[24] and members and former members of Congress.[25]

Willoughby himself testified before the committee early in its deliberation and was the committee's most thorough witness (SBCH, 47–102). His most important theme, in terms of convincing members who were borderline in their support for reform, was that an executive-initiated budget could be implemented without ceding all practical power to the executive, as reportedly had happened in Great Britain.

The faults of the British model were deemed to be the usurpation of legislative authority and the reluctance of Parliament to pare back government estimates. It was this latter tendency that caught the attention of most members of the select committee. At one point, Good noted that a recent study of the British system revealed that "there has not been a single instance in the last 25 years where the House of Commons has refused any estimate submitted to it.... I can not help but feel that perhaps we have gotten along better than the people of Great Britain have under this plan now in vogue" (SBCH, 60). Willoughby agreed with Good, noting that under current practice the House usually cut appropriations estimates, an opportunity that would be missed if the British model were adopted too literally.

Willoughby tried to avoid alienating his congressional patrons further

21 These *Hearings* are abbreviated in the citations as "SBCH."
22 Willoughby, Cleveland, Goodnow, and Warwick.
23 Willoughby and Robert Brookings of the Institute for Government Research; John Pratt and Samuel Lindsay of the National Budget Committee; R. Fulton Cutting and Charles Beard, of the New York Bureau of Municipal Research; and William Allen, Institute for Public Service.
24 W. L. Clause and Elliott Goodwin of the Chamber of Commerce; Charles Norton of the First National Bank of New York; L. F. Loree of the Delaware and Hudson Railroad Company; Jesse Burks, National Industrial Conference Board; Charles Baker, Nelson Lewis, and A. P. David of the Engineering Council of America.
25 John Fitzgerald (D-NY), Swagar Sherley (D-KY), F. W. Mondell (R-WY), James Frear (R-WI), and Halvor Steenerson (R-MN).

by pointing blame for current budgetary problems away from Congress. He contended that the previous two decades of fiscal problems had not been a result of the lack of political will, but a result of a lack of information, brought about from a system fragmented in both the executive and legislative.

Thus, Willoughby and Good tried to steer discussion away from the British model and its overtones of executive dominance toward an argument that cast budget reform in terms of enhanced legislative power. Giving more authority to the president and the House Appropriations Committee was argued to enhance congressional authority, not lessen it, because Congress would be able to cut more quickly and efficiently, and would have access to more useful information. By paying more attention to the peculiar institutional needs of MCs and speaking the congressional language, Willoughby was able to overcome the previous hostility that the Taft Commission had received a decade earlier when it worked for the comparable set of institutional reforms.

After two weeks of hearings, the committee worked for another three weeks to draft the reform package. The reform package consisted of two parts: (1) the creation of a new executive budgetary apparatus, including presidential responsibility for submitting a unified budget, and (2) a change in the House rules to abolish the regime of 1885, returning all spending oversight back to the Appropriations Committee. In drafting this two-part reform package, committee members engaged in a series of compromises designed to please the reform majority and isolate those most wedded to the regime of 1885. These compromises revolved around two points.

First, the committee developed a compromise between the supporters of the legislative budget and of the executive budget. In essence this involved combining the thinking of academic reformers, who favored strong presidential leadership, with the reality that independent legislators would not go along with a system in which, in Frederick Cleveland's words, the only role for Congress would be to serve as the "attorneys" for the presidential budget (SBCH, 528–529).

Out of the compromise the academic reformers, and the president, got the right to shape the budget debate through the use of the executive budget document along with an expert staff to direct the first round of cutting agency requests; they lost the presumption that congressional action would amount to an up-or-down vote on the president's plan. On the other hand, House reformers retained the right to change budget requests through legislative mechanisms, reestablished spending oversight in a single appropriations committee, created a strong "independent" auditing agency (the Accounting Department), and – not unimportantly – received the right to take credit for a popular reform of a chaotic process. The House rank-and-file lost through the shift of budgetary agenda setting away from Congress and individual agencies to the president.

The creation of the independent auditing agency was key to winning support from legislators who feared that the president's added budget expertise would eventually lead to an even greater practical shift toward the president than most preferred. The auditing department was labeled "independent," but the adjective referred to the department's relationship to the president, not to Congress.

Second, the committee decided to bring up legislative reform after the executive budget plan had passed. This tactic was adopted because support for the limited executive budget had reached near consensus in the House, while there was still less consensus in the chamber about who should oversee the president's budget once it reached the House. The Select Budget Committee decided that passing the executive budget first would provide a degree of momentum to get the House rules change passed later.

H.R. 9783 (the "Good Bill" or "Accounting Act"), creating the limited executive budget, was reported out on 8 October 1919. The Good Bill created the Bureau of the Budget in the executive office of the president to assist him in the preparation of the annual budget: Agencies were no longer permitted to submit their requests unchanged to Congress through the Treasury secretary. The budget would contain not only each agency's request, but also a "balanced statements of the revenues and expenditures of the Government" for the relevant fiscal years. As well, the Good Bill created the Accounting Department, overseen by the newly created office of Comptroller General, which would audit expenses after they had been incurred. In establishing the Accounting Department, the committee proposed moving the auditing function from the Treasury Department to an independent agency; the agency's independence from the executive was underscored by the provision that the comptroller general could be removed from office only by concurrent resolution of Congress, and then only for cause.

In its report, the budget committee went out of its way to assure House members that its recommendation did not represent an abdication of legislative power:

It will doubtless be claimed by some that this is an Executive budget and that the duty of making appropriations is a legislative rather than Executive prerogative. The plan outlined does provide for an Executive initiation of the budget, but the President's responsibility ends when he has prepared the budget and transmitted it to Congress. To that extent and to that extent alone does the plan provide for an Executive budget, but the proposed law does not change in the slightest degree the duty of Congress to make the minutest examination of the budget and to adopt the budget only to the extent that it is found to be economical. If the estimates contained in the President's budget are too large, it will be the duty of Congress to reduce them. If in the opinion of Congress the estimates of expenditures are not sufficient, it will be within the power of Congress to increase them. The bill does not in the slightest degree give the Executive any greater power than he now has over the consideration of appropriations by Congress. The proposed plan, if adopted, will unquestionably greatly reduce the drudgery of committees in making inquiry into estimates. (H. Rpt. 362, 66th Cong., 7)

The bill was considered in the House between 17 October and 22 October 1919 and generated almost nothing but supporting statements (CR 66-1, 17 Oct. 1919, 7081–7103; 18 Oct. 1919, 7125–7154; 20 Oct. 1919, 7197–7232; 21 Oct. 1919, 7274–7297). Yet, while there was general support for giving the president more authority to shape agency requests, many questions were raised about the connection between the Good Bill and the anticipated restoration of the House Appropriations Committee. Several members rose to note that they would support the Accounting Act but oppose strengthening the Appropriations Committee.

The floor amendments to the Good Bill did not go to the central substance of the budget reform issue but dealt with matters such as the pay of the comptroller general and the size of his budget authorization. When the bill was finally voted on, the limited executive budget plan passed 285–3 and was sent on to the Senate.

While the executive side of budget reform easily passed, the restoration of the HAC's lost power generated more heat on the House floor. The Budget Committee's strategy in separating the Accounting Act from the rules change ultimately proved effective, although the abolition of the regime of 1885 was not assured at the beginning of floor proceedings.

The House leadership waited until after the conference report of the Budget Act had been completed and the bill had been sent to President Wilson for his signature before bringing up the rules change (CR 66–2, 29 May 1920, 7956). The effect of the rules change, embodied in H.Res. 324, was to create a single appropriations committee composed of thirty-five members to consider all appropriations. The report of the committee emphasized the need for the consolidation in order to reduce expenditures:

The need for this reform has been apparent for a number of years, but never so pressing as now. When revenues to meet expenditures were raised by indirect taxation the people took very little interest in the subject of appropriations....

It is thus seen that in the future by far the greater part of the revenue required for conducting the public business must come from direct taxes. This, coupled with the further fact that the ordinary expenses for running the Government will in the future probably exceed four billions of dollars a year, will cause the public to take a much greater interest than heretofore in appropriations by Congress.

The political issues of the future will not be centered around the tariff, but rather around the problems of economy as reflected in the appropriations made by Congress. If this is true, Congress must place itself in a position where it can meet these problems in the most efficient way. The soundest and most approved methods of business transactions must be adopted by Congress if it is to perform well and efficiently the duties which this new condition creates....

[The adoption of this resolution will mean] that the budget can come before Congress in one measure. The consideration of that measure will involve a full and comprehensive discussion in Congress of the big problem of Government finance. Members of Congress can see at a glance the entire picture. (H. Rpt. 373, 66th Cong., 8–10)

Debate on the reconsolidation began on 1 June 1920 when the Rules Committee called up a special order (H.Res. 527) that provided for the immediate consideration of H.Res. 324. To supporters of thorough budget reform, the previous near-unanimous passage of the Budget Act argued persuasively for the passage of this rules change. In reporting out the special order, Simeon Fess (R-OH) argued:

To me it would be totally inconsistent to go to the extent to which we have already gone, to adopt the budget system in response to an almost universal demand of the country and then refuse to do the one thing necessary to make the system operative. The refusal to make it workable leads to the conviction that those who refrain from openly opposing the system so universally demanded have seized upon this plan to conceal their opposition most effectively. (CR 66-2, 1 June 1920, 8103)

As Fess noted, many members who had previously supported the Good Bill were now organizing to defeat this next step of the reform, by voting to leave the internal distribution of House power unchanged. But, reform opponents also knew that voting against reform outright would be difficult to explain to attentive constituents. Rather than risk the consequences of a direct vote against the rules change itself, opponents of the reform moved to defeat passage of the special order, thus keeping the substance of reform off the floor (CR 66-2, 1 June 1920, 8104–8105).

In the debate that followed about whether to consider the rules change, supporters of the status quo found little to comfort them. The committees that had held appropriating power pointedly received no assurances that they would be guaranteed representation on the new appropriations committee (CR 66-2, 1 June 1920, 8103). The dissatisfaction with this massive redistribution of internal power was angrily attacked by Thomas McKeown (D-OK): "When you put all the power of appropriating money in the hands of one committee of this House, the rest of you may just as well pack up your trunks and go back home and stay there, for they will not have any use for you then" (CR 66-2, 1 June 1920, 8105).

After considerable acrimonious debate over the special order, the votes were taken. On a division (standing) vote, the special order allowing consideration of the reform lost on a 69–69 tie (CR 66-2, 1 June 1920, 8107). A roll call was immediately ordered. In the end, two representatives provided the margin of victory, as the special order was approved 158–154 and the matter of changing the House rules was called up for immediate consideration.

The vote on the special order was structured along partisan, regional, and committee lines (Table 5.1). Unlike the vote in 1885 to decentralize, the vote in 1920 showed a strong partisan cleavage: Republicans and Democrats were split. This is partially attributable to the proposal being brought forward as a Republican leadership measure; Republicans felt compelled to support their leaders while Democrats did not. Plus, the creation of the regime of 1885 had largely been on Democratic initiative. If the fragmentation had aided Democrats more than Republicans, then the vote was also a consequences of material self-interest. Regionally, members from both parties coming from the East, New England, and the Midwest were the strongest supporters, leaving the traditional supporters of fragmentation – the South and the West – more likely to vote no. Finally, and not at all surprisingly, members of the Appropriations Committee were very strong supporters of the centralization while members from the six committees that lost appropriations jurisdiction were, on the whole, strong opponents.

Of course, this did not keep members of the affected committees from undertaking one last push to block the change. Although they opposed this particular reform, supporters of the regime of 1885 still did their best to convince anyone listening that they were reformers at heart and that they differed with the rest of the chamber "not with the principle involved, but in the method of accomplishing it" (remarks of Frederick Hicks, CR 66-2, 1 June 1920, 8113). A motion to recommit the resolution (H.Res. 324) with instructions, offered by Sydney Anderson (R-MN, Agriculture Committee), would have retained the status quo while overlaying a budget committee on top of it, much like the earlier Sherley plan would have done. Anderson's motion lost on a division vote of 79–121. When the final roll call was taken, the consolidation had passed by a vote of 200–117.

The vote on final passage was almost identical to the vote to consider the resolution in the first place (Table 5.2). The healthier margin in the second vote principally came from thirty-nine people who had opposed the special order converting to the cause of reform on final passage.

Thus, the strategic decisions of both sides of the reform issue proved correct. By scheduling the rules change after considering the Accounting Act, reformers got their much-needed leverage. Antireformers were also

Table 5.1. *Effect of committee membership, region, and party*
on vote to call up reform of Appropriations Committee
jurisdiction, 66th Congress, 1920
(logistic regression)

Effect	Estimate[a]
Intercept	0.494
Party (Democrats)	−0.908***
Regions (excluded = East)	
New England	0.913*
Confederacy	−0.169
Midwest	0.869**
Prairie	0.202
Mountain/West	0.092
Committees	
Appropriations	1.719**
Losers	−0.990***

$N = 306$
Proportion voting yes = 52.0
Percent correctly predicted = 67.6

Estimated probabilities that types of members would vote yes:

1. By region and party[b]

Region	Republicans	Democrats
New England	0.803	0.622
East	0.621	0.398
Confederacy	0.581	0.358
Midwest	0.796	0.612
Prairie	0.667	0.447
Mountain/West	0.642	0.420

2. By committee membership[c]

Appropriations Committee: 0.888
Losing committees: 0.347
Committee nonmembers: 0.588

Note: Estimates were produced using only members who were either Republicans or Democrats. The Losers variable denotes members who were members of one of the following committees: Agriculture, Foreign Affairs, Indian Affairs, Military Affairs, Naval Affairs, Post Office and Post Roads, and Rivers and Harbors. For regional definitions, see Table 3.1.
[a]Statistical significance: *, $p < .10$; **, $p < .05$; ***, $p < .01$.
[b]Assuming the member served on neither the Appropriations Committee nor on any of the committees that lost appropriations oversight.
[c]Setting regional and party variables to their means.

Table 5.2. *Vote to consider H.Res. 527 by vote on H.Res. 324*

		H.Res. 324[a]			
		Yes	No	No Vote	Total
H.Res. 527[b]	Yes	145	6	7	158
	No	39	106	9	154
	No vote	16	5	96	117
	Total	200	117	112	429

[a] H.Res. 324 was the substantive reform resolution.
[b] H.Res. 527 was the rule that provided for the consideration of H.Res. 324.

correct in assuming that if they were going to kill this reform, they would have to keep it off the floor in the first place. Once reform was brought up on its merits, the idea was too attractive to defeat.

Reform supporters believed that after two years of intense work and a decade of slow coalition building they had accomplished their goal of comprehensive budget reform, of both the executive and legislative branches. Their hopes were quickly shattered when President Wilson vetoed the Accounting Act. Although he claimed to be "in entire sympathy with the objects" of the bill, Wilson objected to the section that provided for removal of the comptroller general only by concurrent resolution of Congress. He argued that "it has ... always been the accepted construction of the Constitution that the power to appoint officers of this kind carries with it ... the power to remove. I am convinced that the Congress is without constitutional power to limit the appointing power and its incident, the power of removal derived from the Constitution" (CR 66-2, 4 June 1920, 8609).

Because removal power had not been a major issue earlier and because Wilson had been assumed to be a reform supporter, his veto caught most in the House by surprise (see CR 66-2, 4 June 1920, 8609–8613). The vote to override the veto failed on a party-line vote of 178–103. Reformulation and repassage of the Good Bill was caught in the end-of-session crunch, and it died with the close of the 66th Congress.

Wilson's veto left the House in an odd position because the resulting predicament had not been anticipated by reform activists. They had anticipated passage of the Accounting Act without passage of the legislative reform, but the existence of legislative centralization with executive fragmentation had not been foreseen. It was widely assumed that some comprehensive plan would pass in the next Congress, but for the time being final creation of a unified executive budget would have to wait. In the interim, House members began to adapt to a new institutional structure as best they could.

One way of adapting and consolidating support for the rules change was in the appointment of the newly expanded Appropriations Committee. In the Democratic caucus that met after the 1920 election between the 66th and 67th Congresses, party members decided that the new minority members of Appropriations would come from the legislative committees that had lost their spending power. The conciliatory gesture went further when these new Appropriations Committee members were allowed to circumvent normal practice and keep their legislative committee assignments (Democratic Caucus *Journal*, 7 Dec. 1920, 30).

The stage for breaking the executive budget deadlock between the Congress and president was also set after the 1920 election when the Democratic party was swept out of the White House to be replaced by Warren Harding. Harding did not hold Wilson's constitutional objections to the Accounting Act, so Congress could move swiftly to ratify what they had done before. Provision was made in adopting the rules of the 67th House (1921–23) for a Select Committee on the National Budget to consider once again the issue of an executive budget system (CR 66-1, 11 Apr. 1921, 83–84). The Select Budget Committee was again heavily weighted toward the finance committees – this time eight of the eleven members came from either the Appropriations or Ways and Means committees. This committee make up, which did not even pretend to be one that tried to bring together divergent views on the matter, facilitated swift action by the committee.

The committee moved quickly to redraft a budget reform and acted without holding any new hearings (H.Rpt. 14, 67th Cong.). As far as the provision that had prompted Wilson's veto was concerned, the committee argued that it was "so vital to a successful budget system that the House should renew its original position in respect to them" (H.Rpt. 14, 67th Cong., p. 1).[26]

All House members were not satisfied with the provisions concerning the comptroller general's tenure, however. Particularly dissatisfied were southern Democrats, who protested on the House floor against the bill's allowing the comptroller general to hold office "during good behavior"

---

26 The debate over reviving the Appropriations Committee took place in two parts. The first half was on the question to bring up the measure for consideration by adopting the special order reported by the Rules Committee. Special orders are popularly referred to as "rules." However, since the substantive issue here was about the House rules, there is occasion for confusion in this discussion. Therefore, I stick to the technical nomenclature by referring to H.Res. 527 as the "special order" and to the substantive rules change embodied in H.Res. 324 as the "rule."

until a mandatory retirement at age 70.[27] But, a motion by Paul Johnson (D-MS) to change this to a term of seven years failed by a division vote of 35–83 (CR 67-1, 5 May 1921, 1083). At the end of debate, Johnson offered the motion to recommit the bill to the Budget Committee, with the instruction that they report back a seven-year term for the comptroller general. The recommittal motion failed 59–297, with Democrats voting 57–45 to recommit. Most of the Democratic votes for recommittal came from the old Confederacy, which voted 48–30 with Johnson.

This recommittal vote shows that the regional distrust of Republican presidents had not diminished by 1921. Most southern Democrats did not like the prospect of the Republican Warren Harding appointing a potentially strong financial official – the official that would be charged with upholding congressional prerogatives against the executive branch – for life. Still, the prospect of having a life-term Republican comptroller general was not enough to deter southerners and other Democrats from voting to pass the bill, which sailed through on a final vote of 344–9 (CR 67-1, 5 May 1921, 1092). The issue was settled three weeks later when the conference report on the Budget and Accounting Act was adopted (S. Doc 15, 67th Cong.). The final bill provided a term of fifteen years for the comptroller general and was passed by an even larger margin in the House of 335–3 (CR 67-1, 27 May 1921, 1859).

Harding signed the bill, ending the dozen years of efforts by reformers to place stronger fiscal control in the hands of the president. Strict fiscal control continued to be adhered to at both ends of Pennsylvania Avenue for the rest of the decade. On the one hand, the newly enlarged House Appropriations Committee decided that they would not "hear any argument from any chief of any department or any bureau in the Government for the restoration of any item that had been eliminated by the Director of the Budget" and they worked to hold down spending during the 1920s (CR 67-1, 5 Jan. 1922, 836). Harding himself, and later President Coolidge, held annual assemblies with bureau chiefs and budget officers to impress upon them the need for economy and coordination (U.S. President 1922–29). It seemed that the country had finally hit upon a scientific way to design its spending plan undergirded by the progressive ideology of bringing business to government.

Still, it can be questioned whether the legislative and executive budget reforms caused the coming frugality and attention to efficiency, or whether they themselves were products of that attention. As with assessing the impacts of structural changes of 1865 and 1885, the answer

27 While the committee report made it clear that Congress could unilaterally remove the comptroller general, on the House floor Good maintained that any resolution removing the comptroller general would require presidential approval. (See CR 67-1, 3 May 1921, 984.)

lies on both sides. The underlying consensus to retrench following the two great wars of this period was genuine, as was the pressure to expand in the 1880s. After 1920 the reforms served as potent symbolic foci for retrenchment. Some retrenchment would have come without reform, but the reforms provided new mechanisms to effect it.

DISCUSSION

In many ways the politics associated with appropriations reform were different after 1885 than before. The most important, and obvious, difference was the nature of the status quo. Before 1885, the status quo was essentially centralized, giving supporters of decentralization the greater incentive to try to change structure, and giving supporters of centralization added institutional resources to resist change. After the devolution of 1885 the status quo was decentralized, shifting the weight of incentives impelling institutional actors to try to enact reform, and altering the array of institutional resources available for resistance.

There was more to the differences between eras than a shift in the status quo, however. As a way of summarizing and recapping these events, let us review the important factors governing the pace and orientation of reform identified in Chapter 1 as a way to reach some more general conclusions about what transpired between 1885 and 1921.

The preferences of members

Member preferences for outcomes in areas related to appropriations politics changed during this period. First, the rising careerism of House members resulted in more members being concerned about the long-term consequences of their legislative actions. With more members intent upon staying in Congress for a number of terms, attention to constituency service that yielded primarily immediate, localized results had a lower priority. Thus, relatively less attention was paid to facilitating the flow of particularized, pork barrel benefits to constituents, and members were more receptive to ideas aimed at protecting the long-term health of the macroeconomy.

Preferences of members relevant to appropriations structure also changed in important ways on account of World War I and the parallel broadening of income tax incidence. The war and the income tax heightened constituency awareness of costs of government. The Republicans swept into office in the 66th and 67th Congresses truly were "low demand" overall, and that shift in spending preferences tipped the balance toward final enactment of legislative and executive appropriations reform.

While discussing member structural preferences we must finally keep in mind, however, that at no time during this period did structural preferences ever overwhelmingly favor recentralization. The size of the *final* votes approving the Accounting Act and the Budget and Accounting Act have frequently obscured how close the *intermediate* votes were that brought about legislative recentralization in 1919. For instance, the shift of just two votes would have kept committee recentralization off the House agenda at least for one Congress, and perhaps for decades. Thus, at the high watermark of centralization sentiment in the House, support for fragmentation remained substantial.

The nature of the budgetary problem

Unlike the budgetary world that facilitated the rapid movement toward decentralization between 1880 and 1885, the budgetary world after 1885 was one of increasing budgetary constraints. The problem of budgetary aggregation became increasingly prominent, and with the shift of budgetary problems came a shift in the rhetoric associated with budgetary structure. Thus, questions about maintaining or expanding benefits for particular constituents were rarely raised during the reform debates of the 1910s. Increasing budgetary scarcity made any major inclination toward further decentralization unthinkable, and finally made recentralization more likely.

The committee system

While the center of reform activity had been in the legislative committees before 1885, the center of activity shifted to the finance committees afterward. During the 1910s especially, efforts to reform the appropriations process centered in the Appropriations Committee, in keeping with that committee's historic interest in reducing spending.

The legislative committees were important after 1885 not because they fomented reform, but because there were so many people on the legislative committees who oversaw appropriations. Power in numbers made the legislative committees significant obstacles to reform. In the 66th Congress, when reconsolidation back into the Appropriations Committee was effected, over one-third of House members (147 of 435) were on such legislative committees.[28] They were also overwhelming opponents of re-

---

28 The growth in the number of people on the legislative committees with spending jurisdiction during this period was clearly not exogenous to appropriation reform politics. Consider three classes of committees: (1) the legislative committees that had received appropriations power by 1885, (2) the "power" committees (Rules, Ways and Means, and Appropriations), and (3) all of the other legislative com-

form (Table 5.1). With membership on the committees most receptive to consolidation – Rules, Ways and Means, and Appropriations – constituting only 14 percent of the House, consolidation proponents had to win over almost three-quarters of the rest of the House in order to build a majority reform coalition. The necessity for peace with the legislative committees after they lost the reform skirmish led to the appointment of legislative committee members to Appropriations in the 67th Congress without requiring these new members to give up their legislative committee assignments.

The leadership system

While leadership played a prominent role in reform politics before 1885, leadership's efforts to maintain control were rarely successful. After 1885, leadership still played a prominent role, but this time with much more success.

The most important descriptive difference in leadership activity after 1885 was in the amount of unilateral power that it could wield on the floor. This power, associated with the rise of strong party rule through

mittees that were in existence between the 49th Congress and the 1946 Legislative Reorganization Act. The total number of people on each set of committees during the 49th Congress (devolution), 66th Congress (reconsolidation), and 79th Congress (last Congress before LRA) are as follows:

	Number of seats		
	49th Cong.	66th Cong.	79th Cong.
Appropriating legislative committees	81	146	184
"Power" committees	33	60	61
All other legislative committees	198	254	316
Total	312	460	561
Size of House	325	435	435

The percent growth in the number of seats between these time points is as follows:

	49th–66th Cong. (%)	66th–79th Cong. (%)
Appropriating legislative committees	52.1	26.0
"Power" committees	81.8	1.7
All other legislative committees	28.3	24.4
Total	47.4	22.0
Growth in House size	33.8	0.0

the Speaker in the 1890s, helped to keep the floor clear of the endless structural wrangling that had characterized reform politics before 1885.

Yet, although the party leadership system was adept at keeping further fragmentation off the agenda after 1885, the fragmentary pulls of member electoral incentives made bringing consolidation back on the agenda a hazardous enterprise. Even with persistent deficit problems during the Taft administration, party leaders could never get legislative reconsolidation considered. During their eight years in control during the 1910s, Democratic leaders did not fare much better. They were unable to get major leadership factions, personified in the clashes between Fitzgerald and Sherley, to agree on a plan to advance in the first place. Only after dramatic membership turnover in the wake of a major management crisis could leadership navigate reform through the legislative shoals.

This is not to minimize the day-to-day effect that leaders had on the appropriations system during this time. As I argued in Chapter 4, party leaders were adept at altering the pattern of committee appointments to induce the use of more universalistic standards in the making of appropriations decisions. By bringing committee chairs into party councils, Speakers were able to achieve a certain level of spending coordination between programs. And by serving as intermediaries between Congress and the president, Speaker Cannon and Republican leaders in the Senate were able to help achieve a level of discipline in agency requests during the Taft administration that had never before been achieved. As long as party leaders could operate out of the legislative limelight, they could successfully work to effect spending control at the margin. Once they moved into the public eye in an attempt to bring about control, they found themselves in more direct conflict with the jurisdictionally and constituency-induced imperatives of legislative life.

The presidency

This period witnessed the rise of presidential involvement in the setting of national spending priorities. The president first asserted a level of informal control over appropriations during the Taft administration. The level of formal control would never be the same again after the passage of the Budget and Accounting Act.

Looking back three-quarters of a century, this rise seems almost inevitable, and in a sense it was. The events of the turn of the century, culminating in World War I, overtook a system that had been designed to service small, discrete, individual constituencies in an ad hoc fashion and provided a compelling argument that the policymaking system had to be transformed so that comprehensive policies of world war-making and national economic management could be addressed. Congressional debate of this period reveals that most members of Congress knew they could not *govern,* and that in a dangerous world that required swift, effective governmental action, executive discretion would have to be expanded.

Yet while the move toward executive agenda setting and discretion was seen as inevitable at the time, the way in which the transformation was made was also predetermined by how Congress was elected and organized. The electoral realities of legislative life made all House members keenly aware that they would have to find a way to maintain discretion over the particulars of appropriations. The desire to maintain control over budgetary particulars in an executive-led budgetary process also led to the creation of the General Accounting Office, which was to be independent of the president and watchful lest congressional legislative intentions be usurped in the executive branch.

The entire decade of the 1910s saw various congressional and party committees search for a suitable compromise that would convey to the president the right to set the agenda while maintaining congressional discretion in appropriations decisionmaking. By closely associating their visions of an executive budget with the parliamentary practice of enacting a government program, the Taft Commission set back the cause of executive budgets by at least five years. The task of Willoughby and Good at the end was to make the case that an executive budget could be revised downward, thus pleasing fiscal conservatives; and to make the case that any particular item in an executive budget could be changed in the House, thus reassuring all members that the supply of part of their political life's blood would still be in their own hands and not in the hands of the person residing in the White House.

Thus, the movement toward reconsolidation in 1919 and 1921 was a product of the unique constellation of variables defining American political life. Where there was early agreement about the existence of a problem, there was protracted consideration of what the solution should be, followed by a process of perilous coalition building that barely yielded legislative reform. Party structures that still had a spark of life in them were unable to impose their structural wills. The political divide separating Congress and the president left efforts toward an executive budget tentative at their boldest moments: Congress accepted an agenda setter, but a weak one at that, and certainly not a *monopoly* agenda setter. And the power and prerogatives of committees remained the central reality (and obstacle to overcome) in the crafting of budget reform. If the immediate post-World War I era represented the height of the conviction that governing structures should be centralized, rational, and streamlined, can there be any wonder that efforts since 1921 to rationalize legislative budgeting have been so indeterminate?

PART III

Conclusion

6

Budget reform then and now

The story of the development of the budgetary process in the House between the Civil War and World War I is in many ways a stripped-down version of the story of the development of the budgetary process in the House, and in Congress more generally, since 1921. The names and contexts have changed, but the basic processes and themes of reform have remained quite similar over the years. In the last few pages here, I want to revisit the basic theoretical points I outlined at the end of Chapter 1, examine how they expose certain themes in the development of budget reform politics between 1865 and 1921, and, finally, suggest ways that the events of this period can be used to elucidate reform politics during the past two generations.

One general point needs to be reiterated, however, before moving on to conclusions about specific themes of reform politics. That point is this: In order to understand the congressional budgetary system and the politics of its reform, one must begin with a clear definition of what constitutes this system. The analysis in the preceding chapters reinforces the need to define the budgetary system in terms of the relationships among the four major sets of actors that are involved in determining the dynamics of congressional politics – the rank-and-file, party leaders, committee members, and presidents. The major stumbling block in understanding and explaining reform politics over time has been that scholars, journalists, and even members of Congress have focused their attention on only the most visible parts of the budgetary system, mainly the committee system. Failure to seriously appreciate the adaptive relationships among the rank-and-file, leaders, committees, and presidents has caused reform participants and observers to oversell the potential consequences of reform, as did Frederick Cleveland when he promised that passage of an executive budget would reduce appropriations by one-third, and then to be perplexed when outcomes are not as anticipated, as has happened in the aftermath of the 1974 budget act.

By continually keeping in mind that the budgetary process is defined by a *system* of relationships, we can more easily anticipate the consequences of reform. We can assume that a change in any part of the system will elicit changes everywhere else. So long as we understand the goals motivating the participants in the system, we can predict beforehand the direction that subsequent spending politics and adaptations on the parts of others will take. For example, a reform of the committee system, as in 1885, 1919, or 1974, does not change the fact that rank-and-file MCs must still get reelected in parochial constituencies, that the committees still want as much power as possible, that leaders continue to use their plenary powers to pursue independent policy courses, and that presidents strive to institute spending priorities frequently at odds with many in Congress. Thus, while a new committee system might be able to alter outcomes independently in the short term, others in the budgetary system will instantly begin probing ways to overcome the new barriers imposed by the new system or to utilize its opportunities.

It must finally be said that the center of gravity that defines the most significant pairs of interactions in the budgetary system has obviously shifted over time. In the cases examined in most of this study, for instance, the president was clearly less important in determining the fate of the budgetary process than were party leaders and committee members. Since 1921 the significance of party leaders has declined while the importance of the president has increased. It is always dangerous to make predictions in political science, but it does seem clear that the future will see a further strengthening of the significance of the president in budget reform politics (witness the reconciliation revolution in 1981 and Gramm-Rudman-Hollings in 1985) while that of party leadership may or may not continue to wane.

STRUCTURE AND SUBSTANCE

The driving force behind all of the reform politics we have seen has been substance. How does the status quo bias results? How will the proposed plan change outcomes? Between 1865 and 1921 the link between structure and substance was more obvious in certain circles than in others: Retrenchers were continually adamant about the need to centralize, while zealous supporters of regional interests were also adamant about decentralization. But, even among progressive reformers at the turn of the century, who articulated an ideology that equated proper structure with justice, the urgency for reform became more pronounced once they could also justify it as a way to cut federal spending and end chronic deficits.

Although substantive concerns were almost always lurking around the corner whenever reform battles were waged, there was not always a *consistent* relationship between the type of outcomes desired and the type of structure demanded. That is, although retrenchers *usually* agitated for centralization and spenders *usually* pushed for decentralization, this relationship did not hold under all circumstances. For instance, spending control leaders were the ones who supported the split up of the Ways and Means Committee in 1865. Many supporters of enhanced internal improvements, although favoring divesting oversight of the rivers and harbors bill from the Appropriations Committee in the 1870s and 1880s, also opposed the further distribution of the rivers and harbors omnibus into regional committees.

Thus, while there was a general relationship between the desire for spending expansion and the desire for decentralization, whether the general relationship held in any specific instance was still contingent upon the strategic situation. "Retrenching decentralization" occasionally emerged under conditions of system overload and when strengthening or enlarging existing structures would have created an unwanted asymmetry of power in the House. "Expansionary centralization" was occasionally favored when it was clear that further fragmentation would jeopardize the ability of spending coalitions to maintain their logrolling arrangements and agreements on the equitable distribution of federal projects.

Leaving aside the few instances of retrenching fragmentation and expansionary centralization, we are still left with a question about the relationship between preferred outcomes and structures: Why would MCs go through the trouble of changing structure if they already have the majority to alter outputs anyway? Devolution occurred in 1885 at the end of a decade in which demands for expanded government services gradually grew more insistent; reform during 1919–21 occurred in the midst of, not preceding, planning to engage in rapid retrenchment; more recently, Gramm-Rudman-Hollings was enacted even as relevant appropriations actors appeared to have previously agreed with its substance and were moving in that general direction.[1] Why, then, bother with structural reform?

1 The story of the search for a deficit reduction plan in 1985 was one of a move from one simple solution to another. The first simple solution involved some sort of "spending freeze" or "pay as you go plan." Eventually solutions emerged that revolved around exempting Social Security and the "social safety net" (to please the Democratic House) and defense (to please the Republican Senate and President Reagan), and proceeding to cut remaining spending across the board over a period of years. Although various proposed compromises varied in details (and the Gramm-Rudman-Hollings plan allows for military cuts), this was the neighborhood in which negotiations proceeded toward the end of the year. The list of citations to articles

Part of the answer lies in the necessity to guard against reneging: Structural change can provide enforcement mechanisms that help to yield the desired results. Another part of the answer lies in the persistence of structure: Because structural arrangements have been even more stable than substantive agreements over time, a policy majority knows that it has a good chance of locking-in its own policy agreements well into the future. But it should also be remembered that support for structural change provides MCs with the opportunity to take a position on the type of spending that the proposed change is said to represent. At any time, reorienting spending outcomes requires thousands of small decisions over a long period of time made in the executive branch, in committees, and on the floor in order to effect the desired outcome. Support for structural reform, at the same time that outcomes are in fact already changing, gives MCs the opportunity to have one significant action to point to that demonstrates decisively which side of the substantive issue they are on.[2]

These observations about the relationship between structure and substance suggest the two-pronged significance of structural change – as a tool and as a symbol. As a tool, structural change does what its supporters and detractors claim it does: It changes outcomes independently of other factors. But structural arrangements are useful to members more than just because certain arrangements may induce particular outcomes – structural change must also be appreciated for the symbol it frequently is. In both 1865 and 1919–1921, reforms that were interpreted as bringing control to congressional action served as symbols that Congress had realized the difficulties recently encountered in managing previous war efforts. Between 1877 and 1885, the sequence of events loosening the

in the *Congressional Quarterly Weekly Report* that deal with deficit reduction negotiations is simply too long to give here – almost every issue of the year had at least one story about the negotiations.

2 Along the lines of noting the symbolic significance of reform, a historical phenomenon that I term "magic numbers" bears identification. "Magic numbers" are very large budgetary numbers, usually (but not always) integer powers of ten, that draw journalistic, public, and political attention. The closer Congress is to facing a magic number (e.g., a billion-dollar Congress, a $100 million annual budget, a trillion-dollar budget, a trillion-dollar national debt), the more likely reform will be demanded. Thus, the "billion-dollar Congress" was attacked by Democrats in the 1890s, but to no avail. Billion-dollar budgets after the turn of the century, however, helped to prompt people to begin thinking about budget reform. Gramm-Rudman-Hollings was prompted by the coincidence of the first $2 trillion national debt with the first $1 trillion budget. This pattern of coincidences suggests that one could predict the recurrence of reform agitation by predicting when the next "magic number" would appear. For instance, if the 1986 budget is approximately $1 trillion and if spending were to grow at a rate of 6% over the next several years, then using the "rule of 72" we can estimate that the $2 trillion budget would appear twelve years later, in 1998, prompting displeasure with the state of Congress's budgetary apparatus at that time.

HAC's grip over appropriations decisions symbolized the willingness of Congress to end a period of governmental retrenchment and preoccupation with the South and to switch to an active role in the rapid expansion of the country's economy. In more recent years, structural change has served as a symbol that newly won entitlements to the underclass would be maintained into the future (through creating off-budget entitlement spending in the 1960s), that Congress was "resurgent" against the imperial presidency (1974), and that it was serious about efforts to eliminate the deficit (1985).

ELECTORAL GOALS AND STRUCTURAL REFORM

Although the relationship between substantive and structural preferences during the period 1865 to 1921 was contingent upon the strategic situation, a great deal of the time the situation was such that their relationship was easy to discern. Most of the time MCs were seen moving about the House floor trying to alter budgetary structure in the hopes that the end result would be beneficial to their constituents. Pressures to decentralize were usually strong and based on a desire to provide benefits to constituents. Centralization preferences were usually weak, prevailing only at unusual political moments in the nation's history. At all times, however, centralization preferences were most strongly expressed by those who came from areas of the country that had the least to gain from expanded federal spending.

The imprint of the electoral connection on structural politics is easily seen in the general pattern of structural change. It had already begun to have its effects before 1865. By keeping the pension rate-setting process entirely away from the Appropriations Committee from the earliest days of the Republic, the House was exhibiting an incipient form of modern-day entitlement legislation in order to shield popular spending from continual centralized review. True, the Appropriations Committee did oversee the pensions bill that provided for the funds out of which pension benefits were paid, but that oversight was closely akin to the present practice of funding food stamps through annual appropriations bills while keeping entitlement criteria under the purview of the agriculture committees.

Later, after the Civil War, two other federal spending programs that were clearly constituency-oriented, internal improvements and agriculture, were the next to escape HAC oversight. In the third successful move to grant spending programs greater autonomy in 1885, the collection of bills involved was quite different in substance than those that had been affected previously. Except for the post office, these latter bills were generally less useful for servicing particularistic constituency needs than had been the earlier collection of programs.

Although the attempts by the House to control federal spending in the decade after 1865 and in the decade before 1921 have often been explained in terms of simple crisis management, the effects of the electoral connection were also evident in determining how these episodes played out, especially in the case of 1921. The series of crushing defeats suffered by Democrats at all levels of the ballot in 1918 and 1920 can in part be explained as a judgment about Democratic management of the recent war effort (Schlesinger 1971, III:2245–70, 2349–85). Not only was day-to-day management a precarious activity, but the end of the war brought hints of an expanded governmental role that many Americans were unprepared to accept. Before the war, progressives had warned of the dire consequences of running the government according to antiquated methods. Although the incumbent Democratic president was a well-known progressive, management of the government was not an issue that in the end occupied much of Wilson's time; the four Democratic Congresses preceding the 1918 election had continually turned back efforts at progressive reform of the government's business methods. Thus, Republicans could campaign in 1918 and 1920 on a promise to institute governmental reform and expect a good portion of the electorate to be receptive to the message.

Added to this popular acceptance of progressive government management ideology was the palpable change in the direct burden imposed upon citizens and businesses by government during the 1910s. The institution and expansion of the income tax had the predicted effect of exciting more people, especially business leaders, into a concern about what government did with their tax dollars. One consequence of this increased popular concern was the rapid retrenchment of real (inflation-controlled) spending following the war (U.S. Census Bureau 1975, series Y457–463, E135). The rise of business-based agitation for budget reform must have been a key reason why Republicans moved so quickly to enact budget reform after the 1918 election.[3]

The consequences of the electoral connection on budgetary structure continue to be substantial to this day. The secular fragmentation of congressional structure that has been experienced since World War I has had a tremendous effect on the budgetary policy of this century. Although the Ways and Means and Appropriations committees, supported by conservative House leadership, held a tight rein over budgetary politics from

3 It is significant that the first membership referendum that the Chamber of Commerce ever held concerned executive budget reform. The results of the referendum were a central component of Chamber lobbying on the issue (Chamber of Commerce of the United States of America, 1912).

1921 until the 1960s, electoral politics intruded over time to chip away at that control. Thus, as the more expansionary and visionary promises ignited by the New Deal were continually thwarted in the committees of Congress, and as more liberals were elected to the House, the authority of these two control committees was severely challenged.[4] Entitlement, back-door, and off-budget spending became more common during the 1960s, as more and more legislators and the constituents who supported them tried to find ways to circumvent the oversight of these two control committees.

The enactment of a putatively centralizing budget reform in 1974 was, like other centralizing reforms of the century, largely a product of the unusual political climate of the times. Both the popular weakness and the strength of Richard Nixon prodded Congress along the ultimate path of reform. Nixon's strength in unilaterally impounding appropriations and his ability to pin the blame on the Democratic Congress for deficits gave MCs an incentive to spend time finding a way to counter Nixon on the technical issue of impoundments and on the more political issue of who was to blame for deficits. Nixon's weakness on account of Watergate generated momentum for the coalition-building process that resulted in the Budget Act's final passage, and also allowed Congress temporarily to skirt taking their full share of the blame.

But even the 1974 Budget Act was not immune from the more immediate effects of electorally induced fragmentation. Although the Budget Act did restrict future off-budget spending mechanisms, it did nothing to alter the increasingly fragmented committee system, other than to add another layer on top of it through the creation of the Budget committees. Until reconciliation emerged in 1981 as a potent process, the power granted under the act to the Budget committees was essentially hortatory. And, as some have argued, it may have actually added to fragmentary tendencies, by relieving the Ways and Means and Appropriations committees of the necessity to be guardians of the purse (Schick 1980, 441–481). The act succeeded in making "claimants" out of Appropriations and Ways and Means and increased their concern with constituency reactions to their decisions.

Given the weakness of political parties, the increasing significance of political action committees (PACs) in funding political campaigns, and the rise of "entrepreneurial" legislators and candidates, the ability of Congress to enact structural reforms that attempt to counter the fragmentary pull of the electoral process will probably diminish even more.

---

4 Fenno (1966) not surprisingly anticipated these sanctions on the Appropriations Committee's authority by arguing that it was unclear how long the HAC could retain its power if it continued to seriously challenge the median position of the House.

The reform pushed by Alice Rivlin, the first director of the Congressional Budget Office, to abolish the appropriations role of the legislative committees (who still approve dollar amounts in authorizing legislation) seems, therefore, quixotic (Rivlin 1986; Aaron 1987). If anything is to be abolished, the pull of the decentralized electoral process would seem to compel the abolition of the Appropriations Committee and a return to the regime of 1885. Such a turn is unlikely to happen, given the potent symbolism of such a move, but it is also clear that legislators still have few incentives to actively pursue a decrease of each individual's control over small parts of the budgetary pie, and thus reforms such as Rivlin's will no doubt continue to die on the vine.

The increased polarization of spending politics, fueled by continued politics of retrenchment that are exacerbated by the working of the Gramm-Rudman-Hollings process, make it unlikely that MCs will give up what power they have to protect spending programs dear to them, as those programs continue to come under attack. The continued public dissatisfaction with budget deficits also makes it unlikely that Congress will move boldly to loosen what few control mechanisms exist in the House already. The bottom line, then, predicts that stalemate should occur if structural change is seriously floated in the near future. The only possibility for electorally induced structural change would seem to be the appearance of a true fiscal crisis. But, since the recent decade has seen a secular rise in the severity of fiscal crises tolerable to (or ignored by) the political system, it is frightening to contemplate a fiscal crisis serious enough to prompt a cohesion of public opinion on the matter that in turn spurs on congressional action on budget reform.[5]

THE BUDGETARY PROBLEM AND BUDGET REFORM

Although the politics of budget reform has been driven by substantive issues and molded by the realities of electoral politics, there is a real sense in which much debate and behavior surrounding reform has been in response to the budgetary problems facing MCs over time. Substantive biases and electoral exigencies are the lenses through which MCs, when faced with the necessity of resolving budgetary problems, conclude what the proper resolution to those problems is. Recall from earlier discussion that what I call *the* budgetary problem is really one of balancing distributional and aggregational imperatives. One way of interpreting the decades of reform politics between 1865 and 1921, indeed, one way of

---

5 Reaction to the "Black Monday" crash of 1987 reinforces this point. While it prompted a new round of negotiations among budgetary principals, its final results offered no radical departures from the status quo, either substantively or structurally.

interpreting all reform politics since 1921, is that the politics represented the dynamic resolution of this tension between distribution and aggregation.

Most of the time the distributional problem is the one most closely linked to electoral politics. Given this fact, it is not surprising that most reform activity between 1865 and 1921 involved MCs trying to find ways to meet the distributional imperative. The decentralization in the 1870s and 1880s is easily interpreted in terms of the desire to facilitate an equitable distribution of federal largess among regions and economic segments of society. The difficulty encountered in reforming the regime of 1885 also speaks to the importance placed on using the appropriations process to take care of distributional problems before aggregational ones.

The higher priority placed on solving distributional imperatives was demonstrated during the two decades in which the aggregational problem became very acute, the 1900s and 1910s, and in which the House lurched its way toward recentralization. The chronic nature of the deficits encountered at the turn of the century was widely conceded in the House. Yet, Congress spent the first decade of the century trying to find ways to solve the aggregational problem that protected specific appropriations bills from central oversight. First, they granted reporting power to the president and Treasury secretary as a way to curb deficits. When this proved unsuccessful, Congress authorized the creation of the Taft Commission. When the Taft Commission recommended that Congress pay less attention to distribution and more attention to the aggregational consequences of their actions through the creation of an executive budget, the commission was abolished. Study committees of the Democratic caucus tried to fashion some sort of centralized reform, only to fail twice before giving up the enterprise altogether.

Once the Republicans regained control of the House in 1919, reform activity was spurred on largely because the aggregational problems had risen dramatically on account of the war, yet the process of coming to grips with aggregation was still precarious. Although passage of what became known as the Budget and Accounting Act was pretty much assured, abolition of the committee components of the regime of 1885 was not. On the way to building the coalition necessary to pass the rules reform that effected committee recentralization in the House, reform leaders made concessions to distributional concerns: They included members from the legislative committees on the Select Budget Committee and they hinted about, though did not promise, the representation of legislative committees on the newly expanded Appropriations Committee. Even with these concessions, committee recentralization almost never got to the House floor, as the rule to consider the reform passed by a margin of two votes.

Conclusion

Considering what I have already concluded about the actual relation-ship between structure and outcomes, that the direct relationship is in fact tenuous and easily overcome by changes in the general budgetary environment, one might conclude that structure really does not affect the budgetary problem all that much. Yet, while structure is usually not determinative, it is still significant on the margin to predispose the res-olution of conflicts and crises one way or the other. What we see in the history of budget reform between 1865 and 1921 is that even in this less complicated time, before the rise of the activist state, finding ways of assuring that the aggregational problem was attended to was difficult indeed. If it was difficult then, why should we expect any different now?

Since 1921 the aggregate consequences of federal spending have in-creased in significance by several orders of magnitude. The federal budget simply looms much larger in the macroeconomic order of things. But the distributional consequences have grown by leaps and bounds, as well. Thus, the conflict between distribution and aggregation has gotten even more intense over the years, making it even more difficult to address aggregational crises quickly and effectively. The difficulty in resolving this tension has led to increased support for deux ex machina solutions, such as balanced budget constitutional amendments and item vetoes for the president. It is unlikely that such solutions would accomplish the goals of their supporters in the end, in large part because their supporters vastly underestimate the ingrained deference this nation's polity gives to disparate interests, especially organized disparate interests. Thus, it is likely that even if these deux ex machina solutions ever do prevail, the tensions between distribution and aggregation will continue to daunt legislators and impede efforts to reform budgeting.

The problem with finding a way to successfully resolve the tension between distribution and aggregation rests not in the epiphenomenal structures of government, of which budgetary structure is just one among many, but in the deeply rooted political culture of which it is a part. If we did not have our ideological roots in Locke, it would be easier to establish the legitimacy of aggregational considerations. If we had strong political parties, the trade-offs that have to be made between distribution and aggregation might be easier to effect. If we had a long tradition of a Westminster-style parliamentary system, the trade-offs would be easier to institute. But, we have none of these things. What we do have is a deeply rooted predisposition toward decentralization and fragmentation that, while ideologically appealing and practically useful in the days of the Wild West, clashes head-on with economic realities in the days of positive government.

To summarize, the difficulties we have seen in recent years in addressing questions of macrolevel fiscal policy and in resisting the demands of organized interests in budgetary policy are a continuation of difficulties that are at least a century old. That being the case, it is unlikely that a successful remedy to the distribution-aggregation tension will ever be found, short of a dramatic reorientation of national ideology and fundamental governmental structure.

BUDGET REFORM AND THE WHOLE HOUSE

In any age, the actual outcome of reform battles is deeply influenced by the fact that those battles take place in a setting characterized by entrenched institutional interests. Decisions are made about structure in a situation where the Rawlsian veil of ignorance has been ripped asunder. The 1865–1921 era was no exception. At every turn, the preferences and behaviors of rank-and-file MCs on structural questions were significantly affected by the fact that there was already a set of individuals in the House who benefited from the status quo, and who could marshal a significant level of institutional resources to prosecute the defense of that status quo. But these individuals – party leaders and committee members – were not only reactive toward threats to their institutional power. They were also frequently positive actors, leading fights to entrench, or occasionally overthrow, the status quo.

Of the two major institutional subsystems in the House, the committee system was the one that saw more budget reform action during this period. Most of the individual episodes of reform explored here involved questions of committee jurisdiction, while the next largest group of episodes involved questions of committee prerogatives on the floor. The general behavior during these committee skirmishes was pretty much as we expected: All committees desired more power, and the more particular the interest represented on the committee, the more likely its members favored fragmentation.

The zealousness of committee members in asserting a wide scope for their own committees appeared to be a product of committee service itself. That is, whatever predisposition toward a committee that an MC might have had before being appointed to it was enhanced by actual committee service. This committee zeal presented itself in two ways. First, the zeal translated into a willingness to assume active leadership in reform battles. From John Reagan's fight to give the Commerce Committee sole prerogative over internal improvements to James Good's leadership in the reforms of 1919–1921, reform efforts generally originated in the committees.

Second, this zeal subsequently prodded committee members to push for reform even when the institutional odds were against them. In those cases when committee members seemed willing to challenge institutional power centers – other committees and leadership itself – the anticipated gains that the insurgent committee members sought consisted not only of the substantive benefits that would accrue in the future, but also of the benefits that would accrue through using the structural fight itself for symbolic or electoral gain.

The fights about oversight of water projects in the 1870s and 1880s are the best example of this. In these instances, what I called "disloyalty costs" in Chapter 1 were exceeded by anticipated benefits that could be gained by leading the challenge against the status quo. These anticipated benefits included a perceived probability that victory would ensue (usually inflated) and the ability to use the challenge to take positions before attentive constituents. It is inconceivable that these anticipated benefits would have exceeded anticipated disloyalty costs for anybody other than members of interested committees.

Party leaders were not as active during this period in molding reform politics, but they were still forces to contend with. Except for three major instances – the creation of the HAC, the creation of the Rivers and Harbors Committee, and the devolution of 1885 – leadership was often irrelevant in initiating reform activity in the latter part of the nineteenth century. Reform originated in the committees, and the few times that the Speaker-controlled Rules Committee tried to tighten spending control, the committee not only lost the battle, but had to retreat even further. With the devolution of 1885, leadership began to take a more successfully active role in guiding reform. But notice here that the leadership role in 1885 was more one of strategic followership, rather than of the unilateral imposition of their own preferences. Once czar rule took hold, Speakers molded reform behavior in the breech, by keeping unwanted reform proposals off the House agenda all together. Party leadership played an active role during the decade leading up to the 1919–1921 reforms, but by then czar rule had been overthrown, and the leadership role was that of the broker, not that of the despot.

Although party leaders experienced mixed success in taking the initiative on reform proposals, they were more successful in shaping the outcomes of the proposals that reached the House floor from sources other than leadership. This ability to influence the final outcome was crucial when leadership faced a long string of committee insurgencies in the 1870s and 1880s. All throughout this period, majority party leaders could carry a majority of their followers with them in the final votes on reform questions, sometimes winning on the outcome.

This particular pattern of committee insurgency and leadership counterattack led to an interesting dynamic throughout the reform battles preceding and through 1880. In each case, committee insurgency arose during a period of Democratic control of the House, and was led by a

Democratic committee leader. But in every case of committee insurgency, Democratic leadership opposed the committee position. Thus, when the Democratic committee insurgents were successful in changing structure to their liking during the 1870s and 1880s, it was because they were able to generate a level of antileadership voting that could win a bare majority of the whole chamber when joined with votes from Republicans who had little interest in upholding the position of majority party leadership.

The patterns describing leadership and committee influence in structural reform matters have continued and somewhat intensified since 1921. One would be hard pressed to identify a reform in budgeting since 1921 that originated solely from within party leadership ranks in either House of Congress. Party leaders have served as brokers in those cases where reform was actively considered. One exception was 1983 and 1984 in the House, when a leadership-sanctioned task force of the Rules Committee thoroughly considered reforming the Congressional Budget and Impoundment Control Act (CBICA). But, the activity of even this task force was consensus building, and its final proposals simply ratified modifications to the 1974 act's provisions that had already evolved informally. The few marginal innovations that the task force recommended were never seriously considered on their own merits but were finally tacked onto the Gramm-Rudman-Hollings resolution as a rider.

The deference afforded committees, on the other hand, has grown over the decades. Just as the independent influence of party leadership has waned as the significance of parties in the electorate has waned, so too has the independent influence of committees (and now subcommittees) waxed as MCs have been driven to seek independent power bases in the House from which to operate. The most telling sign of the independent influence of committees is the fact that since 1921, no reform of the budgetary process has come close to challenging the existing committee system head on to produce a clearly zero-sum redistribution of committee powers.[6] The Joint Budget Committee created in the 1946 Legislative Reorganization Act (LRA) was simply a "committee of the whole" consisting of all members of the House and Senate Appropriations Committees, the Ways and Means Committee, and the Finance Committee. When the HAC grew out of touch with the liberal Democratic rank-and-

6 The 1946 Legislative Reorganization Act did challenge the *general* congressional committee system head on, but this fact does not negate my assertion here. First, alterations in committee jurisdictions in 1946 were accompanied by granting attractive compensation to those who lost committee leadership positions when the number of committees was drastically reduced (Ripley 1969). Second, and more important, the *budgetary* aspects of the 1946 LRA specifically skirted the issue of spending jurisdictions in the creation of the Joint Budget Committee, which simply consisted of all members of the two appropriations and taxing committees in the two chambers (Ippolito 1978, 97).

file during the 1950s and 1960s, the response was not to challenge the committee directly, but gradually to institute more entitlement and back-door spending. And, the committee aspects of the 1974 CBICA, the creation of the Senate and House Budget committees, simply added another layer on top of the existing committee structure.

Ever since the division of the Ways and Means Committee in 1865, the House has refused to return all real budgetary authority to one committee. The reasons are all too obvious, and they range from the usefulness of independent committees in creating election-relevant benefits to the fact that individual MCs, being the ultimate political animals, simply prefer more power for themselves rather than less. As calls become more insistent for greater centralized control over fiscal policy (leaving aside for the moment the question of whether such centralized controls would actually get the centralizers what they want), it is unlikely that the congressional committee system will be changed willingly by its occupants. Thus, for controllers everywhere, the place on which to focus attention is the presidency.

THE PRESIDENCY AND CONGRESSIONAL BUDGET REFORM

Along with the development of Congress as a complex institution, the period 1865–1921 also saw the rise of the presidency as an independently powerful national political entity. All of the reform events up to 1885 referenced the presidency only indirectly, if at all. The continued maintenance of the regime of 1885 was in part sustained out of a desire to overcome presidential resistance to particularistic spending, but even this relationship between congressional budgetary structure and the presidency was tenuous at best. Helped by the rise of progressive ideology, and by the object lesson of weak tools for executive leadership during World War I, by the end of this period the presidency loomed almost as large as other factors – the economy, party leaders, committees, constituents – in determining the variations of reform politics.

The secondary role played by the president in pre-1900 budget reform politics was in keeping with the ascendancy of Congress in setting national spending priorities. Although the presidency was a relatively weak institution compared to Congress, the president still represented a potential threat in the spending priority-setting game through the veto. Thus, to the extent that the president entered into reform calculations, it was usually as a nuisance that reform was designed to overcome. Democrats especially regarded the usually Republican executive establishment as a collection of saboteurs, intent upon destroying all initiatives passed by Democratic Congresses of the 1870s and 1880s. Thus, the decentralizations of this period can be thought of not only as cases of simple power grabs within the institution of Congress itself, but as attempts by the most high-demand members of Congress to guard spending against the designs of the Republican executive branch and presidents.

By the end of our story, the increasing role of the United States in international affairs, the growth in the executive branch, and the ascendancy of progressive ideology all served to bring the president more centrally into the budgetary picture. But the president was brought fully into the picture slowly. The Republican Houses from 1900 to 1910 were willing to work closely with Republican presidents to solve ongoing deficit problems. Under these relatively benign partisan circumstances, reliance on the president and Treasury secretary to report on budgetary problems, to recommend remedies, and to enforce constraints on overspending was an easy way out of perplexing congressional problems. Yet, before the war marked the clear beginning of the era of presidentially led governing, even Republican MCs were unwilling to consider the next step of granting the president *formal* budgetary agenda-setting authority. It took a national fiscal crisis to convince MCs that the time was ripe for relying even more heavily on the president to guide the nation in budgetary decisions. But, even here, the seeds for ongoing clashes were sown as Congress retained for itself control over the auditing and investigating of federal spending and as Congress refused to consider any reform options that placed the president in the role of anything beyond (non-monopoly) agenda setter.

The continuation of the trend begun during the 1910s, by which more and more budgetary power has gravitated to the presidency, has been one of the more obvious developments in the saga of the relationship between the two political branches of the federal government. Members of Congress, trying to satisfy the many competing demands of reelection, fiscal responsibility, and institutional power, have found the balancing act all too overwhelming and have continually turned over more budgetary responsibility to the president (see Sundquist 1981).

The one major exception, of course, was the events of 1974, when Congress passed the CBICA. One of the many reported, often contradictory, goals of this reform was to create a rationalized budgetary process (formalized by a series of timetables, resolutions, and budget committees) and enhance budgetary analytic capacity (formalized by the creation of the Congressional Budget Office) in order to restore congressional control over the purse strings that had been lost over the past half century.

Yet even the passage of this landmark reform betrayed the dire straits in which Congress as an institution found itself. First, passage only came close to the low point of the modern presidency; the passage of the CBICA and the other major contemporary reform (the War Powers Resolution) was in many ways the political equivalent of kicking someone who is down. Second, the only way in which the reform performed anywhere close to expectations (as varied as those expectations were) was through a constant appeal to "support the process" when the results were substantively insupportable (Schick 1980, 365–377). Eventually, congressional goodwill ran out, and the results under the new process were viewed as being as illegitimate as those produced by the old. Third, any semblance of "congressional control" was vastly overwhelmed once a popular president returned to office. The Reagan budgetary blitzkrieg of 1981 had to be deeply troubling to those who had hoped that the 1974 reform had found a way to make Congress "fast on its 1070 feet" in doing battle with presidential goals.

To many, taking a glance at congressional budgetary reform politics of a century ago is just another lesson in why the secular accretion of presidential budgetary power has been a positive development. Before the rise of a strong presidency that could realistically and consistently challenge congressional spending priorities, the story was generally one of fragmentation and particularism. Congress had a hard time centralizing its own process during the 1910s, and finally turned to the president for a good deal of the structural remedy. The same story can be seen repeating itself in the present: The continuing decentralization and fragmentation of Congress since 1921 has made it even slower on its 1070 feet. Efforts to reach the consensus (in Congress) goal of balancing the federal budget have resembled Keystone Kop routines. And with the passage of Gramm-Rudman-Hollings, Congress has proven once again unable to take positive action on its own to meet problems that all agree are pressing.

There is little in current events to suggest that the long-term ascendancy of presidential budgetary power will abate. Recent court decisions barring interbranch creativity in fashioning cooperative budgetary arrangements (e.g., striking down the legislative veto) will force Congress in the future to choose one of two roads: grant the president more power or take more power to itself. Because the social forces instigating the rise of the powerful presidency at the turn of the century are here for good, the ascendancy of the presidency appears to be here for good, as well. This will bode well for those who are preoccupied with the aggregate consequences of federal spending. This will not necessarily bode well for those who care about the subaggregates and how that spending is distributed.[7]

7 Of course, to those who believe that the presidency is the natural repository of concern about aggregates over distribution, the behavior of Ronald Reagan must be distressing. In dealing with Congress in attempts to reduce budget deficits in the 1980s, President Reagan also arguably showed a tendency to place the distributional problem over the aggregational, at least to the extent that he opposed deficit re-

CONCLUSION: BUDGET REFORM THEN AND NOW

Over the years Congress has found itself continually re-creating its own budgetary apparatus. The sources of that renewal have been many, the pace at which renewal has moved forward has varied, and the lasting effects of particular reforms have been multitudinous. Because the congressional budgetary apparatus does not stand as an impartial arbiter, unchanged by the unfolding of history, but is itself a product of the political conflicts of various ages, it is not surprising that members of Congress have periodically taken great interest in the way that budgeting is done and that political capital has been expended to change the order of things.

The story of budget reform in the House between 1865 and 1921 helps to demonstrate that modern battles over budgetary structure are not rooted entirely in the state of the world as it currently exists. Members of Congress care about budgetary structure because of electoral, policy, and institutional concerns that substantially transcend the idiosyncracies of politics of any given historical moment. A century ago questions of budgetary structure were always addressed with one eye clearly fixed on spending consequences. The budgetary environment over the past century has surely become more complex, the president has taken a more preemptory role in budgeting, and the federal budget is more an integral part of a large, complex, industrial economy. Yet, the budgetary process is still central to members of Congress in achieving whatever goals they might have, and promises a continued history of reform in which the new challenges that face members of Congress will be forced through filters that have remained surprisingly unchanged over the past century.

duction if it meant retrenching his favorite particular spending program, national defense.

235

Appendix: *summary of budget reform attempts in the House, 1865–1921*

As far as can be ascertained, the following list of cases is exhaustive of all reform attempts that reached the House floor between 1865 and 1921 (indeed, several never made it as far as the floor). The cases were derived by thoroughly examining the subject and bill indexes of the House *Journal*, *Congressional Globe*, and *Congressional Record* for each Congress in the time period, as well as the *New York Times Index* for each year and the secondary congressional historical literature.

38th Congress, 1863–65

House Appropriations Committee formed.

43rd Congress, 1873–75

William Wheeler attempts to bring the Army Asylum on-budget (unsuccessful).

44th Congress, 1875–77

First passage of the Holman Rule.

45th Congress, 1877–79

Commerce Committee successfully asserts dominance over rivers and harbors appropriations for the first time.
Railways and Canals Committee challenges the right of the Commerce Committee to report rivers and harbors appropriations.

Appendix

46th Congress, 1879–1881

Rules Committee proposes two rules: requiring three-fourths majority to pass spending bills under a suspension of the rules and granting the HAC jurisdiction over rivers and harbors appropriations (both unsuccessful).

Commerce Committee's exclusive jurisdiction over rivers and harbors legislation is written into the House rules.

Agriculture Committee wrests control of Agriculture Department appropriation from the HAC.

Decentralization of a number of appropriations items is attempted – public buildings, military affairs, patent office, Mississippi River (all unsuccessful).

Railways and Canals Committee challenges Commerce Committee for control over the rivers and harbors appropriations bill (unsuccessful).

Mississippi River Committee challenges the Commerce Committee for control over spending on the improvement on the Mississippi River (unsuccessful).

47th Congress, 1881–83

Mississippi River Committee challenges the Commerce Committee for control over spending on the improvement of the Mississippi River (unsuccessful).

48th Congress, 1883–85

Rivers and Harbors Committee created.

Mississippi River Committee challenges the Commerce Committee for control over spending on the improvement of the Mississippi River (unsuccessful).

49th Congress, 1885–87

The HAC is stripped of most of its jurisdiction over appropriations and the following committees given the power to report appropriations directly to the floor: Military Affairs, Naval Affairs, Indian Affairs, Foreign Affairs, and Post Office.

Bills begin appearing regularly proposing line item veto and the restoration of the HAC's power. Judiciary Committee unfavorably reports line item veto constitutional amendment.

Budget reform attempts in the House, 1865–1921

51st Congress, 1889–1891

Reed Rules passed.
John Bynum attempts to change House rules to tie pensions increases to
tax increases (unsuccessful).

58th Congress, 1903–05

Congress prohibits planned agency deficiencies (successful).

59th Congress, 1905–07

Congress strengthens prohibition enacted in 58th Congress and author-
izes Treasury secretary to allocate agency funds in monthly
installments.

60th Congress, 1907–09

Congress directs the secretary of the Treasury to estimate revenues for
the upcoming year and to make suggestions for retrenchment if a deficit
is indicated.

61st Congress, 1909–11

The Commission on Economy and Efficiency (Taft Commission) is provided for in the sundry civil appropriations bill.

62nd Congress, 1911–13

Holman Rule reinstated.
House refuses to fund the Taft Commission any further.
Taft submits the first "executive budget."

63rd Congress, 1913–15

Creation of a budget committee killed in Democratic caucus.

64th Congress, 1915–17

Democratic caucus budget study committee reconstituted but fails to
come to a recommendation on budget reform.

66th Congress, 1919–21

Appropriations centralization is reestablished in the House, with the HAC regaining authority lost in 1885.

The Budget and Accounting Act is passed but fails to withstand President Wilson's veto.

67th Congress, 1921–23

The Budget and Accounting Act is passed and is signed by President Harding.

References

Frequently cited congressional publications and newspapers are abbreviated in the text as follows:

CG   *Congressional Globe*
CR   *Congressional Record*
NYT   *New York Times*
SBCH U.S. Congress. House. Select Budget Committee. 1919. *Hearings on the establishment of a national budget system*. 66th Congress.
WP   *Washington Post*

Aaron, Henry (ed.). 1987. *Economic choices 1987*. Washington, DC: Brookings Institution.

Alexander, De Alva Stanwood. 1916. *History and procedure of the House of Representatives*. Boston: Houghton-Mifflin.

Arnold, R. Douglas. 1979. *Congress and the bureaucracy*. New Haven, CT: Yale University Press.

Arrow, Kenneth J. 1951. *Social choice and individual values*. New York: Wiley.

Barclay, John. 1874. *Digest of rules of the House of Representatives of the United States and the joint rules of the two houses*, 43rd Congress, 2nd sess. Washington, DC: U.S. Government Printing Office.

Barnes, James. 1931. *John G. Carlisle: Financial statesman*. New York: Dodd, Mead.

Barnett, V. M. 1939. Contested congressional elections in recent years. *Political Science Quarterly*, 54:187–215.

Bauer, Raymond, Ithiel De Sola Pool, and Lewis Dexter. 1963. *American business and public policy*. Chicago: Atherton Press.

Bogue, Allan, Jerome H. Clubb, Carroll R. McKibbin, and Sandra A. Traugott. 1976. Members of the House of Representatives and the processes of modernization. *Journal of American History*, 63:275–302.

Bolling, Richard. 1968. *Power in the House*. New York: Dutton.

Brady, David. 1973. *Congressional voting in a partisan era*. Lawrence: University of Kansas Press.

References

1978. Critical elections, congressional parties, and clusters of policy changes. *British Journal of Political Science,* 8:79–99.

Brady, David and Mark Morgan. 1983. Reforming the structure of the House appropriations process: The effects of the 1885 and 1919–1920 reforms on money decisions. Paper prepared for presentation at the annual meeting of the American Political Science Association.

1987. Reforming the structure of the House appropriations process: The effects of the 1885 and 1919–1920 reforms on money decisions. In *Congress: Structure and policy,* Mathew D. McCubbins and Terry Sullivan (eds.). Cambridge: Cambridge University Press.

Buchanan, James and Gordon Tullock. 1962. *The calculus of consent: Logical foundations of constitutional democracy.* Ann Arbor: University of Michigan Press.

Bullock, Charles. 1972. House careerists: Changing patterns of longevity and attrition. *American Political Science Review,* 66:1295–1300.

Bullock, Charles and David W. Brady. 1983. Party, constituency, and roll-call voting in the U.S. Senate. *Legislative Studies Quarterly,* 8:29–43.

Busbey, L. White. 1927. *Uncle Joe Cannon.* New York: Holt.

Cain, Bruce, John Ferejohn, and Morris Fiorina. 1987. *The personal vote.* Cambridge, MA: Harvard University Press.

Calvert, Randall L. 1987. Coordination and power: The foundation of leadership among rational legislators. Paper prepared for presentation at the annual meeting of the American Political Science Association.

Cancian, Francesca M. 1968. Varieties of functional analysis. In *Encyclopedia of the Social Sciences,* pp. 29–43. New York: Macmillan and Free Press.

Cannon, Clarence. 1935. *Cannon's precedents of the House of Representatives of the United States.* Washington, DC: U.S. Government Printing Office.

Chamber of Commerce of the United States of America. 1912. On the question of the plan for a national budget. *Referendum Pamphlets: I.*

Cleveland, Frederick A., 1912. *The budget as a means of locating responsibility for waste and inefficiency.* New York: Academy of Political Science.

Cleveland, Frederick A. and Arthur Buck. 1920. *The budget and responsible government.* New York: Macmillan.

Coletta, Paolo E. 1987. *A survey of U.S. naval affairs, 1865–1917.* Lanham, MD: University Press of America.

Collins, Charles W. 1915/1916. Constitutional aspects of a national budget system. *Yale Law Journal,* 25:376–385.

1917. *The national budget system.* New York: Macmillan.

Committee for Economic Development. Research and Policy Committee. 1983. *Strengthening the federal budget process.* New York: Committee for Economic Development.

Congressional Quarterly. 1982a. *Budgeting for America.* Washington, DC: Congressional Quarterly Press.

1982b. *Origins and development of Congress.* Washington, DC: Congressional Quarterly Press.

Cooper, Joseph and David Brady. 1981. Institutional context and leadership style: The House from Cannon to Rayburn. *American Political Science Review,* 75:411–425.

Davis, Otto, M. A. H. Dempster, and Aaron Wildavsky. 1966a. A theory of the budgetary process. *American Political Science Review,* 60:529–547.

References

1966b. On the process of budgeting: An empirical study of congressional appropriations. *Papers on Non-Market Decision Making,* 1:63–132.

1971. On the process of budgeting II: An empirical study of congressional appropriations. In *Studies in Budgeting,* R. F. Byrne, A. Charnes, W. W. Cooper, Otto A. Davis, and Dorothy Gilford (eds.). Amsterdam: North-Holland.

Dempsey, John T. 1956. Control over the seating and disciplining of members. Ph.D. Dissertation, University of Michigan.

Downs, Anthony. 1957. *An economic theory of democracy.* New York: Harper.

Economist, The. 1982. *World business cycles.* London: The Economist Newspaper Limited.

Ellwood, John and James Thurber. 1977. The new congressional budget process: Its causes, consequences, and possible success. In *Legislative reform and public policy,* Susan Welch and John Peters (eds.). New York: Praeger.

1981. The politics of the congressional budget process re-examined. *Congress reconsidered,* 2nd ed., Lawrence Dodd and Bruce Oppenheimer (eds.). Washington, DC: Congressional Quarterly Press.

Evans, Rowland and Robert Novak. 1975. Lyndon B. Johnson: The ascent to leadership. In *Congress in change,* Norman Ornstein (ed.). New York: Praeger.

Fenno, Richard. 1965. The internal distribution of influence: The House. In *The Congress and America's future,* David Truman (ed.). Englewood Cliffs, NJ: Prentice-Hall.

1966. *Power of the purse.* Boston: Little, Brown.

1973. *Congressmen on committees.* Boston: Little, Brown.

Ferejohn, John A. 1973. *Pork barrel politics.* Stanford, CA: Stanford University Press.

1986. Logrolling in an institutional context: A case study of food stamp legislation. In *Congress and policy change,* Gerald C. Wright, Jr., Leroy N. Rieselbach, and Lawrence C. Dodd (eds.). New York: Agathon Press.

Ferejohn, John A. and Morris Fiorina. 1975. Purposive models of legislative behavior. *American Economic Review Papers and Proceedings,* 65:407–14.

Fiorina, Morris P. 1977. *Congress: Keystone of the Washington establishment.* New Haven, CT: Yale University Press.

Fiorina, Morris P., David Rohde, and Peter Wissel. 1975. Historical change in House turnover. In *Congress and change,* Norman Ornstein (ed.). New York: Praeger.

Fisher, Louis. 1972. *The president and Congress.* New York: Free Press.

1975. *Presidential spending power.* Princeton, NJ: Princeton University Press.

1984. The Budget Act of 1974: A further loss of spending control. In *Congressional budgeting,* W. Thomas Wander, F. Ted Hebert, and Gary W. Copeland (eds.). Baltimore: Johns Hopkins University Press.

1985. Ten years of the Budget Act: Still searching for controls. *Public Budgeting and Finance,* 5:3–28.

Ford, Henry Jones. 1898. *The rise and growth of American politics.* New York: Macmillan.

Frank, Arthur D. 1930. *The development of the federal program of flood control on the Mississippi River.* New York: Columbia University Press.

Galloway, George. 1955. *The legislative process in Congress.* New York: Crowell.

1962. *History of the United States House of Representatives.* New York: Crowell.

References

Galloway, George. 1976. *History of the United States House of Representatives*, 2nd ed. New York: Crowell.

Garfield, James. 1879. National appropriations and misappropriations. *North American Review*, 270: 572–586.

Glass, Andrew. 1975. Mike Mansfield, Majority Leader. In *Congress in change*, Norman Ornstein (ed.). New York: Praeger.

Glasson, William H. 1918. *Federal military pensions in the United States*. New York: Oxford University Press.

Haines, Wilder H. 1915. The congressional caucus of today. *American Political Science Review*. 9:696–706.

Hartz, Louis. 1955. *The liberal tradition in America*. New York: Harcourt Brace Jovanovich.

Havemann, Joel. 1978. *Congress and the budget*. Bloomington, IN: Indiana University Press.

Hinds, Asher. 1907. *Hinds' precedents of the House of Representatives of the United States*. Washington, DC: U.S. Government Printing Office.

House, Albert. 1940. Northern congressional democrats as defenders of the South during Reconstruction. *Journal of Southern History*, 6:46–71.

Huitt, Ralph. 1965. The internal distribution of influence: The Senate. In *The Congress and America's future*, David Truman (ed.). Englewood Cliffs, NJ: Prentice-Hall.

Ippolito, Dennis. 1978. *The budget and national politics*. San Francisco: Freeman.

  1981. *Congressional spending*. Ithaca, NY: Cornell University Press.

Josephy, Alvin. 1979. *On the hill*. New York: Simon and Schuster.

Kendrick, M. Slade. 1955. *A century and a half of federal expenditures*. New York: National Bureau of Economic Research.

Kernell, Samuel H. 1977. Toward understanding 19th century congressional careers: Ambition, competition, and rotation. *American Journal of Political Science*, 21:669–693.

  1986. The early nationalization of political news in America. *Studies in American Political Development*, 1:255–278.

Kernell, Samuel, and Gary Jacobson. 1984. The relative standing of legislatures and executives as news in the nineteenth century. Paper prepared for presentation at the annual meeting of the Southern Political Science Association, Savannah, GA.

Key, V. O. 1940. The lack of a budgetary theory. *American Political Science Review*, 36:1137–1144.

Kiewiet, D. Roderick and Mathew D. McCubbins. 1985a. Congressional appropriations and the electoral connection. *Journal of Politics*, 47:59–82.

  1985b. Appropriations decisions as a bilateral bargaining game between president and Congress. *Legislative Studies Quarterly*, 10:181–202.

Kimmel, Lewis. 1959. *Federal budget and fiscal policy, 1789–1958*. Washington, DC: Brookings Institution.

Kinder, Donald and D. Roderick Kiewiet. 1981. Sociotropic politics: The American case. *British Journal of Political Science*, 11:129–161.

Leloup, Lance. 1980. *The fiscal Congress*. Westport, CT: Greenwood.

Levy, Marion J., Jr. 1968. Structural-functionalist analysis. In *International Encyclopedia of the Social Sciences*, pp. 21–29. New York: Macmillan and Free Press.

Lindblom, Charles. 1959. The science of "muddling through." *Public Administration Review,* 19:79–88.

Luce, R. Duncan and Howard Raiffa. 1957. *Games and decisions.* New York: Wiley.

Lustick, Ian. 1980. Explaining the variable utility of disjointed incrementalism: Four propositions. *American Political Science Review,* 74:342–353.

McConachie, Lauros. 1898. *Congressional committees.* New York: Crowell.

Manley, John F. 1970. *The politics of finance.* Boston: Little, Brown.

Martis, Kenneth C. 1982. *The historical atlas of the United States congressional districts, 1789–1983.* New York: Free Press.

Masters, Nicholas. 1961. Committee assignments in the House of Representatives. *American Political Science Review,* 55:345–357.

Mayhew, David. 1974. *Congress: The electoral connection.* New Haven, CT: Yale University Press.

Mooney, James. 1947. *The principles of organization,* rev. ed. New York: Harper.

Morres, Merrill. 1917. *A historical and legal digest of all the contested election cases in the House of Representatives, 1901–1917.* 64th Cong., 2nd sess., H. doc. 2052.

Niskanen, William. 1971. *Bureaucracy and representative government.* Chicago: Aldine-Atherton.

Noyes, Alexander D. 1909. *Forty years of American finance.* New York: Putnam.

Oleszek, Walter. 1978. *Congressional procedures and the policy process.* Washington, DC: Congressional Quarterly Press.

Olson, Mancur. 1965. *The logic of collective action.* Cambridge, MA: Harvard University Press.

Orloff, Ann and Theda Skocpol. 1984. Why not equal protection? Explaining the politics of public social spending in Britain, 1900–11, and the United States, 1800s–1920. *American Sociological Review,* 49:726–750.

Panning, William. 1985. Formal models of legislative processes. *Handbook of legislative research.* Gerhard Loewenberg, Samuel Patterson, and Malcolm Jewell (eds.). Cambridge, MA: Harvard University Press.

Penner, Rudolph (ed.) 1981. *The congressional budget process after five years.* Washington, DC: American Enterprise Institute.

Pitkin, Hanna. 1967. *The concept of representation.* Berkeley and Los Angeles: University of California Press.

Polsby, Nelson. 1968. The institutionalization of the U.S. House of Representatives. *American Political Science Review,* 62:144–168.

Polsby, Nelson, Miriam Gallagher, and Barry S. Rundquist. 1969. The growth of the seniority system in the U.S. House of Representatives. *American Political Science Review,* 63:787–807.

Price, Hugh D. 1971. The congressional career: Then and now. In *Congressional behavior,* Nelson Polsby (ed.). New York: Random House.

   1975. Congress and the evolution of legislative "professionalism." In *Congress in change,* Norman Ornstein (ed.). New York: Praeger.

   1977. Careers and committees in the American Congress: The problem of structural change. In *The history of parliamentary behavior,* William O. Aydelotte (ed.). Princeton, NJ: Princeton University Press.

Priest, Loring Benson. 1942. *Uncle Sam's stepchildren: The reformation of United States Indian policy, 1865–1887.* New Brunswick, NJ: Rutgers University Press.

References

Ratner, Sidney. 1967. *Taxation and democracy in America.* New York: Wiley.

Richardson, James, (ed.) 1913. *A compilation of the messages and papers of the presidents.* Washington, DC: U.S. Government Printing Office.

Riker, William. 1962. *The theory of political coalitions.* New Haven, CT: Yale University Press.

Ripley, Randall. 1969. Power in the post-World War II Senate. *Journal of Politics,* 31:465–492.

Rivlin, Alice. 1986. The need for a better budget process. *The Brookings Review,* 3:3–10.

Roady, Elston E. 1951. Party regularity in the sixty-third Congress. Ph.D. Dissertation, University of Illinois.

Robinson, James. 1963. *The House Rules Committee.* Indianapolis, IN: Bobbs-Merrill.

Rothman, David. 1966. *Politics and power.* Cambridge, MA: Harvard University Press.

Rowell, Chester. 1901. *A history and legal digest of all the contested election cases in the House of Representatives, 1789–1901,* 56th Cong., 2nd sess., H. doc. 510.

Rudder, Catherine. 1978. The policy impact of reform on the Committee on Ways and Means. In *Legislative reform,* Leroy Rieselbach (ed.). Lexington, MA: Lexington Books.

　　1985. Tax policy: Structure and choice. In *Making economic policy in Congress,* Allen Schick (ed.). Washington, DC: American Enterprise Institute.

Saunders, Charles. 1966. *The Brookings Institution: A fifty-year history.* Washington, DC: Brookings Institution.

Schick, Allen. 1980. *Congress and money.* Washington, DC: Urban Institute.

　　1981. The three-ring budget process: The appropriations, tax, and budget committees in Congress. In *The new Congress,* Thomas E. Mann and Norman Ornstein (eds.). Washington, DC: American Enterprise Institute.

　　1984. Legislation, appropriations, and budgets: The development of spending decision-making in Congress. *Congressional Research Service Report,* 84–106 GOV. Washington, DC: Congressional Research Service.

Schlesinger, Arthur, Jr. (ed.) 1971. *History of American presidential elections,* 3 vols. New York: McGraw-Hill.

Seip, Terry. 1983. *The south returns to Congress.* Baton Rouge: Louisiana State University Press.

Select Budget Committee. *See* U.S. Congress. House. Select Budget Committee.

Seligman, Edwin R. A. 1921. *The income tax,* 2nd ed. New York: Macmillan.

Selko, Daniel. 1940. *The federal financial system.* Washington, DC: Brookings Institution.

Shepsle, Kenneth. 1978. *The giant jigsaw puzzle.* Chicago: University of Chicago Press.

　　1984. The congressional budget process: Diagnosis, prescription, prognosis. In *Congressional budgeting,* W. Thomas Wander, F. Ted Hebert, and Gary W. Copeland (eds.). Baltimore, MD: Johns Hopkins University Press.

　　1985. Prospects for formal models of legislatures. *Legislative Studies Quarterly,* 10:5–19.

　　1986. Institutional equilibrium and equilibrium institutions. In *Political science: The science of politics,* Herbert Weisberg (ed.). New York: Agathon Press.

References

Shepsle, Kenneth, and Barry Weingast. 1981. Structure-induced equilibrium and legislative choice. *Public Choice*, 37:503–519.

Shuman, Howard. 1984. *Politics and the budget*. Englewood Cliffs, NJ: Prentice-Hall.

Simon, Herbert. 1950. *Public administration*. New York: Knopf.

　1957. *Administrative behavior*, 2nd ed. New York: Macmillan.

Sinclair, Barbara. 1983. Purposive behavior in the U.S. Congress: A review essay. *Legislative Studies Quarterly*, 8:117–31.

Sklandony, Thomas. 1985. The House goes to work: Select and standing committees in the U.S. House of Representatives, 1789–1828. *Congress and the Presidency*, 12:165–187.

Skowronek, Stephen. 1982. *Building a new American state*. Cambridge: Cambridge University Press.

Smith, Steven S. 1985. New patterns of decisionmaking in Congress. In *The new direction in American politics*, John E. Chubb and Paul E. Peterson (eds.). Washington, DC: Brookings Institution.

Smith, Steven S. and Christopher Deering. 1984. *Congressional committees*. Washington, DC: Congressional Quarterly Press.

Sprout, Harold and Margaret Sprout. 1939. *The rise of American naval power*. Princeton, NJ: Princeton University Press.

Stanwood, Edward. 1903. *American tariff controversies in the nineteenth century*, 2 vols. Boston: Houghton Mifflin.

Stewart, Charles III. 1985. The politics of structural reform: Reforming budgetary structure in the House, 1865–1921. Ph.D. Dissertation, Stanford University.

　1987a. Does structure matter? The effects of structural change on spending decisions in the House, 1871 to 1922. *American Journal of Political Science*, 31:584–605.

　1987b. Budget reform and its consequences: Agencies, the committees, and the House, 1865–1921. Paper prepared for presentation at the annual meeting of the American Political Science Association.

　1988. Budget reform as strategic legislative action: An exploration. *Journal of Politics*, 50:292–321.

Stouffer, Samuel A. 1966. *Communism, conformity, and civil liberties*. New York: Wiley.

Studenski, Paul and Herman Krooss. 1963. *Financial history of the United States*. New York: McGraw-Hill.

Sullivan, Terry. 1984. *Procedural structure*. New York: Praeger.

Sundquist, James. 1981. *Decline and resurgence of Congress*. Washington, DC: Brookings Institution.

　1983. *Dynamics of the party system*, 2nd ed. Washington, DC: Brookings Institution.

Taft, William Howard. 1916. *Our chief magistrate and his powers*. New York: Columbia University Press.

Taft Commission. *See* U.S. President's Commission on Economy and Efficiency.

Tawney, James. 1910. Federal appropriations: Their rapid increase. *Review of Reviews*, 42:343–348.

Treasury Secretary. *See* U.S. Secretary of the Treasury.

Truman, David. 1949. *The congressional party*. New York: Wiley.

U.S. Census Bureau. 1975. *Historical statistics of the United States*. Washington, DC: U.S. Government Printing Office.

U.S. Congress. 1880. *Report of the Mississippi River Commission.* 46th Cong., 2nd sess., H. exec. doc. 58.

1912. *National budget system.* 66th Cong., 1st sess., H. Rpt. 362.

1984. *The line item veto: An appraisal.* 98th Congress, 2nd sess., House Budget Committee print.

U.S. Congress. House. Appropriations Committee. 1912. *Hearings before the subcommittee of the House Committee on Appropriations...in charge of the sundry civil appropriations bill for 1913.* 62nd Congress.

U.S. Congress. House. Select Budget Committee. 1919. *Hearings on the establishment of a national budget system.* 66th Congress.

U.S. President. n.d. *Compilation of the messages and papers of the president.* New York: Bureau of National Literature.

1922–1929. *Addresses of the President of the United States and the director of the Bureau of the Budget at the meeting of the Business Organization of the Government.* Washington, DC: U.S. Government Printing Office. [A typescript account for the first meeting in 1921 is bound with this volume in the library of the Brookings Institution, Washington, DC.]

U.S. President's Commission on Economy and Efficiency. 1912. *The need for a national budget.* Washington, DC: U.S. Government Printing Office.

U.S. Secretary of the Treasury. 1909. *Annual report.* Washington, DC: U.S. Government Printing Office.

1910. *Annual report.* Washington, DC: U.S. Government Printing Office.

1922. *Annual report of the Secretary of the Treasury on the state of the finances.* Washington, DC: U.S. Government Printing Office.

Wander, W. Thomas. 1982a. Politics of congressional budget reform. Ph.D. Dissertation, Stanford University.

1982b. Patterns of change in the congressional budget process, 1865–1972. *Congress and the Presidency,* 9:23–49.

Wander, W. Thomas, F. Ted Hebert, and Gary Copeland (eds.). 1984. *Congressional budgeting: Politics, process, and power.* Baltimore, MD: Johns Hopkins University Press.

Weaver, R. Kent. 1986. The politics of blame avoidance. *Journal of Public Policy,* 6:371–398.

White, Leonard D. 1958. *The Republican era: 1869–1901.* New York: Macmillan.

Wiebe, Robert. 1967. *The search for order.* New York: Hill and Wang.

Wildavsky, Aaron. 1964. *Politics of the budgetary process.* Boston: Little, Brown.

1979. *Politics of the budgetary process,* 3rd ed. Boston: Little, Brown.

1984. *Politics of the budgetary process,* 4th ed. Boston: Little, Brown.

Willoughby, William F. 1918. *The problem of a national budget.* New York: Appleton.

Willoughby, William. 1934. *Principles of legislative organization and administration.* Washington, DC: Brookings Institution.

Wilson, Rick. 1986a. What was it worth to be on a committee in the U.S. House, 1889 to 1913? *Legislative Studies Quarterly,* 11:47–63.

1986b. An empirical test of preferences for the political pork barrel: District level appropriations for river and harbor legislation, 1889–1913. *American Journal of Political Science,* 30:729–754.

Wilson, Woodrow. 1887. The study of administration. *Political Science Quarterly,* 2:197–222.

1956. *Congressional government.* New York: New American Library.

References

Woodward, C. Vann. 1966. *Reunion and reaction: The Compromise of 1877 and the end of Reconstruction*. Boston: Little, Brown.

1971. *The origins of the new south, 1877–1913*. Baton Rouge: Louisiana State University Press.

Young, James Sterling. 1966. *The Washington community*. New York: Columbia University Press.

Index

Index

Index

Index